RAMALA

"A School on Earth
teaching
The Truth of The Heavens"

THE REVELATION
of
RAMALA

JERSEY
NEVILLE SPEARMAN

Published in Great Britain by
Neville Spearman (Jersey) Ltd
PO Box 75, Normandy House, St Helier, Jersey
Channel Islands

Distributed by Neville Spearman Ltd
The Priory Gate, Friars Street, Sudbury, Suffolk

First Published April 1978
Second Edition June 1979
Third Edition October 1982

3/96

Printed in Great Britain by offset lithography by
Billing & Sons Ltd, Guildford, London and Worcester

'And I saw a new heaven and a new earth: for the first heaven and the first earth were passed away; and there was no more sea.'

Revelation
Chapter 21 Verse 1

ACKNOWLEDGEMENT

We would like to express our gratitude to all those who have given so generously of themselves in order to make this book possible. Its production has truly been a combined effort, with many individuals contributing in thought, word and deed. To all of them we would like to say a heartfelt 'Thank you'.

DEDICATION

We dedicate this book to all who serve.

CONTENTS

FOREWORD

From the records of early British history we learn that, after the Crucifixion of Christ, His Disciples arrived on the swampy shores of Avalon, where Glastonbury Abbey now stands. The Druids welcomed them and presented them with tithes of land, gifted in perpetuity.

On that same land now stands Chalice Hill House. From within its walls fresh inspiration has issued forth in the form of this book, to invigorate the seekers of today. Such seekers are emerging everywhere in the world at this time, in their hundreds. They bear the stamp of a new race, who refuse to be conditioned, who wish to ascertain the purpose and potential of their own lives, both as individuals and as the forerunners of a new civilisation. Under their influence thousands of Groups of every grade are forming around the planet, linking together in a common purpose: that of discovering the rightful way of evolution and the part which each can play in it as an emerging 'Son of God'.

Humanity is awakening from its deep stupor of materialism and is becoming aware of the great step which lies before it — of implementing and building the Aquarian Age and Ideal — and it is demanding help, training and a more mature knowledge than it so far possesses. This demand is being met by a succession of fascinating new teachings which are proving the subject of the Inner Truths to be inexhaustible, and are the prelude to a revolutionary expansion in human consciousness. This new book contains many indications of what such consciousness will produce in new standards and in new ways of living. It could constitute a valuable help and a stimulating challenge to those who intend to press forwards.

Humanity has still a very long way to go before it even begins to realise the amazing development which lies before it. Apparently, to get to the moon is easier than to find the heaven which lies so near — within oneself! We have allowed ourselves to be robbed of our vitality, which is corroded physically and mentally by unwise, even primitive, ways of living and thinking, and their production of pollution on all planes. The needed regeneration can be much helped by such a book as this. Not only does it sum up many of the essentials of the Ageless Wisdom, but it offers thought-provoking postulates which may be new even to the seasoned spiritual seeker. We feel that the courage and dedication which has gone into it should evoke our gratitude, and ensure a life of joyful service both to this volume and to its originators.

VERA STANLEY ALDER
Bournemouth 1977

INTRODUCTION

We live in exciting, if turbulent, times, because this planet is being transformed and made ready for a New Age of Man. In recent years many people have spoken and written of the significance of the Age of Aquarius which is now dawning. In almost every language inspired writings are to be found which predict what is going to happen to this Earth, and to Humanity on it, during the next few decades. From the Revelations of St. John the Divine, through Nostradamus to Edgar Cayce, one can discover many predictions which all point to the fact that the next twenty-five years are exceptionally critical years in the Earth's evolutionary process.

As we look around the World today we cannot help but notice the violence and conflict that are prevalent on every level. Our modern western society is sick, and what we are witnessing are the symptoms of a fatal disease. Hand in hand with this has come the questioning of many of the accepted beliefs and values upon which that society is based. This has led, in turn, to a loss of personal direction, to uncertainty and to escape into materialism, apathy, drugs and so on. Many people are finding that they cannot cope with the conditions of life as they exist today. The pressures of life have now become so great that Man cannot even recognise the insanity of many of his own actions.

Nevertheless, there are people from all walks of life who are positively seeking an understanding not only of the meaning and purpose of their lives in society today but of the purpose of Man himself. They are seeking answers to questions which neither the politicians, the scientists nor the Churches can provide. These people have recognised that science and religion, because they are largely based on Man's own divisive thought, far from leading them into an understanding are in fact separating them from the reality of physical life today. They have realised that modern science and religion are not capable of conceiving of the perfect whole, of seeing the complete picture. Some of them have, therefore, turned to the esoteric teachings of past generations, but only a few can understand their terminology and symbology and even fewer are capable of relating them to everyday living in this materialistic age in which we live. Here, in the Western World, some people are turning to the spiritual traditions of the East hoping to find there the answer which present-day Christianity cannot provide, but the way of the East has not transformed the East, so why should it suddenly have the power to transform the West with its totally alien culture and different evolutionary patterns? Others have been attracted to the many cults and 'gurus' that have mushroomed in response to Man's demands for a new concept of creation. However, the danger with any form of secondhand knowledge or wisdom is that it is so easy for Man to believe in something but not to live it, to profess something but not to practise it. No matter how great the wisdom, if Man does not accept it into his being and live it then it becomes nothing but a mental exercise leading to illusion. For many today the dogma of no-God has great appeal, and here in the West, where the intellect reigns supreme, it has required only a short step to proclaim that Man is God, that Man is the master and controller of all that is.

For most people the reality of life today is that which they are aware of with their five senses — the physical plane of Earth — and anything which points to an existence above or below this plane is ignored or derided. However, in recent years more and more people have begun to recognise and to use extra-sensory powers. For reasons as yet unknown to them they have become aware of levels of existence beyond that which Man recognises and understands. They have begun to exhibit talents and skills which they cannot logically explain in terms of physical evolution alone. All they know is that suddenly a corner of the veil is lifted and they become aware of a source of wisdom and knowledge beyond the physical which can best be referred to as Universal, or Infinite, Consciousness. Depending on the individual this Consciousness takes many forms. It has, however, always been present around the Earth to help and inspire Man. Whereas in the past It might have been identified as a father figure, as God, because Man's thoughts always projected outwards and needed an external reference, today It is becoming recognised as a voice within, as a part of Man's being.

Throughout the history of Man one can read of the intervention of this Divine Force to implement a Plan of which Man cannot conceive. Furthermore, at critical times in Man's evolution great souls have incarnated on the Earth to ground this Consciousness for all Mankind to witness.

Today, all over the World, there are people who are in contact with this Universal Consciousness. Through various forms of self-development they have learnt, some quite quickly, others over many years, to tap into this source of Infinite Knowledge and Wisdom. Many channels of communication have been established, especially in recent years, and from this it would appear that a greater Will is preparing the Earth for a new revelation, for a new Age of Man. Various individuals have a deep inner conviction that they have incarnated to act as messengers, as channels for the release of new knowledge. Many of them feel a strong guiding force within controlling their lives. They sense the hand of the divine leading them along a path which they agreed to walk they know not when. Like attracts like, and to these channels have come people who intuitively feel that the wisdom which the channels ground and display, the life-style which they advocate, truly reflects that Universal Consciousness. As a result all over the World little groups or communities have been forming to share this new release of consciousness. Although such groups are situated all over the World, and although the inspiration which each group receives reflects the personality of that group, the underlying message is the same, and is universal in its application. This book contains the inspiration received by one such group — Ramala.

This book is published anonymously. The name Ramala was taken from the soul, as opposed to the earthly, names of the husband and wife team who were the channel through which the teachings came, and was used only as a title to which the general public could write when asking for the teachings. The identity of the channel through which the inspiration has come is not important. When one listens to a radio one is not concerned with the station but with the programme. We have no desire to attract people to the group, for we are only the instruments through which the teachings have come. The events leading up to the establishment of the group and to the subsequent development of the channel would probably make fascinating reading, but they can be of significance only to the individuals concerned and, if published here, might lead the reader into forming unnecessary and distracting opinions about the teachings, which should stand or fall by themselves. The sole purpose of this book is to make the teachings which the group received available to as wide an audience as possible.

Inevitably the personality and the soul consciousness of the channel is imprinted on the teachings, for in this form of communication Universal Consciousness has to work through the mind of the channel. Therefore the teachings are shaped and coloured by the nature of the channel's mind and experience. This explains the background to many of the teachings, for the channel was brought up as an orthodox Christian. As the consciousness of the channel developed under the influence of Universal Consciousness so the level of the teachings changed markedly. The first and the last teaching represent a time interval of almost five years. The teachings were all received during periods of meditation. The inspiration would appear in the channel's mind and he would then speak it into a tape recorder, from which it was later transcribed into the printed word. It must be remembered that originally the teachings were intended to aid in the development of the group and so the subject matter reflects the interests of the group. It was only later that they were found to have a much more universal appeal and were made available in pamphlet form to anyone who asked for them.

The group has been in existence for several years and during that period has received and recorded several hundred inspired teachings on a wide variety of subjects. Of necessity we have had to select, on a purely personal basis, the teachings to be included in this book. Many of them have been edited and condensed, but always with strict regard to the original meaning. We have tried, however, to represent the various stages of development through which the group passed. As the titles perhaps suggest, the teachings were closely associated with the growth and everyday problems of the group and thus they have been presented chronologically in the book in order to reflect both the evolution of the group and of the channel. In consequence, although each stands by itself as a complete statement, the later teachings will be found to differ markedly both in content and consciousness from the earlier ones. We have also tried to establish a balance between what could be called the esoterical and the practical teachings. Nearly all of them, however, in some way cast a fresh light on the problems of today. Whilst they might not necessarily provide the answer to all the many questions about the purpose and meaning of life today, they do offer an answer to some of them. It is for you, the reader, to judge.

These teachings have proved to be a source of inspiration to our little group. They have transformed our lives in many ways, not so much as a result of their content but of their consciousness and of their subtle effects upon us. The teachings came at a time in our lives when we were questioning the whole meaning of Man's material and social way of life, and enabled us to arrive at some understanding of life today. It is our hope that they may be of similar value to the reader. However, what is truth for one person may not be for another. Hence it is for you, the reader, to discover the truth of the teachings through right practice and by exercising your spiritual intuition. If the teachings bring forth a response, a spark of recognition, from within you, then accept them, but if they do not then place them aside for the time being. What is important is not that the contents be memorised and repeated ad infinitum for the benefit of others, but their effect upon you as you read them. Our earnest desire is that they will act as the spark which will ignite the flames of your own intuition, and that they will help you to develop your own personal and unique link with that great Universal Consciousness.

RAMALA
Glastonbury 1977

The Ramala Centre,
Chalice Hill House,
Dod Lane,
Glastonbury,
Somerset BA6 8BZ, England.

THE CYCLE OF LIFE
DEATH

Death is of no greater importance than birth. They are both of equal significance. They merely entail the transition from one body to another, from the physical to the astral or from the astral to the physical. That is all. Whereas Man can perhaps comprehend the transition of birth because it is from the unknown to the physical, which he understands, death, being the transition from the physical to the unknown, he finds more difficult. So while Man accepts birth, and the meaning of birth, he cannot do the same for death. He thinks of death in a different way depending not only on his individual soul evolution but also on his emotions — for death, after all, is an emotive subject. What else does death mean to a man today but a stirring of the emotions, a fear of loss, a feeling of pity either for himself or for others who are dying or about to die? If Man was to understand the true significance of this transition and realise that it is merely an act of Natural Law it would not arouse the emotive feelings that it does.

Because some people consider that death is a finality, and not a transition, they think from their emotive centre of what it means to them. Because someone is dying they think that they are to lose that person forever and will never see that person again, that life will not be the same when that person has died, that they are to be permanently separated and that the way of life they have led in the past cannot continue. Fear of death is, basically, a selfish emotion, for what else is concerned with death except the self? It is the little 'I', the ego, thinking of how life will change because someone has died. "How will my life change?" you think when you are faced with the death of a friend or someone in the family. You feel sorrow, perhaps, not so much because they are dying and changing their bodies, but, rather, because they will no longer be around you, that a way of life will change. Even if someone dies whom you do not like, whom you hate, you still consider death from the same

16

viewpoint: "How does it affect *me*?"

Now, as I have already said, birth and death are of equal significance. They should concern you no more than going to sleep every night and waking up every morning. As you go to sleep, you die. As you wake up, you are born. Every day is a life. It is as simple as that, with no more significance. Man fears death primarily because of his lack of spirituality and also because of the way in which he leads his life and treats his fellow-men. If Man does not accept that his life on Earth is merely a journey between one form of existence and another, but thinks rather that he is only here for his short three score years and ten and then perishes forever, then the whole import of his life, and the values by which he leads it, are of necessity different. If he thinks that this is his only life, then he will surely try to get the most out of it for himself. He will think that once somebody has died and has gone from his life, then that person has gone for good, and that there is no need to think about that person any more. So, by his very concept of death, Man adjusts his views of life. If Man is not aware of Natural Law then he will lead his life outside that Law and, even though it does affect him, he will be unaware of that effect. He denies it because he does not see it, and does not recognise it.

Death, then, is a transition. For many less evolved souls it is the beginning of the holidays after going to school. They have been to school on the surface of this planet and now they have their holidays, when they rest from their labours to consider what they have experienced whilst they have been at school, to organise and assess in their own minds what they have learned and to refresh themselves before they go back to school again to learn more lessons.

Now it is not possible to convince anyone who comes to you demanding proof that there is life after death. It is something you will never prove to anybody, because proof is impossible. What you know you feel from your own soul-consciousness, and if the soul-consciousness of the man who stands before you has not yet advanced to that point of evolution when he can consider death in its true light you will never convince him of life after death. He will not appreciate what is involved. So do not waste your time in discussion with any man who wishes to argue about life after death. It is pointless. Either you know there is life after death, or you do not. It is not for you to convince any man. That discovery

17

must come from within. What you may do, however, is to invite a man to consider that if he believes that there is a life after death then his physical life must have a purpose. If he is to live on after he has died there must be other planes of existence, there must be a greater meaning to life. This must surely affect the way he leads his present life. Let him then consider that his thoughts, his words, his deeds, are written forever, and that what he has done will have an effect not only while he lives in his physical body but also on other planes of existence after his death.

It would seem to be inbred in Man that he fears death. Let us consider this for a minute. Everyone of you, even the most evolved soul, is aware of this fear of death. If you were to analyse this emotion, whilst for some it would be a genuine fear of dying because it meant the loss of the pleasure of living, for the more evolved soul it would be a different fear, a fear of needlessly losing its life. You might think that they are the same but, in reality, they are not. In the latter case it is your soul telling you from within that you have a destiny to fulfil, and that you must not throw away your life and so fail to fulfil that destiny. Your fear is not really a fear of dying. It is, rather, a fear of not fulfilling your destiny, for the whole purpose of your living in a physical body on this planet is to fulfil your destiny, the plan which you yourself agreed to and mapped out before you were born. You are here to learn certain lessons and to experience certain vibrations and, therefore, as with a child going to school, it would be pointless to take you away in the middle of your studies. Your soul, therefore, tells you to take care that you do not leave before you are supposed to, and it is this protective instinct of the soul that prevents you from needlessly risking your physical body in acts of the personality — when you drive too fast, when you climb a high tree or risk your body in some foolish venture. That protectiveness is your soul guarding your destiny.

The more evolved the soul the greater is the certainty of that soul fulfilling its destiny, not only because the unseen Guides and Masters from the Higher Realms strive to ensure that it does so to enable it to carry out the responsibility associated with it but also because there is less chance of accidental death. Each one of you is born at an appointed time in spiritual time, and is destined to die at an appointed time, also in spiritual time. Nevertheless it is possible for a soul to die before its appointed time, but this can only happen due to the actions of a more evolved soul. There is a

18

Natural Law which states that a less evolved soul cannot take away the physical life of a more evolved soul. So as you advance and progress on the upward spiral of evolution the numbers who can touch and affect you become fewer. It takes an equally or a more evolved soul to take away your physical life. Therefore an evolved soul will usually fulfil its destiny. It is the less evolved soul who stands the greater risk of not fulfilling its destiny, but because the destiny of a less evolved soul is not of the same importance as that of a more evolved soul nothing is lost. The experience of death itself is a valuable lesson for a young soul to learn, for, until death means nothing more to it than the simple transition that it is, it has much to learn from the process of death. The actual transition is shattering for a young soul whereas for an evolved soul it will be like going to sleep and waking up the next morning on another plane of existence. That is all. So a young soul may go before its appointed time. It may not fulfil its destiny, but the Law of Karma, the Law of Cause and Effect, demands that the more evolved soul who was responsible for this must pay the effect. You cannot change a destiny without good cause.

One form of death is suicide. This can occur when a person decides to end his life because he cannot face his destiny. This can either be because the emotions are completely controlling the body to the exclusion of the soul influence so that the personality, out of self-pity, wants to destroy the body because it can no longer face life, or because of the influence of one of Man's stimulants, either alcohol or some form of drug. In such cases, as the soul is not protecting the body because it has been forced out, the body can be made to do things which it would not do if the soul was in control and so, for example, a man who is drunk might needlessly risk his life. There are many ways. Once the protective forces of the soul are removed the emotions can run riot. Because you have no fear, you may drive too fast or you may walk too near the edge of a cliff.

There are other occasions when a person can die before his appointed time. I will give two examples. The first is when, in order to assist another soul which needs help in its earthly progression, of its own volition the soul decides to make a sacrifice by withdrawing. If the soul decides that by leaving the physical it can help another soul to progress further, to overcome a challenge it has not already faced, to learn a lesson it has ignored in other lives, then it can, within Natural Law, decide to return, and the process of death takes place. The second example is when, if the soul has strayed so far from the destiny path which it came down to follow that no other lessons can be learned from its present incarnation and the way of life that it is leading, and if every known way of guidance has been ignored or rejected, then the soul itself may decide, again voluntarily, that as nothing more can be gained in this incarnation it will return to start that life again at a later stage in the Earth's evolution. Once more the process of death takes place. All such decisions are, of course, made on levels of consciousness above the physical.

You may well ask, "What happens in time of war?" It may be difficult for you to accept, but Natural Law works even in war. A less evolved soul cannot kill a more evolved one unless the more evolved soul allows it. Even someone dropping a bomb from many miles high onto a city cannot destroy a more evolved soul below. That is the Law. That is why there are these so-called miraculous escapes where one person in a house is saved and the remaining people die. The same Law applies to combat in the field of battle and, again, decides how one man dies and another does not.

Under the stress of war Man has to make many important decisions. It is indeed a testing time. It is a time, perhaps the only time, when Man truly considers the values of life. Because he is faced with death Man has to consider the purpose of life, the purpose of what he is doing and, nightly, he examines his soul. War, for a young soul, is a refining process, but very few evolved souls are to be found taking part in it. They may be there, however, for a specific purpose, as instruments of Divine Will, to combat a certain course of events or to ensure that a country's destiny is fulfilled. There were many evolved souls in the last World War who had incarnated for the purpose of preventing what was liable to happen. This they achieved. But very rarely are evolved souls to be found in combat because they do not need to learn that lesson. They have already reached the point of consciousness when they recognise the sanctity of life, when they understand what is involved. Many of them would rather sacrifice their own lives than go through the process of killing another to serve a purpose, or a cause, in which they might not even believe.

Death is, in reality, no more than a moment of transition, and for those who have fulfilled their destinies it is a pleasant one.

They have passed their examinations at school and are returning triumphant for their holidays. It is a time for rejoicing. However, if they have failed their examinations then the feeling will not be the same, and for those who die unhappy this is what has happened: they have not fulfilled their destinies. But for those who have, there is much joy and reward in the transition. They pass over to meet the Guides and Masters who have advised them during their lives in physical matter, and for the few who were already in communication with these higher beings there will appear to be no difference. Before they die, all evolved souls should be able to communicate with the Higher Vibrations, even to see them on certain planes of existence, so that for them death will be as nothing. It should be something of which they will hardly be aware. It is as simple as that.

After the moment of death has taken place you will merely look down on the physical life you have just left from one of your higher bodies and life will appear just the same as it does now. There will be no change except that the limitations of the physical body will have been thrown off and you will then be able to travel to the places of which you have only dreamed. You may study in the Halls of Learning about which you have heard but which you never visited in your physical body. You may see and listen to the great Masters about whom you have read but never met. It is not a stage of your life to fear. It is not a stage about which to worry.

The transition from life to death takes three days. That is the time it takes your soul and your spirit to leave your physical body and to withdraw from the shell it has inhabited into a higher body. That is why at Easter the Christian Churches talk of the Nazarene rising on the third day. He was not fully in a higher body until then, but after that time he could travel and appear as he so desired.

So in conclusion, I would ask you to place death in its proper perspective. Value the life of all your fellow-men as you do your own. The more evolved you are, the more aware you will be of death and of its meaning, and therefore the greater will be your responsibility to your fellow-men and to their lives. Do not needlessly take away the life of a lesser brother. It is a painful karma to incur. Remember that all life is sacred. It is not yours to take or to give. It belongs not to the individual but to that Infinite Spirit that controls us all.

THE CYCLE OF LIFE
BIRTH

Man is as much preoccupied with birth as he is with death. The reason for this is that birth, like death, is a transitional stage on the Wheel of Life. Whilst the purpose of death might perhaps intrigue Man more, the purpose of birth, because it is a stage from the unknown into reality as opposed to death which is a stage from reality into the unknown, Man accepts more readily. The result of birth can be seen. A child is born and is present in matter, and therefore everything that has gone into that child seems justified: the love, the act of creation, the preparations and the dreams are all present in that child. Therefore Man can more readily understand the purpose of birth than he can the purpose of death. Death to Man is, for the most part, purposeless because, considering it a finality, he regards it as the end of a useful life in matter, whereas he thinks of birth as being the beginning of life with a baby having everything to live for and enjoy. Birth, to Man, is the first step on the ladder of a fruitful life.

I do not intend to discuss the physical process of birth, as it is peculiar to this planet alone. It is, for most women, a small initiation when the child which is being born is a destined child: that is, a child which the parents were destined to have. You may consider that this is a strange thing to say, but many of the children who are born into matter are not destined children, and if they were you would not have so many of the problems that you do in your World today. Conception, and the child which comes from this act, should be as a result of a true spiritual marriage. From this true union a spiritual, or destined, child is born, and in that birth the mother will have an initiation. What so often happens in your World today is that children are created for entirely the wrong reasons. They are created when they are not wanted. They are created out of the wrong emotions, the lower emotions: out of lust, out of self-pity, out of pride, out of greed. From such a union no spiritual, no destined, child can result.

Many of the children who are born today are, of course, unplanned. This is because Man has grossly distorted the original purpose of the sexual act and now uses it for pleasure instead of for what it was intended, the procreation of children. Although Man commits the sexual act many times, even today he still does not understand the function of creation. The result is that even in the most careful of relationships a child can be conceived, and can be born unplanned. It is a sad thing to say but many of the children who inhabit this World are unplanned, and that is why those of you who are aware, when you see a child of a true marriage, when you see a child who is born out of parents with the correct motivation, when you see a child who has been asked to come, you see a child who stands out from its fellows. You are seeing a true spiritual child, which is what every child who is ever born into matter should be. If a child is not, then it labours under a great disadvantage and, apart from the creation of karma for the parents who have brought it into matter with such a liability, it places the child itself under a great burden in that life. Man today is not aware of the importance of the vibrations of matter on a child during its formative years.

As I said earlier, I am not going to discuss the physical process of birth. For those who have seen and experienced it the birth of a baby is indeed a wonderful and a beautiful happening. There are many forms of birth on the different planets within your Solar Body. Physical birth, as you know it, is peculiar to the Earth, but creation, the growth and the life of a baby inside the mother's womb, is almost as mysterious and as unknown to Man today as is the position and the size of the soul. It is a miraculous happening which occurs within the mother's womb and, even now, medical scientists are not completely certain as to what decides the build, the size, the features and the condition of a baby. But that is another story. What I wish to talk about in this lecture is the spiritual side of birth, of which there are three major divisions.

Firstly there are the children who are born to chosen parents for a specific reason. The souls concerned are usually souls of advanced evolution. The parents, therefore, deliberately incarnate for the purpose of allowing these special children to come through them. The birth of such children is the result of an agreement that the souls made before they all incarnated into matter. There is no doubt but that the obligation will be carried out, as the destiny of nations, even the World, can be affected. An example of this would be the birth of the Nazarene.

The second division of birth is what I would call karmic: when a child comes through its parents for a karmic reason. This means either that the parents have a debt to pay to the child who is coming through them, or else that the child itself has a debt to pay to the parents who have conceived it. This can either be the result of actions in previous lives or it can be the offering of the child to help the parents to learn certain lessons by coming through them, even if the child has not known the parents in other lives. The soul of the child is exemplifying the lesson of this planet, sacrificial service, even before it enters into matter. It agrees to help its parents to learn certain lessons, and so comes through them even though it has no lessons itself to learn from them. Likewise, two evolved parents can agree to let a soul come through them which has no debt to them, or them to it, but which through past experiences, usually unhappy, needs the benefit of balanced parents to experience certain lessons in its life. So the two spiritual parents agree to allow this soul to come through them: again a sacrifice.

The third division of birth is that which unfortunately contains the largest number of children born on this Earth. It is the result of Natural Law: namely, that when man and woman cohabit, depending on the functions of their bodies, which are again ordered by Natural Law, they will create. They will create not because they desire it but because they cannot control the functions of their bodies. In your World today it is considered natural for every married couple to have children. A woman is not considered to have fulfilled herself unless she has had at least one or two children. How wrong this is! To have children is not, as is so often imagined, the sole function of womanhood. Women carry the child: that is true. They give birth to the child, but that is not their sole function in incarnating on this planet. They are the balance for the male: that is their true reason for being here. They are the wisdom aspect to balance the power of the male, and a woman can fulfil herself completely without having children by showing and using the wisdom that she possesses to the full. If women had only their destined children the World would not be as over-populated as it is today, and you would not have all the problems associated with too large a population: the shortage of food and raw materials, and the wars caused by Man trying to acquire new lands to accommodate his people. All these

24

problems, basically, are caused by the one root problem, and that is too many people. Again, too many people strain the natural resources of the Earth and destroy the balance that Natural Law strives to preserve. In that Man is too populous he affects the Animal and the Vegetable Kingdoms as well. Man's imbalance leads to imbalance in them too.

So a birth, as you know it, should only be a destined birth. It is hard to believe, but it is true. This means that a man and a woman should come together only when they are sufficiently inspired by Divine Will, when they know that the time has come for them to bring into matter this child that they have agreed upon. Only then do they cohabit and unite the seeds which will produce this spirit child. Inspired by Divine Will, inspired to conceive at the right time, conception is assured. There is no need to worry about whether it is the correct time to conceive a child or not, whether it will be born at the correct time or not, because falling within Natural Law there will be no failure.

The soul, then, which has decided to incarnate has already asked and been accepted by the souls of its intended parents in matter. Before the time of conception, because it knows when it is to be conceived, it draws close through its astral body to the aura of the Earth, and in particular to the auras of its parents. It awaits in its astral form its moment of conception. It watches its intended parents as they live their lives in matter. At the moment of conception the three souls unite on the astral plane. It is rather like a reunion, a time of celebration. But there are very few people in your World today who can say when their children were conceived. They do not know because they are not aware of the importance and significance of this moment. Every parent knows the moment of birth, but only a few know the moment of conception. How strange that so important an event should remain lost to Man. In the New Age to come Man will become aware of this: it is just as important as the birth.

At the moment of conception, therefore, this reunion of the souls takes place. A very small fraction of the soul that is to be born thereafter resides within the seed of that union. During the following months, as the body of the unborn child grows within the mother's womb, so that small fraction of the soul begins to increase until, at the moment of birth, one seventh of the soul is in the child's body. At the moment of birth, as the child leaves the aura of the mother and its cord is cut, through the ether to that

25

child comes the Divine Spark which energises the child and starts it on its path. The soul has begun to fulfil its destiny and the lessons which have to be learned are now set in motion. The life which that soul has agreed to lead has now begun.

Many people today ask why birth for some is a happy event and for others a tragedy, why some have perfect children and others do not, why some who seek boys have girls and why some who seek girls have boys. Why cannot Man decide and produce what he wants? All these questions involve an understanding of Natural Law. As you are, so you will create. A balanced marriage will produce a balanced child. The way of life that the parents have lived in their present incarnation will affect their child. That is The Law. The way the parents live while the child is being formed also affects it. That is The Law also, for the child is formed while in the mother's womb from the vibrations of both parents. It gets its shape and its earthly characteristics from its parents while it is being carried in the womb. If the parents live a balanced life throughout the pregnancy a balanced child will result, and by balanced I mean balanced in physical terms, for the parents cannot influence the child's soul or its associated personality. They are unique to the child, but its physical body and associated characteristics they can, and do, influence. Therefore, if a soul wishes to acquire certain characteristics in order to learn certain lessons, and I am thinking now in terms of race, colour or creed, then it will choose its parents most carefully to ensure that it will incarnate into conditions where it can learn the lessons it has to learn.

Man must learn that nothing happens by chance: there is no such thing as luck. If one mother has a beautiful child and another does not, then look for the reason. At the moment of conception that child was perfect: it had to be. That is The Law. What has changed it has happened during the nine months whilst it was being formed in the womb. All children should be born perfect in form, for it requires a perfect body to fulfil a destiny. Only on very rare occasions does a soul deliberately choose to incarnate with a physical deformity, and when I use the word deformity I do not mean it to include those babies who you call mongoloid: that is not a deformity. Children born with deformities usually have acquired them because of the parents' behaviour. There are, however, a few instances when a child is born deformed for karmic reasons, either because that particular child has to learn the lessons associated with a deformed body, or else because the parents do.

The difficulties that some mothers experience in trying to have children in your World today is because they should not be having them. The vast lengths to which your scientists go to ensure that women have children is breaking Natural Law. If a couple cannot produce a child in natural union then that is what is intended. To artificially conceive an unspiritual child through the use of drugs or other such means is totally wrong and opposes Natural Law, and no spiritual, or destined, child will result from such a conception. You would be interested if you could see these children who have been artificially conceived by the time they reach the age of thirty-three.

As with all forms of evolution, the more advanced one becomes the more one is aware of, and obeys, Natural Law, and so children born through evolved souls are usually evolved themselves. Natural Law decrees that evolved souls cannot be born through unevolved parents and, of course, evolved parents do not normally have unevolved souls. However, on a few rare occasions evolved parents will make a sacrifice and allow an unevolved soul to come through them in order to help that soul to learn a lesson it has failed to learn in previous lives, or to help it onto a new evolutionary spiral.

Mongoloid children, as I mentioned earlier, are not deformed. They are the first incarnation of a soul on the surface of this planet. They have evolved from another planet, the one below the Earth in evolution, and have fully learned the lessons of that planet. Now they are appearing on the second rung of the ladder of evolution as they incarnate on this Earth, and so they appear in the form to which they have evolved in their previous lives. The soul builds a mongoloid body because it is the most evolved body that its consciousness knows: the soul knows no better. Then the soul lives on the surface of this planet for its first incarnation and is introduced to factors it has not yet met — such as light, colour and emotion. It records these factors so that when it incarnates a second time it remembers what it has learned and adjusts its concept of the perfect body. Therefore the vehicle which the soul chooses for its second incarnation will be different to that of its first. This refining process will go on for many lives until it evolves the body most desirable for this planet.

Birth, like death, is a transition. For the soul it is merely a changing of bodies: no more, no less. As death is going to sleep, so birth is waking up. You have done it many time and will doubtless do it many more. Birth, as opposed to death, is significant only in that it is the beginning of an incarnation rather than the end. It is the beginning of the cycle of life rather than the end. As you enter into the world of matter you enter full of hope for all that is to be achieved and learned in that life ahead of you. You enter full of excitement for the life that is to be led and to be experienced. Your soul enters with the knowledge of all that is to happen to you if you walk your true path. It is this air of excitement, of anticipation, which the parents catch. It is, of course, an emotional moment when one has one's child and brings into reality what one has desired and longed for in one's dreams. The excitement of birth, however, is not purely for the parents: it is also for the child, for that spark of Infinite Spirit as it starts its path, in pure form, as yet unsullied by the personality. It is beginning its walk in life. It is ever hopeful and full of anticipation for the joy of the life that is to come.

THE CYCLE OF LIFE
LIFE

As I have already talked about the transitions which occur at either end of life, namely birth and death, let us now consider life itself. Life does not apply only to the period which exists between birth and death whilst you live in your physical body on the surface of this planet, for life is eternal. Life does not cease when you die, it does not begin when you are born. Although most people are not aware of them, there are seven stratas of life, and you live on these stratas in seven different bodies. Most of you are, of course, aware of only your lowest body — the physical — and therefore you cannot conceive of life in another body on another level. You are not aware of the fact that you do indeed live on other levels of existence even whilst you are in your physical body, and that when you leave it at the end of your incarnation in matter you simply move to another body, to another life. Life does not stop when you die: death is merely a transition into another body and a continuation of life on another plane of existence.

Where Man has gone wrong today, and in this he has been encouraged by many of the World's religions, is in that either he believes that he has only one life and that that life can exist only on the surface of the Earth, or he believes in reincarnation, or he hopes that after death he will reside in some benevolent place called 'Heaven'. If you think in such terms, then it must affect your attitudes and beliefs to a considerable extent. If you think that what you are doing is never to be repeated and will pass away forever, that there is only one life and, therefore, that you must get the most out of it even at the expense of your fellow-men, then this will undoubtedly affect your attitude towards life. Today, therefore, we find Man living on the Earth basing his whole attitude to life on wrong beliefs, leading in turn to a whole pattern of wrong thinking and wrong action which his religious leaders should, but do not, correct.

Like everything that exists in the Cosmos, life is planned. What you call destiny exists on all levels of expression. You have a destiny in your physical body, you have a destiny in your astral body, and so on. On whatever level you exist, in whatever body you exist, according to your evolution you have a destiny to fulfil. This destiny is decided by your soul before it incarnates into a particular body. Let us take the example of the physical body, which is the body of which people are most aware. Before you incarnate you decide on your destiny, and the fulfillment of that destiny is the purpose of your life in the physical. Now you may well say, "Why do I incarnate?" That is a different question altogether. You incarnate with a destiny designed to teach you certain lessons, and to enable you to repay debts incurred in other lives. Depending on the destiny you have to fulfil, you choose the year and the time of your birth, the country of your birth and your parents. When you are born, the destiny of your life begins. When you die and return to another body you begin another destiny in that body until such time as you are reborn again in yet another physical body. Destiny is not applicable only to living on the surface of the Earth. Everything that exists has a destiny, a life, a purpose for existing. You are born to fulfil your destiny, but because of the stage of most people's evolution very few are aware of what their destiny is. Only a few, when they have reached a certain stage of spiritual development, begin to become aware of what it is.

To many, then, destiny is an unseen force. Your destiny is controlled by your soul which is always struggling to maintain you on the path which it agreed to follow before it incarnated on the Earth. Your destiny path in life could perhaps be likened to a journey around the surface of the Earth. You are born, shall we say, in England, and during the course of your life on the surface of the Earth you have to travel around it completely and arrive back in England where you were born. Now obviously your soul would desire that you follow a previously planned path around the Earth in order to arrive back where you started. If you could listen to your soul and be ruled by it you would follow that path, but because you are not, and because you have that divine gift of free choice, you can go wherever you choose. From your start in England you may follow whatever path you desire. You may even go backwards, which means you have to return to where you began in order to begin your path in life. Many people do this.

Now, obviously, as you wander from your paths the more aware of you will begin to feel certain subtle influences on your lives. You will feel that you are not doing what you should be doing, that you are not living where you should be living, and you will respond to that wisdom and return to your path. If you do not, then perhaps warnings will be given by your soul and by the Guides and Masters who look after you while you are on this Earth, and these you may heed. Normally, an evolved soul is sufficiently aware of its destiny not to drift too far away from its path. However, a young soul which has much to learn, having free choice, can proceed where it desires hence, no matter what restrictions are placed upon it, it throws them aside because it does not wish to respond to guidance. Now for a young soul this does not matter, because whatever path it treads to get back to that point from which it started would mean that lessons were being learned. Some souls never return to their paths: they go so far from their destiny paths that they cannot regain them again in their present life-times. That being the case, when the soul, in consultation with the Higher Masters, decides that no more can be learned, it then completes the transition of death into another body and another destiny in order to prepare itself for another incarnation. That soul loses nothing because the experience of the transition of death when it is away from its destiny path has a very strong influence upon it. It takes many incarnations to balance out that experience.

All of you, then, incarnate to experience physical life and to learn certain lessons. These lessons may be ones you are learning for the first time or they may be lessons that you failed to learn in other lives. They may be the result of powers you have misused in other lives which you have to learn to use correctly in this life. As you proceed along your destiny path you will meet certain people, souls who you have agreed to meet, for the purpose of paying off karmic debts. However, do not think that all relationships in life are karmic, for they are not. Many relationships are there for the development of the souls in unison, each having something to give to the other. For most people there will be marriage and, for some, children. This again is all planned. Your partner in marriage is chosen by your soul before you incarnate. Your children, too, are chosen. If you follow your destiny path, everything in your life will have been planned.

Throughout your early years you are an infant helpless in your parents' arms. Unlike animals, human beings take a long time to mature. Indeed, almost a third of an average lifespan is spent in just preparing for life. Gradually, throughout the early years, as the body grows and the capacity of the mind and brain develop, so the soul capacity is increased until, by the age of eleven, in most children the soul is fully inside the body for that incarnation. Until that age the soul can still, if it so desires, if it feels that certain factors are not desirable, terminate that incarnation. But once the soul is fully inside the body, beyond the age of eleven, then it is committed to that life, that destiny, and the lessons which must be learned from it. After the age of eleven a child then has ten years until the age of twenty-one for it to develop fully the capacity of its physical body in every respect so that it is ready to learn the lessons which must be learned from its life. Obviously it will learn many lessons in the art of living before the age of twenty-one. It will learn the laws of the society in which it lives and how to live with its fellow-men, but in actual fact it will not learn many of the real lessons of life, many Natural Laws, many Spiritual Laws, until it is past the age of twenty-one. Some evolved souls may, however, start to learn before this age, some from the age of eleven onwards, but most souls do not learn the lessons of life until they are past the age of twenty-one. They are given these ten years to develop their bodies to their full potential, to develop their minds, their brains, their hands and the facilities for the lives which they are to lead. It is a period of preparation for life. When the age of twenty-one is reached a person is then assumed by Natural Law to be at full potential, the soul is ready to learn the lessons it has incarnated to learn, and from that moment onwards the actions of that soul are permanently written in the Book of Records and cannot be erased.

The nature of the lessons and experiences which are to be learned during the life are decided by the actual evolution of the soul. If a person follows his spiritual path certain power centres within the body will develop and open, doing so on average every ten years, provided that the soul has coped satisfactorily with the source of power opened ten years earlier. So, during one's twenty-first year a power centre is opened which the soul then has to learn to master and use. If the soul masters it then it will progress to the next power source; if the soul does not, a halt is called until it has learned to use it. Some souls never open more than one power centre in an incarnation. Now depending on which power centre you have opened, you have to learn the lessons of that centre, because lessons and experiences are associated with the centres in the body. When you meet with these lessons, if you understand and accept them then you progress onward and upward, but if a lesson is not learned it is repeated.

Obviously when I use the word 'lesson' I do not mean a lesson as it is held in a classroom, but rather something which could perhaps be best described by the term 'soul-experience'. By this I mean that if, for example, you have to learn that your parents who allowed you to come into matter, who made that sacrifice, who were responsible for your upbringing, who have given so much of their time and love to you, as they grow old need that same love and care and protection which they gave you in your childhood, then this soul-experience, or lesson, will be presented to you in the form of you being required to help your own father or mother. This is what I mean by a soul-experience or lesson. One must learn to give as much as one takes, and as your parents have given you love and protection, so you must now give them the same love and protection in their old age. Another lesson you may have to learn is that of being poor and of living in poverty, without greed for money, without stealing from others who have it, accepting the state of poverty and realising that poverty is merely an earthly value, and that provided one has faith and that one's body is in good health it is only a state of mind. Another lesson you may have to learn is that of being rich. The lesson of wealth is a difficult lesson to learn, for with wealth inevitably goes the responsibility for the destinies and karma of people, and perhaps even countries.

So these are the lessons of which I talk, and as you live life so you will meet with them according to the path you have chosen for yourself. Normally, unless karma has been incurred in the life in which you are now living, by the time you reach the age of fifty-five you will have learned the lessons you came to learn, and from that age onwards you will then be giving back to the World that which has been given to you in your first fifty-five years. You will become a teacher, teaching what you have learned in life to the young and to your fellow-men. You will be teaching your soul-experiences to those around you, and helping others. Again, certain power centres will be opened to enable you to do this. If you do not reach this stage, then the appropriate power centre is not opened and you do not become a teacher. But normally from around the age of fifty-five onwards you open up this power centre and the 'wisdom of the old', as it is called, is revealed. You continue on this path, teaching to the world, still learning the lessons which you have to learn about teaching, until you reach the age when you agreed to leave the physical plane. On reaching the stage when you have achieved what you set out to achieve in your destiny, when you have arrived back at the point from which you started, the full circle is made and you then return to another body.

Now Man should normally live out his expected life-span, but as he has free choice he can shorten that life considerably. He can shorten it through the abuse of his body, by what he eats or drinks, by how he lives or where he lives. If he does this, then a karmic debt has been created. Unless you have to learn the lessons of living in a deformed or imperfect body you are given a perfect body at birth, and you should return an equally perfect body to your Creator when, at death, you transition into another body. That is The Law. The body is the temple of the soul, and any abuse of the body is also an abuse of that spark of Infinite Spirit within you.

If you are in the least spiritually aware you will follow the life that was destined for you. You will fulful the destiny to which you agreed before you incarnated into a physical body. You will accomplish what you set out to achieve. However, in the world in which you live today many of the souls who incarnate into matter do not achieve their destinies — they do not live to the age they should and they do not learn the lessons they came down to learn. Unfortunately, the conditions which exist on your planet at this time are such that the search for, and the following of, one's destiny, is difficult. As materialism now controls every facet of life, it has transformed the meaning of life. Life for most people today means material things, and it will require the removal of material things before Man understands the true meaning of life. Life is not possessing, life is not owning, life is not achieving something at the expense of your fellow-men. Life is love — sacrificial love. Life is giving rather than taking. Life is helping rather than ignoring. Life is blessing rather than cursing. Life is sacrificing rather than seizing. Life is thinking of your fellow-men before yourself. If you eliminate the self, you are living life. That is why you are here in matter on this planet. To learn to be selfless is the lesson, the basic lesson amongst the many little ones, that you all have to learn as you incarnate on this Earth.

So now take stock of your life. Consider according to your earthly age where you are in life, what you have done, what you have yet to achieve and what is expected of you — your soul knows if you will but listen to it. Look for the true meaning of life in everything which you do and say, and, finally, remember that this life which you lead is not the totality of your existence. Try to be aware of your life at this moment, of your life on levels of existence beyond the physical, and try to follow the example that has been given to you by the great Masters who have incarnated on Earth. See in their lives the soul expression which you should strive to attain.

UNIVERSAL MAN

The American astronauts, during their journeys to and from the Moon, had the privilege of viewing the planet Earth from their space craft. They took a remarkable series of photographs with the result that the people on the Earth could be aware, as they were, of the beauty and splendour of the Earth. It would be true to say that, without exception, all the astronauts were greatly affected by the sight of the Earth as they viewed it from a distance. The view of the Earth in totality, no matter whether it was from the Moon itself or from a space craft travelling to or from the Moon, had a profound effect upon all of them, and on their return to the Earth many of them were changed men. If it were possible for you to view the Earth from a distance, or even for you to be able to stand outside your own physical body, you would probably obtain a new perspective, a new vision, not only of the Earth's and your body's purpose but also of their perfectness and of their beauty, and from that you might realise more of the nature and purpose of their Creator.

Looking at the Earth from a distance you would be forced to look at it as a single unit. You would not think of the individual countries that you knew existed on its surface but rather of the Earth as a whole, comparable with the other planets, the other stars and the other universes that you could see around you. You might almost consider yourself a god, for you would be standing above all the countries of the World, all the happenings, all the events that were taking place, and then, perhaps, you would begin to realise how those Higher Beings who control the destiny of this Earth look down on it in a similar fashion. They too see the perfectness of the Earth. They see its beauty. They feel the emanation of its expression: Universal Love. However, as you descended towards its surface, so the Earth, which before you could see as a single unit, would now have to be split up into segments and eventually into continents. Soon you would begin to see only individual countries and to think only in terms of those countries. The vision of the whole would be lost and you would once more return to your physical casing with its limited vision.

Man is born on the surface of the Earth with an individualised consciousness. When, after many incarnations on the one planet within the Solar Body which is less evolved than the Earth, Man first incarnates on the Earth, he struggles to establish his identity in the human physical body. Once he has established his own individuality, his personality, he then has to learn to control it. Man has to learn to control his own will and to subjugate it to the will of his Creator in order to fulfil the destiny of the Earth. The basic lesson which Man has to learn is to sacrifice the self, his own individuality, to sacrifice his personal desires and wants, and to consider the other people around him, not only in his own country but in the World as a whole. He has to learn to think not only of his own race, of his own creed, of his own part of the Earth, but of the Earth as a whole. It is in this particular field that Man experiences the utmost difficulty for, at present, although Man has firmly established his individuality, he finds it very hard to sacrifice that individuality for people around him, still less for his country, and even less for the World.

Great motivation is needed to make Man unite together, to make him think of his country as a single unit and be prepared to sacrifice his self for his country. This usually occurs only in times of conflict, of war, when the emotion known as patriotism moves Man to think not of himself but of his country, and to join together with his fellow country-men to defend his country in the face of aggression. Indeed, were it not for this emotion of patriotism he would not unite together. In times of peace Man finds it difficult to make the sacrifice of his individuality even for his neighbours, let alone for his country.

If Man will not look after the people in his own country then, of course, he will not concern himself with those who live in other countries, and no matter what reports he hears of disasters, such as famines or earthquakes, he will usually ignore those events which are far removed from his own country. Because they are not happening to him or to his country, he thinks they are not his concern. This is one of the great lessons which Man has to learn, and until he has learnt the lesson of total responsibility for every human being who lives on this planet, no matter what their country or their creed, he will not advance along the path to higher things, to Mastership. Man has to learn to sacrifice, to help all the people who live on the surface of this Earth, to give freely no matter what the cost and to share what his country has with the countries that do not. Remember that matter does not belong to Man. Just because one country is capable of growing food and another country is not that does not mean that all food belongs to the country that grows it, for all the countries in the World cannot grow food and it is the duty of those who can to share with those who cannot.

As he advances along his path Man has to learn to sacrifice the self, firstly for his community, then for his country, then for his race, and finally for the Earth. It is only when Man regards himself not as an Englishman, a European or a white man, but as a man of the Earth, that he may be said to have truly evolved to his Earthly potential. When you can say that you are a man of the Earth, that you regard every man on this Earth, no matter what his colour or his creed, as your equal, when you show as much responsibility towards him as you do to your own family, then it may be said that you have progressed to the level of an evolved soul.

All of you must try to think not in terms of division, of comparing one country with another, one way of life with another, one race with another. Try not to divide the World into countries and races. Try not to compare national customs and characteristics but regard every human being as an individual spark of your Creator, the equal of you in every respect, merely walking along a different path in life. Remember that all of you, being at different points of consciousness, chose to incarnate onto the Earth into varying families, into varying ways of life, into varying countries, into varying races, in order to experience the lessons and the vibrations of those countries and of those races. You chose all these factors before you incarnated knowing that you would advance your consciousness to a greater understanding along the path that you had chosen. The path that is right for one soul is not necessarily right for another.

Where Man goes so wrong today is in his thinking that one race is superior to another, that one race is more civilised than another. The countries in the World today that are more advanced technologically consider themselves to be the more civilised countries, and they seek to impose their way of life, their conditions of life, upon all the other countries in the World. No country, no person, has the right to impose their will, their way of life, upon another no matter how correct they might think their way of life to be and how wrong they think another's is. It is up to the individual countries and their inhabitants to change of their own free choice without the interference of any other country.

The Masters who watch over you as you live in a physical body on Earth do not interfere with you. They know when you are wrong, when you make mistakes, but they let you make those mistakes, they let you advance your consciousness through your own actions and decisions. There is no 'Big Brother' to come and make you do something in the correct way. So, mindful of the wisdom of those more evolved Beings who allow you to act as you choose, allow other countries to make their own decisions too.

When he first incarnates on this Earth Man will obviously not exhibit as high a state of consciousness and evolution as those who have incarnated for many thousands of lives. Therefore do not try to impose on unevolved Man a way of life that he does not understand, comprehend or even need. Respect the individuality of all men. Regard them as your brothers and help them as best you can. Ensure that with the responsibility of a more evolved soul you help them as befits their point of evolution and that in no way do you disrupt their path towards consciousness.

One of the greatest errors of the nineteenth and twentieth centuries has been the imposing of western ideas, western religions, western beliefs, on the natives, as they were called, of the colonised countries. Great karma has resulted, which will have to be repaid. Just as individuals incarnate with a destiny, so do countries, and just as individuals create karma for themselves, so do countries. That is why, as a whole, some countries suffer and others do not, why some countries are involved in great wars and others are not. The Law of Karma applies as much to countries as it does to individuals, and therefore the effect of what a country does in one generation will be experienced by those who live in the next. For example, the present generation of Americans is having to pay the karma for the error of those who shipped many thousands of black slaves from the coast of Africa to America, who took them away from their true environment, from the country of their evolution, and placed them in a false and hostile environment.

39

I mentioned earlier that the one force which can seemingly unite people in time of war is the emotion known as patriotism. In war, people are prepared to make great sacrifices for their country. They are, perhaps, not prepared to die for much else, but they will sacrifice their lives to preserve their country. Patriotism, like a diamond, has many facets, many aspects. I am not going to say that patriotism is an undesirable emotion, although one can point to many examples where it has been abused and used to persuade people into sacrificing their lives in the name of their country. It is interesting to note, though, that the people who sacrificed their lives usually believed in the cause for which they were fighting. They died, believing in their cause or their country, even though others standing outside the actual conflict could see the error in the actions of those countries who were fighting.

Patriotism, sometimes called nationalism, has often been used as an excuse for much evil. When a country sets out to conquer another country, to enlarge its empire, to gain new possessions, the emotion of patriotism is often generated. You can kill for your country, you are told, because your country demands it. It is not your responsibility. You are only doing what is expected of you. You are fighting for your country. Likewise, when a country is being attacked, the men and women of that country, who normally would not fight or kill anyone, unite together and are prepared to kill to defend it. They can now justify what, before, they would never have considered or approved of. Moreover, the few people who say they are not prepared to fight, the people whom you call conscientious objectors, people who are not prepared to kill, are despised and held up as objects of ridicule and, indeed, are usually imprisoned.

You will judge patriotism according to the level of your soul-evolution. If you are truly an evolved soul and recognise the Earth as a whole and all the peoples on it as one, then you will not be influenced by that emotion. You will not be influenced by lower feelings of patriotism and nationalism, especially when they are used as a means of comparing one race with another, of placing one country above another, of dividing men, of creating hatred and distrust between them.

You will view the emotion of patriotism according to your level of consciousness. If you cannot identify with the Earth as a whole, with your Creator and with the Higher Beings who influence this Earth, then you will of course try to identify with your country. You will say that you are an Englishman, a Frenchman or an American, and that will give you a feeling of security, of belonging. Yet, even within a country, you can still have people who regard themselves as not belonging to that country but only to a small part of it. They will say that they come from Wales or Scotland, from the Northern or the Southern States of America, from the East or the West coast. They will think of themselves as belonging only to the smaller unit and will not recognise the whole. You can also have people who regard themselves as belonging only to a city. You can even find people who will not identify beyond their own family.

So you see how important it is that, whilst recognising the significance of the individuality of each and every being, you should also recognise that together you form a greater whole. Every one of you should look at what you consider to be the whole and then take one step further beyond that, for as you evolve you will realise that your concept of the whole is limited. As you advance so you will begin to think not of your town, of your state, of your country, of your race, but of your Earth, and when you think of your Earth then you will begin to think of the Solar System and of your Creator, and of Solar Systems beyond it.

Realise that World Government actually exists within your Solar Body. The other members of the Solar Body practise World Government. Because Man on the Earth has not yet evolved to the required state of consciousness he will not, and cannot, participate in it. He is still struggling to identify as a one, to realise that he is a one. When that day comes when the Earth as a whole unites in one harmonious vibration and takes its seat in the Chamber of the Representatives of the Solar Body, then it will be fulfilling the purpose which its Creator intended and will be displaying the power of its true vibration: Universal Love.

THE POSITION AND PURPOSE OF THE EARTH
IN YOUR SOLAR BODY

In this lecture I wish to talk about the position and purpose of the Earth in your Solar Body. The teachings which I am going to give you are very simple, so do not think that what I say represents all there is to know on the subject. I have greatly simplified them so that you may more easily understand, for this subject is a very complex one and unless you are very evolved and are aware of the Laws of Nature and of the Cosmos you will not readily appreciate all there is to know about your Earth.

Obviously, the Earth is the planet on which Man lives when he is in his physical body — but that is not its sole reason for being. The Earth is part of a much greater whole: the Solar Body. This Solar Body, like your own physical body, consists of various vital organs linked by matter. Within the human body are the major organs, of which you are aware, linked by the matter necessary to hold and sustain them while the body is alive: the tissue, the muscles, the bones, etc. Holding the organs of the Solar Body together is another form of matter which obviously does not take the form of the flesh and bones of the human body. The vibrations of which I am now talking are much higher and, therefore, these organs are encased in a much finer matter. If you could stand outside the Solar Body and were of a sufficient evolution to see, you would recognise the Solar Body from afar as an outline, a shape, just as you recognise a physical body on Earth. Within this Solar Body the vital organs are the twelve planets of your planetary system. Although some of them have still to be discovered, there are twelves planets in the Solar Body, and these correspond to the organs in your own physical body. Each of them has a vital function to play within the Solar Body.

One of the Natural Laws which will help you to understand what I am talking about can be summed up as, 'As above, so below'. This has many levels of meaning, but the important one in connection with this lecture is that everything is a replica of a larger design, only on a smaller scale. Within your own physical bodies exist living organisms, and just as you in your physical bodies live within the Solar Body so the Solar Body lives within what I will call a Galactical Body, and the Galactical Body lives within yet another Body beyond your comprehension. Everything is a replica of your physical body only on a smaller or larger scale.

In the same way that Man incarnates on the Earth to fulfil a destiny so the Solar Body also incarnates to fulfil a destiny. As Man incarnates and passes over into other bodies so does the Solar Body. The more evolved the vibration of a body the longer the incarnation of that body in spiritual time, and the less evolved the vibration the shorter the incarnation. Thus, on the planet within your Solar Body which is less evolved than the Earth, physical incarnations are much shorter than your normal three score years and ten, and on the more evolved planets within the Solar Body the souls incarnate for much longer.

In the same way that Man is evolving so are the beings living on the other planets within the Solar Body, and just as you all evolve so does the whole, the Solar Body. However, unless all the organs of the Solar Body evolve together the Solar Body itself cannot evolve. As you in your physical bodies strive to become more aware, and try to refine your bodies and raise your vibrations, so you have to harmonise the organs within your bodies. It is no good having some organs vibrating at a higher frequency than the others for, if they do, disharmony and imbalance occur. So with the Solar Body there must also be harmony and balance, with all the organs evolving at the same rate.

What is happening at present, however, is that all the other organs in the Solar Body are evolving according to The Plan, but, alas, the Earth is not. It is the Earth which is slowing up the progress of the Solar Body, and so the Masters who are responsible for the evolution of the Solar Body, knowing the conditions of the Earth, are trying to heal the Earth. As you would treat a part of your physical body which is ill, so they are seeking to treat the Earth so that it may return to its true path, evolve at a higher rate and maintain its correct place in relation to the other organs of the Solar Body. Just as a soul evolves by raising its vibrations, so, in order to quicken the Earth and to aid in its evolution, the Masters responsible for the evolution of the Solar Body are to raise the vibrations of the Earth by uprighting it

43

on its axis and allowing it to spin faster. Of course, as you must realise, this event will necessitate changes in the structure of life on the Earth.

When you are incarnating in a physical body your spirit dwells within your heart. In the Solar Body, the Sun is the equivalent of your heart, and within the Sun dwells the spirit of your Solar Logos. It is He Who you would call in your earthly terms 'God'. Although He is, obviously, a very evolved and special Being, in the chain of evolution even He is only a small part of a still more evolved Body, and He in turn would look to the centre or the heart of that Body, the 'God' who He strives to emulate. Life is an ever upward spiral interlocking between the various bodies and their degrees of vibration, but for the moment I feel we need concern ourselves only with your little Solar Body. It is hard for Man in his physical casing to be aware of anything beyond his Earth. He can perhaps just conceive of the planets, but what is beyond is incomprehensible to him. It is not for me to reveal what exists beyond Man's comprehension except to say that something does exist and that it is his birthright to discover it when he has evolved further.

So the organs in your Solar Body are the planets. As with the organs in your physical body so the organs in the Solar Body perform a specific function and, just as your heart is different from your kidneys, so the Sun is different from Venus. The Solar Body could not exist without each of them functioning and, at the moment, all the planets are functioning efficiently except for the Earth. Each of the planets has a particular vibration which it radiates onto all the other parts of the Solar Body. You will discover, in time, the power or the ray of each planet. Although the Earth itself has a power which it radiates onto the other members of the Solar Body at the moment that power is very weak.

In the same way that Man incarnates on the Earth and at death passes into another body so do the beings who inhabit the other planets. They incarnate into matter, not matter as it exists on the Earth but into matter according to the nature of their planet, and, after a period of spiritual time, they too transition into another body and move onto another level of existence. All the beings who dwell on the other planets may, if they are evolved enough, move from planet to planet, but the structure of the Solar Body precludes them from moving outside that Body. They can move only within the Solar Body. There is only one being who can leave the Solar Body, and that is the Solar Logos, your 'God'. This ensures that no unevolved vibrations can spread to where they could do harm in the Universe.

I ask you, therefore, not to think of Man only in terms of his incarnating in a physical body on the planet Earth, then passing into a higher body and then incarnating again, but to think of Man in terms of his being a part of a whole, as a part of the Earth. Think of all the millions of souls who exist either in physical or in higher bodies as being part of the Earth, and of the Earth in its turn as being part of a greater whole which is more important than Man and his little Earth. Although because of its destiny and of its higher rate of vibration the soul in your physical body is of more importance than, shall I say, your kidneys, nevertheless Man cannot live without his kidneys. They are indispensable to one another. You need the lower vibration to allow the higher one to fulfil itself. In the same way the Earth is needed by the Solar Body so that the Solar Body may fulfil its destiny.

When you go outside at night and look up at the sky do not just think that space is a meaningless void of stars and planets. They are bodies like your own, and what you see, apart from the planets, are the Suns, the Lords, of countless Solar Bodies. It is rather like you standing in front of a large crowd and looking at the people in it yet seeing only their souls. That is what happens when you look into space although, of course, your view of space is limited to what you can see with the physical eye. Everything is in its place. Everything is in The Plan. Everything is evolving. I do not expect Man to comprehend the nature of what he sees in space: I ask only that he becomes aware of its existence and purpose and that, in his ignorance, he does not harm other members of the Solar Body of whom he is not aware.

At present there exists on the Earth a feeling of supreme egoism. Man believes that he is perfection and that, because the conditions on the planets cannot sustain life in a physical body as he knows it, only an inferior form of life can exist on them, whereas, in fact, Man's physical body is the second lowest form of life in the Solar Body, for ten of the planets are more evolved than the Earth. The physical body in which Man lives whilst on Earth is a wonderful body. It is a replica of the Solar Body. It is magnificent in its design and construction, but it has its limitations which you will gradually discover as you become

45

spiritually aware. It is a very dense body. It is a limiting body, for you cannot live in it outside the atmosphere of the Earth. Above all, it is subject to forces to which your higher bodies are not, such as the personality and the physical emotions. The beings who live on the other planets do not have physical bodies like your own. They have, with the one exception, all evolved further than the souls on Earth and have passed the stage of using physical bodies. They live on far higher levels, although, if they so desire, they can present themselves in a physical body. However, the reasons for doing this are very special and it happens very infrequently.

Man, at present, believes himself to be king of all he surveys, and because of his own imbalance, caused by material growth at the expense of spiritual advancement, he thinks that in his pioneering efforts in space he is benefitting Mankind whereas, in reality, he is not. He is incurring karma for the Earth which will have to be repaid, for when he fires his space probes and rockets at the planets he is harming the other members of the Solar Body. The impact of Man's rockets on the Moon, for example, threatens the existence of the beings living in the Moon who are there to be of service to him. What Man does, in his ignorance, is to risk the very structure of the Solar Body. He does this without even considering his motives for going into space. It is right that he should look into space and inquire about the nature of the other planets, the other parts of the Solar Body, but there is no need for him to go there or to send his space ships to find out. That is not the way to meet the other members of the Solar Body. Man can do that on the higher levels of existence through his higher bodies. Finally, is it not hypocritical of Man to spend his energy and time and money on sending rockets into space when so much needs to be done on his own Earth?

I will conclude by asking you not to think of the planets and of space as a mystery. They are as real as the people around you in your everyday life. Do not condition yourselves to purely earthly terms. What you see, what you feel, what you think, is entirely related to your own environment and is peculiar to the Earth alone and, as it is the Earth, is of a very low vibration. Let us hope that Man soon recognises his place in the evolving pattern, that he struggles to regain his position in the Solar Body and that he once again becomes the force for good that he should be. That is what the Higher Vibrations are striving to achieve by coming to the Earth in the way that they do: to inspire Man to correct himself.

ASTROLOGY

In this lecture I wish to say a few words about the science of astrology. I use the word science, although on your Earth today there are few who would apply the term 'science' to this subject. Why is this? Firstly, you live, as you know, in a very materialistic Age. You have been through the Piscean Age and, as you now enter the Aquarian Age, so the traits, the habits and the ways of life of the Pisceans are still with you. The Piscean, if he could not see, touch, or otherwise obtain physical proof of something, was not easily convinced of its existence, and therefore his awareness of life was limited to the surroundings of his Earth. He might have been aware that the stars and the planets were above. He might have been inquisitive enough to wonder why they were there, to measure their brightness, to estimate their size, to compare one with another and to calculate their distance from the Earth using earthly measurements, but that was all. He did not, because he could not conceive of it, think of the influence that the vibrations of those orbs which he viewed from the Earth could have on him.

Nevertheless, there are some who live in this World today who, even though they were born in the Piscean Age, through the use of astrology in past lives have incarnated again in this life bringing with them that wisdom, that belief in the influence of the Cosmos. They have kept the science of astrology alive throughout their incarnations in the World during the past two thousand years for, truly, astrology has not been in the forefront of Man's consciousness during those years. Now, with the New Age dawning, things are to change, and astrology will once again take its correct place and assume its rightful importance alongside all the other factors in Man's life. Man will realise the importance of, the need for and the effect of astrology.

Let us begin then by trying to define what astrology is. Astrology is the science of the vibrations of the Cosmos on the

Earth. Everything that exists vibrates and, depending upon the strength of the source from which the vibration comes, the effect of that vibration is felt by everything within its range which is receptive to its frequency. Even as you sit reading these words you are being influenced not only by the other parts of your Solar Body, the planets, but by influences beyond them. The most recognisable influences which are felt on Earth are obviously the vibrations of the planets within your Solar Body.

The influences that come from the other planets of your Solar Body are important. You live within that body and, just as the organs of your own physical body affect you, so the organs of the Solar Body, the planets, affect the Earth most strongly. You are linked within the casing of the Solar Body and its influence, especially the influence of the Sun, the dwelling place of your Creator's spirit, is important. If the astrology of the ancients was known today Man would know, as is his birthright, the correct influences and the importance of the planets and the part that each of those organs plays in the Solar Body. He would know how, and when, they acted, the manner in which they acted and how their power and influence could be used or, if it was not desired, avoided. The true science of astrology disappeared centuries ago, and Man has to rediscover it in the New Age. This he will do.

Many people in your World today think of the most important part of astrology as being a means of foretelling the future. This is not so! It is only a very small part which Man, with his inate curiosity and because he lacks true spirituality and seeks to find answers without rather than within, seizes onto as a means of discovering his future. So perhaps we had better examine this approach to astrology.

The time when you are born is important. You are not born by chance. If the parents of the child permit it, and if modern medicine does not intervene, a child is born at a precise moment in time, in Solar time that is, not Earth time. That child, after it has evolved and grown to manhood or womanhood, will also die at a precise moment in Solar time, again, if Man does not intervene. The coming and going are important, and in as much as astrology, as you call it, defines them it is worthy of attention.

As you live each day of your life you are subject to the influences of your Solar Body. These can be forecast and mapped out. Your actual position on the Earth also affects the degree to which you receive the influences of the planets, and this too can be forecast. With regard to the mathematical side of astrology, Man can be fairly accurate and can predict the movements of the planets and stars around him. He can predict when they will appear and disappear, and when they will influence him. Man has advanced in this respect because it is the simple side of astrology. Where Man has not advanced is in his understanding of the powers, or influences, of the various celestial bodies, knowledge which is sometimes referred to as the Ancient Wisdom.

Now you will appreciate that astrology today, as it does not recognise the existence of twelve planets within the Solar Body, since Man still has to discover three of them, must be inaccurate. Some of the varying influences, the signs of the zodiac, as you call them, are in consequence attributed to wrong planets. There are twelve planets and there are twelve signs of the zodiac, one to each planet. You are born at a definite time depending upon the lesson which you wish to learn and the planetary influence which you are attempting to master in that incarnation. This influence will vary throughout the period of the zodiacal sign depending on whether you are born early or late in the period. At the beginning you are under the influence, to a degree, of the last sign and towards the end you are receiving the influence of the next.

Therefore when, before you incarnate into matter, you choose your birthday you choose not only the calendar day but also the astrological day in order to receive the influences you desire, for at the moment of birth through the ether there comes to the child not only the spark that starts its path in life but also the astrological influences of that moment in time. What Man today does not know are the actual influences of all the planets. He might understand some correctly, but not others. Therefore when he tries to cast a horoscope certain influences will be missing, but most important of all, he does not know of the influence of what I will call soul wisdom, by which I mean the evolution of the soul that is born, the lives experienced previously, the state of consciousness attained. As you can readily appreciate, you can have two people born at the same second in time alongside each other in the same room and yet they will both lead vastly different lives. How is this possible, you may ask, since they were both born under the same sign? You may now begin to appreciate how small the significance of the planets is in this respect and how much greater is the significance of the individual's consciousness. As you evolve and become more aware and are more receptive to the planets so you vibrate to them more fully. You become a finer instrument. A coarse instrument would be less aware of the power and would respond less. Consequently the use which you can make of planetary powers differs according to your point of consciousness.

Let us therefore place this aspect of astrology in its correct position. It can help you to predict the destiny of a person. It can help you to realise the influences under which you yourself vibrate and can point to certain significant periods in your lifetime, but it cannot tell you with any degree of accuracy.

As you live your life on the surface of the Earth you are subject to the influences of the planets and, here, Man can be more accurate in his predictions for, depending on your location on the Earth, as the planets come into view and vibrate their influence so their power will be felt. Man can predict the appearance of Mars and Venus, of Jupiter and Saturn, and he knows when they will shine upon him. If he knew their powers he could also say that he would be influenced between certain times, on certain days, by the powers of those planets. No matter what the soul consciousness of the individual, all are affected. People may not react in the same way to the powers, but they are all affected. So astrology, in this respect, can predict the pattern of the planets and the stars and the influences that they will have on Man. If he was to realise that the planets do have influences, if he was to learn about those influences, Man would be able to run his life more smoothly by anticipating, by using or by avoiding, if he so desired, the influences of the planets at certain times during the course of the year.

The one factor which I have not mentioned so far, as I do not wish to confuse what is already a slightly complicated subject, is the all important question of time. Now all astrology on the Earth is computed on Man's time. He bases his calendar year on the Earth revolving around the Sun and, as Man knows, this is not accurate. As he refines his measurement of time, so he has had to refine his year. Therefore in a subject so precise as astrology to use Man's time must lead to inaccuracies. Man's time is not true time or, as I would call it, spiritual time. If Man, who is perhaps aware that the Earth is quickening on its evolving spiral and that time is speeding up, could measure time correctly, he would know the true influence of the planets and could predict what is to happen. But, because he is unable to conceive of any time outside of Earth time, he is unable to do this. This again — the inability to see beyond his Earth — is a trait of the Piscean.

So, as you walk your path in life, it is important that you realise that the planets do influence you. Seek in your own meditation to find what the influences of the planets are; as knowledge is released to you seek to draw out the meaning and the influence of each planet. Then, when the almanac tells you that a planet is to appear, if you look for the influence, and expect it, you will find it and recognise it, and can then use it or avoid it as you so choose. But you must be aware of it and look for it. It is no good standing outside at night and saying "There is Venus; I wonder what it is doing to me", for truly it is doing very little to you!

Yet another factor which I have not mentioned so far is the influence of Solar Bodies beyond your own. Your Solar Body is influenced by other Solar Bodies which, as you are a part of your Solar Body, must, of course, also affect you. So you are subject not only to planetary influences but also to influences beyond the planets which, although Man is barely aware of them, are of just as much importance. When you consider the power of your Solar Logos, and as you look up in the sky and realise that even with your little physical eyes you can see thousands of Suns, you will begin to appreciate the complexity of astrology. It takes a great mind, an open mind, an inspired mind, to comprehend the nature, the boundaries, the importance and the correct use of astrology.

For the time being, therefore, you on Earth should concern yourselves with the most important influences on your physical body as you lead your everyday lives, and these are the influences of the Sun and the planets. Also, do not forget your own satellite, the Moon, which revolves around you, for it also influences you. It is difficult, I know, but try not to be conditioned by the particular power which Man has ascribed in the past to a planet. As you have been told many times, do not live in the past. The past is not necessarily correct. More evolved Man will see a more evolved influence. For example, if Man was to say that the influence or power of a planet was love, think of how many interpretations you all can place on the word love.

Remember that planetary influences, whilst indeed they have been responsible for some of the great happenings in your World, have also been wrongly attributed as being the cause of other events. Remember that astrology influences, but cannot change,

Man's will; it impels but does not compel, for you all have that divine gift of free choice. Remember that the influences of the planets are important. They do influence the glands and the spiritual centres in your body, they do affect your physical casing, they do affect your spiritual work and life, but, like any other powers that exist in the Cosmos, they have to be understood, learnt, tested and, moreover, invoked.

The problems that Man has in his little World today would be halved overnight if only he would understand the influences of the planets on him. If only Man would not scoff and make fun of the one source of knowledge that could truly help him, if only your governments, which spend so much money on making weapons, were to spend just a little on researching into the planets, not by sending rockets to them but by measuring their vibrations and their influence on the Earth, you would achieve a great deal. It is a fascinating Universe in which you live. It is so immense that you cannot conceive of it. You can hardly conceive of your Solar Body. You may, perhaps, in your more evolved bodies be aware of life on the other planets, but what lies beyond them? In astrology, if you did but know it, you have the key to Creation.

LOVE

In this lecture I wish to talk about what is, perhaps, the most magical and mysterious subject of the Western World — Love. If you were to ask any individual to define what love is, you would get many answers. Even evolved souls would have many ideas, and would express many degrees, of love, some of which would be due to their conditioning by the environment in which they lived, but only a few of which would truly reflect the correct interpretation of that word. You can no doubt think of many kinds of love. You love your husband. You love your country. You love your child. You love your food and drink. All these activities involve the use of the word love, and so perhaps we had better begin by examining the use which Man makes of this word.

You would perhaps agree that the use of the word love as applied to food and drink would not be correct, for after all these are personal likes, personal desires, and as such they are not worthy of being included under the term love. You like: it is a personal gratification, and that is not love. So one should not apply the word love to physical functions such as those which occur in your everyday life.

It can be said that a man loves his country, loves the area in which he lives or loves his house, but when one speaks of this kind of love is not this, again, a personal gratification of what one seeks and desires? You love a particular area or you love your country because it reflects the way of life that you like and with which you are content. If it was not as you desired, not as you wanted, you would not love it. Therefore this, again, would not be the correct use of the word love.

It can be said that a mother and a father love their children but, in reality, is this love? They have established a physical relationship and from this has come a child. But it is not their creation. It is not their child. It has come through them, and has honoured them with its presence. That is all. Just as any animal

53

looks after its own, a mother and a father look after their child. They feed, protect, educate and give it affection, but is that an act of love? No! A parent's love for their child is a love for creation. It is the recognition of perfection in creation before the child develops its personality and is influenced by physical life. It is easy to love a young child, but is it not more difficult to love a grown-up child which has developed its personality and knows what it does or does not want, and will not always comply with the parents' desires and wishes? The parents do not necessarily stop loving their child, but if they are honest with themselves they will admit that their love moderates with the child's growth. So perhaps here we have a clue as to what love really is. The love of the parents for their child is the love of perfect creation, the recognition within them, not by their personalities but by their souls, of a perfect spark of creation. It is the recognition of the power, or the love, of their Creator.

Let us now turn to the question of love between husband and wife, between brother and sister or between friend and friend; and you will notice that I include husband and wife in this group. May I say immediately that love, although your world today would have you think otherwise, is not what you call the sexual act. That has nothing to do with love whatsoever. The sexual act is not, and was not, intended to be love. It is simply a natural function intended solely for the procreation of children, for the bringing through of souls into physical matter. It is only your society today and Man's lesser self that have raised the sexual act up out of all proportion and have placed it upon the pedestal on which it now stands so that it governs many, many functions of society. The sexual act is not love, and anyone who thinks that it is is fooling themselves and should analyse it most carefully. However, a husband and wife can love each other, just as a brother and sister or two friends can love each other. Can there be degrees of love? Do you love completely or do you love with limitations? What is it that places these limitations? Why do you love someone with a greater intensity than you do another? What governs the degree of this intensity? Why should you love one person more than another? Let us examine this aspect of love a little more closely.

The same power of love can join together a man and a woman whether they be husband and wife, brother and sister or strangers who have met and grown to know one another. It can join together woman and woman, and man and man. Your society today would perhaps frown upon this, but there is nothing wrong in love between man and man, or between woman and woman. It can be just as strong, just as natural, just as binding, as love for the opposite sex. It is only Man who has placed a sexual connotation on the word love, and who seeks to limit love in this way. In the days of old, as is written in the Bible, David and Jonathan loved one another deeply, and nothing wrong was thought of this. However, today, if two men or two women love each other society frowns upon them, but, truly, it is possible and quite natural for two people to be together and to love one another without any physical relationship.

The fact that a brother loves a sister is not because they are brother and sister, for truly you can have a brother hating a sister. It is not the family link that creates the bond of love. Again, the fact that a man has married a woman does not automatically create love. Part of the mystique that your society today has created around the act of marriage is that there must be this magical expression of love. One must marry for love, you have been told, and if there is not love there should not be marriage. So everywhere young people are seeking love because they have been conditioned to think that love is the essential part of marriage. If you were to ask them what they were seeking they could not tell you, for truly love, as they would have it, does not exist in marriage and neither does it exist between brother and sister or between friends.

Here, may I mention two other aspects of love. You can say that you love God and that your God loves you. Again, the word love, but what a difference in the meaning of the word here. You could also say that you love life, the act of living, of being. The love for life is strong within all of you. So here again is a different aspect of love. What common factor is there, then, which ties together all these forms of love into one recognisable force? What is it that has established this belief in the power that you call love which can exist between the relationships that I have mentioned? Is it not the act of recognising what, for want of a better word, I will call the spirituality of the person with whom you have the relationship? Is it not the recognition of the reflection of your Logos, your Creator, in that person? By this, I do not mean that you love a person because he is good, or because he supposedly leads a spiritual life. That is not the quality of which I am talking. It is the recognition in a person of the very essence of our Creator, the very breath of His life and of that person's expression of his Creator's gift.

As you well know, a person can hurt you mentally or physically and yet you can still love that person. Such an act does not destroy the feeling, the recognition of what you see in that person. Two people may be said to be in love when they walk a common path with a spiritual recognition of each other. Two people walking for a moment in spiritual time, which may be an incarnation, a part of an incarnation or only a few days, can create the bond of love through their mutual recognition of that something which exists above and beyond the physical casing. It is the recognition of their Creator in each other.

As you come together to fulfil a common destiny, to fulfil a destined work, a destined deed, or as you come together to fulfil karma, love can be created. The very act of spiritual love does not require a reward, does not require a reply. True love, as it is known on this planet, is the giving of the self to another person, and in the giving of the self you are giving not of your personality but of your soul-consciousness. It is the true 'you' recognising in another person their soul quality so that, no matter what their little personality may do, or may seek to do, you can ignore it knowing that that is not the action of the true soul but merely the surface response.

Love is power. Love is the power of your Creator which is sent out in millions and millions of rays to each of you and to every being that exists. How you tap into and use that power depends on your individual consciousness. Do not think that you have to love, or that you can create love. You cannot build up love. You cannot establish love. You cannot work at love. Love is an act of being.

When two souls come together in marriage that love which joins them together, which motivates their marriage, is not a physical love, is not a personality love. It is the recognition by two souls that they agreed to come together in marriage before they even incarnated into matter. It is said that some people fall in love on sight. This is true, for there are people who can know in an instant that they are meant to marry. The bond of love is created before a word is spoken. The same is also true of two men or two women who meet each other in the passing currents of life. When you meet someone, sometimes you know instantaneously that you love that person and, no matter what happens in subsequent days or years, that link will not be broken. It will, indeed, be strengthened.

I ask you, therefore, to try in your own minds to separate what I would call the spiritual side of love — spiritual is not the correct word, but it is the nearest approximation in your language — from the personality side of love. The personality creates its own kind of love because it needs it. It creates love for the wrong reasons and, as such, it fails, because while a personality love may last for many years, if the personalities change then the common link has gone. All of you can remember people whom you thought you loved and yet, when you meet them years later, you are amazed that you could have loved them. Such is the nature of the change in you as you live your everyday life. A love that is based on personality desires is not true love, and will not last. The love that lasts is the love of creation. If you see a person performing an act of spiritual goodness then you feel love for that person. That is the true emotion of love. If you were to experience the emotion of having a person sacrifice his or her life for you, and if you knew that that person was doing it for you, you would then experience the highest feeling of love that exists. Some of you retain that feeling in your soul memories. Some of you have sacrificed your lives for your fellow-men in other incarnations, and that is why a bond of love as great as that survives, incarnation after incarnation.

What you love, what you truly love, is the spirituality of life, of people, of places, of the deeds that go on between those people and in those places. If all of you examine your emotions of love with this new insight you will then begin to appreciate what love is. You will appreciate the love of your Creator. You will appreciate the love of the many Masters who have come down onto the Earth to serve Humanity. You will appreciate the many great souls who have come and gone on your Earth with the sole purpose of helping people who neither recognised them nor, on a personality level, even wished to know them. You will recognise love by the act of a man who, when nailed to a cross in the most painful of deaths, could still say "Father forgive them for they know not what they do". If you understand those words, and that emotion, then you will understand the true meaning of love.

A DAY IN YOUR LIFE

As you live out your life-span you live many days. In order that each day may be lived correctly, so that the maximum benefit be obtained from it, it is essential that you become aware that each day is an act of spiritual existence. As the months and years go by what is it that makes a day stand out for you? How do you distinguish between one day and another? Why do you remember one day and wish to forget another? As you wake up each morning to a new day, do you think of living that day or do you merely think of existing during that day? Of course, you have to eat and drink and provide clothes and shelter for yourself, but these are only a means to an end — to maintain the physical body in a balanced and healthy state. Their whole purpose is to enable the soul to function within the body so that it may fulfil the destiny it chose before it incarnated into physical matter. Therefore the purpose of life, the purpose of waking up each morning, is not merely to exist, to feed and drink, to worry about the material aspects of life or society: it is to fulfil the spiritual destiny of each day.

In the society in which you live today it is so easy to forget completely what a day is for. The days merge one into another. Life becomes a continuous struggle to live with material things, or to obtain more material things. You desire to eat to the fullest extent, to live in a superb house, to have the latest car or to obtain the pleasures which you think you need. But that is not the purpose of a day. You did not incarnate to live a life of pleasure, although that is not to say that you should be without it. You incarnate to learn the lessons of this planet. That is the reason for your existence on Earth.

If you knew that you were to die tomorrow and that today was to be your last day in a physical body in this incarnation, how would you lead your life? Would you not be completely aware of the day? As every minute, every hour, went by, as the Sun rose, as the Sun set, as life revolved around you, would you not be completely aware, perhaps for the first time, of life and what it meant? Would you not smile and welcome everyone you met, even your enemies? Would you not perhaps forgive them for anything they had done? Would you not strive to help people? Would you not look at your surroundings with a new awareness of what they meant to you? Would you not think more of life, of its purpose, of why you are here, of why you are to die, of where you will go after death? Would you not think of what you have achieved in this life and in particular of what you wish to achieve today knowing that you are not going to be here tomorrow? You would plan every second of the day to get the maximum benefit from it. You would wake up in the morning knowing it to be your last day and you would live that day as your Creator meant you to live a day. But, of course, this pressure is not upon you, for even if you are to die tomorrow, you do not know it.

Those of you who are aware of the spirituality of the day, of the Sun that is there to give you warmth and light, of creation all around you, realise that each day is given to you for a purpose. You are here to fulfil the will of your Creator and, therefore, as you arise in the morning consider what the will of your Creator is for each day, and then consciously strive to fulfil it. The lesson of life on this planet is sacrificial service in love, and that is exactly what should motivate all your actions during each day. So as you live each day render service to all around you, not only to your family but to everyone you meet. This means helping and not rejecting. It means sacrificing. It means serving. It means controlling the little ego that does not want to help because it is inconvenient or because it desires other things. It means being aware of all the lower forms of life — the Animal, the Vegetable and the Mineral Kingdoms — and of being responsible towards them.

As you live each day look with new eyes and not with the eyes of memory. Strive to live each day anew. Be reborn every morning. Forget what has gone before. Begin each day as you would begin a new life. Consciously try to control your personality. Try to hold back that sharp tongue, that evil thought. Shower goodwill and love on everyone and everything that you meet. Try to help your fellow-men. If you do this you will be surprised at the change in your life. If everyone on this planet gave the power of love every minute of the day, your World would become the paradise it is meant to be.

As you walk around your home, in the countryside or in a town, observe life around you as if it was your last day. For the first time really look at things you have accepted before. You will be amazed how you will notice things which you have never seen before, and how aware you will become of life around you. For example, if you drive to work through slum areas where your less fortunate brothers live do not close your eyes and say that this is something you do not want to see. Look, observe and be aware. Recognise that people live there, people less fortunate than you, and consider what you and society can do to help them. Do not live in a little world of your own making to the exclusion of those around you, for if you create your ivory tower it will soon be tumbled down.

Life should mean more than going to work every day to earn money for your family, more than the housewife working all day looking after her home and children. They may be necessary parts of life, but they are not the totality of life. You have created homes, you have had children, you have worked in various trades during your many past incarnations, and in your incarnations to come you will do just the same. What you must all look for is the spirituality of life which exists beyond that.

Life should involve giving in every respect, sacrificing the 'I' to help your fellow-men, blessing them when you would rather curse them, helping them when they ask for help, even offering to help when they do not ask. You should think not only of the people in your village, in your town, in your country, but of all the people in the World. Do not support a government if it advocates a way of life which is contrary to what you know to be true. Do not ignore a problem and assume that the government will take care of it. Remember that it is how you think and what you say that will change people. Show that you care, show that you are concerned, and you will arouse that spark in others.

If you wake each morning intending to do that, then you will truly live each day. Do not worry about tomorrow or what is to happen in a year's time. Concern yourselves with living each day as if it was to be your last, so that in the evening when you review what you have learnt from each day, you may truly look back and say "I have done everything that my Creator would wish". If you can say that, then you have a lived a day for the purpose for which it was given to you.

THE TRUE MEANING AND SIGNIFICANCE OF CHRISTMAS

Man is by nature conservative. He is loath to give up the customs and practices that he has adopted. He is reluctant to reject the traditions, the beliefs, the ideologies of the World into which he has incarnated and which have been instilled into him as he has grown from childhood to adulthood. However, as you approach the period of the year which you call Christmas, I ask you to look for once with a new eye, with a new vision. Try to erase from your memories everything that you have been told concerning the meaning of Christmas. Forget what your Churches have told you. Forget what your parents have told you and have handed down to you. Forget the commercial aspects of Christmas. Place all that aside and try to examine Christmas for what it is, not for what you would like it to be, not for what you have been told it should be, but for what it was intended to be by your Creator.

It would be true to say that in the Western World today the spiritual significance of Christmas is lost on most people. There are only a few who think it necessary even to recognise the event, and those who do, because they are so bound up in the dogma of their respective churches and beliefs, fail to see what was intended by the birth of the Christ Principle. So I ask you all, no matter what creed or tenet you hold to, or even if you hold to none at all, to consider the spiritual meaning of Christmas with me.

Christmas should not be looked at in isolation and considered only for a few days around December the twenty-fifth, then to be forgotten with the coming of the New Year. It is Man alone who limits Christmas to this short period of time and who then ignores it for the rest of the year. Christmas, the Christ-mass, is meant to be celebrated on every day of the year. The importance of the period known as Christmas is that the astrological influences which affect the Earth, the vibrations of great Beings not only from within your own Solar Body but from Solar Bodies beyond your own, flow down upon the Earth to revitalise the Christ Influence, the Christ Principle. It is a time when you should all consciously strive, more so than in your normal everyday lives, to consider what is meant by the Christ Principle, to remember why It was sent down onto this Earth and to examine the extent to which you are following it. Christmas is meant to act as a yearly reminder to all of you to measure your spiritual progress in the year that has gone, to examine your consciousnesses, to assess how far you have evolved, to consider the ways in which you have lived, and to prepare yourselves for the year to come.

You may well say, "What has this to do with the Christmas story which I know so well, of the man born almost two thousand years ago in a stable amongst the animals, of the shepherds who came to visit him, of the wise men who came to herald his arrival, of the star that shone over Bethlehem, of the whole story that is written in the Bible?" I am not going to say whether or not this particular story, as it is written in the Bible, is entirely true. That is not to say that the events mentioned in the Bible did not actually happen but rather that, because the writers of the original manuscripts wrote in an ancient tongue, as the years have passed by much of the meaning has been lost in translation. Therefore, as Man's consciousness has expanded or diminished, as he has failed to understand or desired to expand upon the story in the Bible, he has changed it to suit the Age in which he has lived. So I would advise you not to place absolute faith on anything that is written in the Bible. Read it, yes. Meditate on it, yes. Extract from it that which your consciousness permits, but do not slavishly adhere to every phrase that is written in it. Do not make it into a dogma, a creed, that separates you from your fellow-men, for that was never intended by its writers.

The true history of the Earth is complex. Scientists have still to discover how this planet was formed and the evolutionary changes that have taken place on its surface. To comprehend the true evolutionary processes of this Earth demands a high degree of consciousness. If, therefore, I do not delve too deeply into them at this time, I do so not to avoid this issue but merely to simplify this lecture for the benefit of all those who will read it.

This Earth on which you dwell was created by the Being Who in the Western World you call 'God'. However, you do not really comprehend what that term means. Each of you understands it according to your own consciousness or according to the way you have been taught by your religious teachers, for with your limited consciousnesses you cannot comprehend your God, your Creator, Whose spirit dwells in the Sun, the one true star in your planetary system. You cannot comprehend His power, His majesty, His wisdom or His love, but it was He Who created the Earth, just as He created the other parts of the Solar Body, the planets.

The Earth was the last of the planets to be created. As a child born on the Earth comes from the womb of its mother, so the Earth came from the Sun, as indeed did all the other planets. Your God created this Earth with His Love. He created it through His consciousness for the purpose of reflecting Universal Love. With the aid of His servant, the Lord of the Earth, who dwells within the Earth, He created all the creatures and the conditions of life which exist on the Earth, and everything was perfection. Into this state of perfection your Creator placed Man. When, in the Christmas story, you are told of the Virgin Birth, it is to the birth of Man that the story refers, not to the birth of the Nazarene. The Nazarene was not born outside Natural Law: he was born from the union of man and woman.

On Earth perfect Man, if I may call him that, lived and dwelt with the angels, with those beings of perfection who transmit the will and love of your Creator around His Universe. For aeons of time Man dwelt in perfection with the angels. Then, for reasons which I will not go into now, for you cannot conceive of them, it was decided by the Lords of the Solar Body that to further Man's evolution, to enable him to advance his consciousness, to be a perfect imitation of his Creator and to exemplify His wisdom and His knowledge, he was to be given the divine gift of free choice. He was to use this gift to advance his consciousness. He would, by exercising his free choice, learn. He would learn right from wrong, light from darkness, joy from sadness, goodness from evil, and through aeons of time he would advance his consciousness along the slow path of evolution.

Whilst recognising that this was not an easy task, not something which could be accomplished in the twinkling of an eye, but at the same time remembering that spiritual time is timeless, Man was reborn on the Earth possessing the inherent qualities of his Creator. He had to develop them, he had to perfect them, but he possessed, just as each of you do today, the potential of his Creator. It was up to Man, as he incarnated on the

63

various levels of existence within this Solar Body, to advance his consciousness. Because of the nature of his task, Man was not to be alone. He had the angel hosts to guide and advise him. He also had those beings who dwelt on the other planets of the Solar Body who had been in existence long before him. They may not be fulfilling similar functions to those of Man on the Earth, they may not have the same forms of life as Man, but in their particular evolutionary fields they have advanced a long way and so are able to help Man if he so desires.

When he was given free choice Man was also given the gift of creation. He was one of the few sparks of consciousness in this Solar Body who was given the right to reproduce himself. Man could create when he wished. This was a gift to which the angels, who were sent to guide him and who walked hand in hand with him, were attracted, for they do not possess it. So, as you read in Genesis, the first sin took place when some of the angels cohabited with Man and created from their own consciousnesses rather than in imitation of their Creator. From that moment erroneousness, imbalance and disharmony were introduced onto the Earth and Man lost his spiritual purity.

Aeons of time went by as Man slowly evolved and developed his consciousness. Civilisations rose and fell. There were periods of great spirituality followed by periods of darkness when the love of your Creator was not reflected by His servants on the Earth. As great civilisations came and went Man, through his greed for material possessions and desire for power over his fellow-men, through his lack of understanding of the true nature of both his and of the Earth's existence, through his inability to see beyond his present life, reduced the vibratory level of the Earth to the stage where it was so much out of balance that it was affecting the other members of the Solar Body.

As a consequence, the Lords of the Solar Body met with the Lord of the Earth to decide what should be done so that Man could be shown the error of his ways and could be redeemed, so that Man could see the purpose of his existence on the Earth and could see what he had to achieve and the way in which he could achieve it. Your Creator, Who so loves this planet, this reflection of His love, then made the supreme sacrifice by offering to send a part of Himself onto the Earth to show those who dwelt on the Earth the example they had to follow. This spark of life, this aspect of consciousness, the wisdom of your Creator, was called

The Christ. So you will see that the term Christ does not refer to a man. The Nazarene was not The Christ. The Christ is a principle, a reflection of the wisdom of your Creator.

Throughout the Ages, as civilisations came and went, as the astrological influences on the surface of the Earth changed, as the four major races came and went and fulfilled their functions, so the Christ Principle was sent down at intervals onto the Earth through the aid of great Masters, such as the Nazarene. These great Masters offered to come down to ground the Christ Principle upon the Earth so that Man could see It demonstrated for him. The Nazarene is not the only Master who has demonstrated the Christ Principle. Western Civilisation is not the only civilisation to have had the Christ Principle demonstrated to it. It has been grounded many times, for with the birth of every new Age the Christ Principle is demonstrated so that Man may be presented with the example which he may follow according to his point of consciousness. Obviously, today, you are aware of only the Christ expression as It was displayed by the Nazarene for the Piscean Age. You are rapidly approaching the end of that Age, and with the dawning of the Aquarian Age the Christ Principle will be grounded once again. There will be a return of the Christ.

The Nazarene, overshadowed by the Christ Principle, demonstrated, even if it was almost two thousand years ago, the way in which Man was expected to live, how he was to treat his fellow men, how he was to discipline himself, how he was to evolve as he lived in his physical body on Earth. Piscean Man was given the example to follow if he so chose. Above all, the Nazarene demonstrated the Natural Laws of the Universe in which you live. His 'miracles', which are described in the Bible, are all examples of Natural Law at work. You, too, could perform such acts if you possessed his wisdom and knowledge.

So the Nazarene is not to be placed upon a pedestal and worshipped as a God. His teachings should not be turned into a creed, a dogma, for he would not want that. He came as a servant to ground the Christ Principle for others to follow. He did not decree that his birth should be made into a celebration as your churches have done today. He did not ask you to celebrate his birth. It is Man since then who, because he did not understand why he came and what he tried to do, has created this mystique, this aura, around the birth of the Nazarene. Look at the

65

Nazarene's life. Read what he said, meditate on it, and then from within your own consciousness bring out its meaning. For each of you it will be different, for you are all at different stages of consciousness as you walk along the path of life.

As you approach Christmas do not think of the Nazarene himself but of what he demonstrated. Think of what he taught and, by looking at his life, think of what he has revealed for those that follow. It is obvious that souls of a limited consciousness will not be able to walk his path. For most, that lies far in the future, but all of you can strive, each to a limited degree, to follow that Christ Principle. Christmas, the Christ-Mass, is the anniversary of the birth of the Christ Principle, and I ask you to try for the first time in your lives to re-establish the true meaning of Christmas. It is the time when, helped by the influences of the planets, the Masters and High Beings around you, you can establish how you are to live for the rest of your lives.

You are told that Christmas is for children. It is not. Christmas is only for children in that they see the example of their parents. It is the parents who must demonstrate the meaning of Christmas. If, on Christmas Day, the parents indulge in gross materialism as they have done throughout the rest of the year, then their children will follow their example. Christmas is not all decorations and lights, the receiving and giving of presents. This is merely what Man has made of it because of his limited consciousness.

As Christmas approaches stop and look within. See if there, in all humility, you can see the Christ light, that light of self-sacrifice. See if you can discover there the recognition of your life as a part of the whole as opposed to the recognition of your life as being purely self-centred. Can you begin to sacrifice to that greater whole, to say that it is not what you want but what your Creator wants, it is not what your family wants but what the World wants? Can you begin to recognise that Christ light and to accept it? Perhaps you could begin by recognising that the physical manifestation of Christmas as created by Man — the glamour of the decorations, the tinsel and the lights, the giving of presents, the over-eating, the over-drinking, the creation of pleasures for the self — is in complete contrast to the true expression of Christmas. Nevertheless, underlying all this superficiality and self-gratification there is a feeling of goodwill which Man finds hard to explain. All he knows is that it comes at

Christmas, it lasts for a short period of time and then disappears. But for a few priceless days Man has unknowingly known of the Christ, for by changing the outward expression of his very being, by altering his views on life, if only for a few days, he has begun to understand the meaning of the Christ and how It can transform not only his own life but also this Earth on which he lives. What you all feel at Christmas should not be the exception but the rule, for in those few days you may know how life on this Earth should be lived throughout the whole year. That feeling of goodwill towards men should exist not only at Christmas: it should be eternal.

Therefore be aware that at Christmas you have the responsibility of saying that you will make the Christ-Mass live not for a day, not for a month, but for a year. It is for you to so motivate your beings that, enhanced by the Christ light, you will recognise that the spirit of Christmas should exist not only at this time but throughout the whole year. Be aware that it is *your* evolution and no one else's, that it is *your* consciousness and no one else's that is responsible for determining the way you lead your lives throughout the rest of the year. Next Christmas can you begin to lead your life as it should be led throughout the year and, once you have reached that pinnacle, once you have reached and experienced that point of understanding, can you maintain it so that in future you may look back and say truly that you have been worthy of that which has been given to you in a sacred trust: the Christ light?

I ask all of you to think of how you can change your Christmas so that it will not be a Christmas of the past, so that it will not be a Christmas of indulgence, of excess. Let it be a Christmas of real giving, of real helping, of real consciousness. Try to use the influences that rain down upon you at that time so that you may all increase your consciousnesses, reflect the love of your Creator, and then goodwill will indeed return to this Earth.

MONEY AND POSSESSIONS

If you were to ask almost any adult in the Western World today about which factor in their lives they worried the most, which factor most concerned their conscious minds, they would probably say money. Therefore in this lecture I am going to talk about money and possessions. As the lecture progresses you will see that the subject of money cannot be taken in isolation from all the other aspects of life around you. Why is this? It is because money is the motive power of society today. If the value of money was to disappear overnight, then the whole structure of western society would collapse. On an international level, as the strength of a country's currency rises or falls, so its status and position in the World varies also. A wealthy country has influence and power in an international conference, whereas a poor country does not. On an individual level, a wealthy person usually has more influence in society today than a poor person. Man has created a material society, the basis of which is possessions, and he supports it with his monetary system. Therefore it is difficult, even for those who do not wish to join in this system, to avoid it.

In the world of money there is, of course, usually very little room for spirituality, for the very act of possessing has in itself an unspiritual vibration. But what, in fact, can you really possess? Nothing ever belongs to you. Every aspect of matter on this Earth, no matter whether it be a piece of land, a stretch of water, a plant or an animal, is not yours to buy and sell. You might think that because you have paid money to buy something from another person you now possess it, but that person had no right to sell it to you, neither had you the right to buy it, for the matter of this Earth does not belong to you but to the Lord of this Earth. It is only lent to you in a sacred trust.

Truly, you possess nothing, for even when you think you possess something you possess it only until another man takes it away from you, or until it is destroyed, or until you leave your physical body at death to pass on to another level of life. The act of possessing can never be final. Man should appreciate this and realise that all the energy and time which he spends on trying to possess material things are wasted because, although it might bring him temporary benefit, or so he thinks, his possessing can never be permanent. Moreover, Man should examine the responsibility of possessing because he must handle everything that comes into his possession, and for which he assumes responsibility, correctly and according to Natural Law. If he does not he then risks the chance of incurring karma for himself and for those around him with the Lord of this Earth and the Lords of Matter. Truly, a man who possesses very little may well lead a more fruitful life than a man who possesses a great deal.

The whole structure of society today is based on money. People work to earn money. Most people would agree with me if I was to say that they would not work if they could earn or obtain money in another way. Therefore their very motivation for working is wrong, for they work not because they want to but because they have to: they need money. In society today you, of course, have to have money. No one could deny this, and because society is established in this way you have to earn money to live in society. You have to buy your clothes and food, you have to buy or rent a home, and therefore you must earn money. I would just like to say at this point that although you might think that this is normal, and that money is an essential part of any civilised society, it has not always been so. In fact, in some ancient advanced civilisations, as yet undiscovered by Man, money was not used in any form. It is quite possible to live without money — indeed, it is desirable to do so — but today it is obvious that you cannot, and therefore you must concern yourselves with how to use the money that you have and to decide how much you really do need.

The way in which your society is structured at this time has caused money to become a drug. Whether you earn one, two or even a hundred thousand pounds a year you always need, or rather you always think that you need, more. A person who earns a thousand pounds will perhaps be happy with five thousand. A person who earns five thousand will perhaps be happy with ten thousand, and so on in progression. Few people are ever satisfied with the money that they earn. Why is this? Because, to them, money means possessions. With more money they can obtain more possessions, more things they can call their own: bigger and better houses, more expensive cars, more clothes than they need. They can go on more expensive holidays and buy more expensive decorations both for themselves and for their homes. How often does Man think about how much money he really needs just to live on, and for nothing else? If Man had only just enough money to live on and did not have any extra to spend on possessions and therefore worrying about what he possessed, how would he spend his free time? Would he not, perhaps, begin to appreciate more his fellow-men and Nature around him? Would he not begin to think of spirituality, of God, of Creation, of the Earth on which he lives? A man who has many possessions finds it difficult to think on spiritual matters because his mind is totally absorbed with his money and possessions. Those that have money worry about losing it and investing it to produce more, and those that do not have money are constantly seeking to obtain it for the pleasures that they think it will bring them.

Obviously these remarks are not directed at the relatively poor people in society who exist in real poverty and who need money not just to maintain but to improve their standard of living so that they may live at an acceptable level for humanity. The people who earn a great deal of money should be helping those who do not, those who really need money. Your governments, who have this responsibility, should be doing this automatically as a function of it. These comments then are directed at the people who earn a great deal of money, who have money to spare.

There is a story in the Bible about a rich man who asked the Nazarene "What do I have to do that I may inherit eternal life?" The Nazarene replied, "Obey the commandments, sell everything that you possess, give it to the poor and then follow me". But the rich man could not do this because he valued his possessions above his spirituality, and he departed sadly. All of you should heed this story, for it is relevant no matter whether you possess a large or small amount of money. If you place your possessions above your God, above your responsibility to your fellow-men, then your possessions will rule you. You may worship God or Mammon, and that is what Mammon is, the idols of Man, and, truly, the idols of the present Age are money and possessions. There have been Ages in which no one possessed anything, but Man today has his possessions and, once he has paid money for them, believes that they are his and that no one else may use them.

Let us now examine your responsibility towards your money and possessions. Firstly, let us examine how you obtain your money. If you perform a fair day's work and you are paid a fair wage by your employer, then that money having been fairly earned will have a spiritual as well as a material value. In the field of industrial relations today, where so much blackmail and pressure is used by both sides, although one side may think they have gained, such gains are not true gains for any money, any conditions of service gained through wrong motivation, against Natural Law, are worthless. You may think they are of value, but they are not. In the short term you may think that you have gained something, but in the long term the Law of Karma will always equal it out. There are those who earn their money immorally; and by this I mean through exploiting one of the Kingdoms of Nature. Money gained in this way is of no spiritual value.

You should examine why you work. Do you work just to make money for yourself and your family, or do you work to help others? Do you run a business for the good of your fellow-men, or for the good of yourself? It is most important that all of you in business firmly establish your motivation, for anything gained with the wrong motivation is worthless in spiritual values and will reap the effect of Natural Law. It may not be an immediate effect, but in time it will come about, for as you sow, so shall you reap. For those of you in society today who earn a great deal of money, who have power and influence, the responsibility is ten times as great as for those who earn very little. If you control a big factory employing many men then you stand a great chance of incurring karma if you do not treat them with responsibility.

If the great nations do not treat the small ones with responsibility, and if the rich countries do not share with the poor, then again karma is incurred. As you look around your World today you can see countries hoarding their natural resources, their minerals and their food, and not sharing them with other countries unless they receive payment for them. There are countries which produce food and destroy it to maintain an artificial price whilst people in other parts of the World are starving. This is incurring a painful karma in lives to come for both the countries and the individuals concerned, for it shows

71

that they value their possessions more than their Creator. The Creator is in all men, and therefore if you do not value the Creator, Who created you, the Earth and everything on it above your own little possessions you still have a great deal to learn, and the learning will be painful.

You may well say, "How can I change my attitude towards money? I would like to live a life based on true values but I find it difficult in the society of today". Firstly, you must begin by recognising that money is merely a possession and that it does not matter if you gain, or if you lose, possessions. The important thing is how you gain them, and how you lose them. Unless you are amongst the very poor, be satisfied with your present standard of living and strive not to improve it, for by striving to improve your standard of living you are supporting the very system which you wish to change. If you continually want more possessions, then you are supporting the structure of society which you have already decided does not aid the spirituality of Man.

Always remember that your possessions are not really yours. You may think that you own them, but you only own them while you are incarnating: that is all. You cannot take your possessions with you beyond the grave, so why do you attach so much importance to them while you are living? Do not therefore hold onto any possessions as if your life depended on them, for they are not that important. Remember that you need money to provide a home, to buy food and to clothe yourself but, once you have done that, what else do you really need? If you were a spiritually motivated person then after you had housed, clothed and fed yourself you would give all that was remaining to those who needed it more than you. Indeed, an evolved person, one who truly exemplified the Christ Principle, would give his money to the poor before he even considered himself. If you all were to do this then you would be surprised at how your Creator would look after you.

It is said, in the Bible, that if you ask, you will receive. You will say, of course, that there are people in this World who ask but do not receive, who even starve to death. At this moment I am not going to go into the karma of nations, or of individuals, who suffer in this way, but just as even the hairs on your head are counted so their deaths are numbered too. Everything happens for a reason.

It is up to you to help your fellow-men. If you live in a land of plenty, then help in the lands of scarcity. If your country has plenty of money, then it should give help to those countries that need it. If your country has plenty of natural resources, then it should share them with any country in the World that needs them. Remember that the Law of Karma, of Cause and Effect, will repay you much more than you would receive in currency for, as you help others, so you will be helped yourselves. Examine your motivation in everything that you do with your money and possessions. Remember that some of the wisest, the happiest and most spiritual people that have walked this Earth have possessed nothing. The Nazarene was of a poor family, possessing nothing but the clothes he walked in, and was fed by those with whom he stayed: yet he exemplified the Christ Principle for the World. There is the example. You do not need money or possessions to be as the Christ. Indeed, it is best to be without them. Societies have existed where people lived together in a community, growing and making what they needed, without money. It could be done today. All over the World New-Age children are striving to do just this, to establish little communities which are not based on money and possessions. Until you have tried this, do not despise it. If you have had possessions all your life, is it not difficult to give them up? In the end possessions possess you and, in that they possess you, they deny you your full spiritual birthright.

So to those of you who have money and possessions I say beware, for you could be creating great karma for yourselves. You must handle all your money and possessions with responsibility otherwise one day the Law of Karma will decree an incarnation for you where you too may be one of the millions of people who live in poverty and die of hunger in a far-off country.

The structure of society today is such that the monetary system of the World is soon to collapse. The money on which you place so much faith and security will become worthless. The present situation, where the rich countries keep on getting richer and the poor countries poorer, cannot be allowed to continue. The value of money and possessions will change. How much better it will be if you have changed your values before that happens. If you can look at your bank account, if you can look around your house and truly say that you could give them up, if you had to, with no pain or remorse, then you have the right amount of money and possessions. But if you say that you could not do this, for you needed them, you had to have them, then you have too much.

I ask you all to examine the motive force on which you base your lives. Is it to be money, or is it to be spirituality? That is not to say that the two cannot go hand in hand, but that the balance must be there. The balance of spirituality is that you do not possess or strive to possess more than your Creator intended for you. If you possess a great deal while others possess nothing, then obviously the balance is wrong. The fact that you have so many problems in your World today, between both races and individuals, can nearly always be traced to money and possessions. What you have, another wants. What you are striving to possess, another will try to prevent.

Remember that you are the children of God, that you are living on His Earth along with the matter of the Earth and that nothing whatsoever belongs to you. All that you possess is your consciousness. That is the only thing that you will take with you when you leave the physical body. How much better, therefore, to advance that consciousness.

MEDICINE

In the Western World today Man has placed the medical profession on a pedestal and has surrounded it with an aura of infallibility. He is reluctant to challenge or attack it, or to accept that it can indeed be gravely at fault. However, in this lecture I am going to ask you to consider that the medical profession is in error in its beliefs and practices and is indeed misleading Man. In the great civilisations which have existed in the past many of the beliefs which it supports today would have been rejected out of hand as being totally un-Christlike and unspiritual. But Man today accepts what the medical profession stands for and is largely content with its judgements because it has gradually evolved to its present position throughout the centuries of the Piscean Age. As you are now entering the Aquarian Age, however, much of what is accepted as normal today is to be rejected, and I would like to present just a few thoughts for you to consider so that, especially the next time you are ill, you may explore different approaches to treatment.

One of the big differences between medicine today and medicine in Ages gone by is that medicine today is called upon to help Man only when he is ill, whereas in the past its purpose has been to prevent illness. Man today does not usually go to his doctor until he is really ill, until he is in so much pain that he cannot fulfil a useful function in life. He then goes as a last resort and expects the doctor to work the 'magic' of his profession and to cure him, whereas in actual fact, although the doctor might be able to alleviate the pain, and in some instances of minor illness to effect a cure, any major illness cannot usually be healed. Man then has to resort to other means, for example to surgery, to having the illness cut out, to removing a diseased part from the body, for once a disease has firmly established itself in his physical body Man cannot usually heal it.

The medicine of the future is to change in its attitude towards illness in that the emphasis will shift to prevention as opposed to cure. Man will understand that he must go once or twice a year to a doctor no matter whether he is ill or not. This doctor can be compared to your family doctor or general practitioner of today. He will place a patient in a special room and, by examining the electromagnetic aura emanating from the patient's body he will be able, with the use of certain instruments, to tell at a glance whether that person is in good health or bad health. Before disease actually manifests the doctor will be able to tell a patient where it is liable to occur, where there are deficiencies in his body, perhaps caused either by his diet or his manner of living, and then the patient will be able to take action to prevent disease occurring.

If you could see the auric emanations of Man, you would see him surrounded by many colours, for every vibratory level manifests as a different colour. The experienced eye can tell the nature of a person's illness at a glance. It can tell if a person has an illness in the head, the heart or the bowels by the emanations of colour around them. Moreover, it can detect disease before it manifests, for it sees the pre-physical rather than the physical with which your present-day doctors have to contend. All over the country there will be, in the future, doctors whose function it will be to prevent illness and, for the few who actually suffer illness there will be a specialised group, very small in number, who will attempt to cure an illness once it is established in the body. Far from being medical, as it is today, this group will consist of people of great spirituality. They will understand the Natural Laws of the Universe and the healing properties of cosmic rays, and will be able to heal people through using these rays. The Nazarene, for example, who performed many cures which are beyond the power and understanding of medicine today, was not a doctor.

The surgeons and their operating theatres, then, will not be present in the New Age, as they will not be needed. Man, if he is ill, will go to a spiritual person who will be able to heal by using the rays of colour and light from the Sun reflected through prisms to play upon the parts of the body requiring healing. However, there will always be a few people who have illnesses for karmic reasons and these, of course, will not be healed.

If you compare what I have just talked about with medicine today you will see how vastly different they are. The way in which the medical profession has advanced over the last hundred years has resulted in all its ideas and expertise being directed into a very narrow channel. The emphasis has been placed mainly on research into disease, on how to identify and destroy it, rather than on how to prevent disease by using methods other than vaccination, which involves a violation of the body. Man has perfected means of surgery, both external and internal, which seek to cure by destroying, by cutting out parts that are diseased and replacing parts that are worn out. It is not for me to say that these methods are wrong and that Man should not practise them, for how can he replace a system that has been tested and tried and is practised by the medical men of today if there is no other substitute readily available?

For every disease known to Man on this Earth today there is an antidote, a cure, which exists in the Vegetable Kingdom, in the flowers, herbs, berries, fruits, grasses, bushes, roots and trees. Every disease affecting Man today can be cured through a knowledge of these aspects of Nature. Even uncivilised tribes which Man calls primitive — which of course in some respects they are — can effect the most amazing cures using barks of trees, roots of plants or certain berries, which modern Man could only achieve by the use of extensive surgery, by cutting out organs and stitching. Obviously Man cannot immediately change over to healing by herbs because the necessary knowledge is not readily available for, although there are some books on the subject, this art has not been widely practised in the Western World. However, in the years to come certain souls are going to incarnate who will re-establish the art of herbal medicine. In time, of course, this too will be replaced by the more advanced methods of healing which I mentioned earlier, but the first step towards achieving them will be for Man to cure by natural as opposed to artificial methods.

If you are ill today you really have little alternative but to accept the advice of the medical profession, but I would like to give a few words of caution, for the medical men of today do not really recognise the spirituality of Man. If they did, they would never cut the body with their knives or introduce into the body some of the drugs which they do. When modern medicine seeks to cure a certain disease or illness in the physical body it introduces drugs of such strength and variety that, although they might cure the illness which was present, they destroy much else, often leading to further illness and disease, which may not become evident for many years.

You would say to me, "It is all very well to criticise modern medicine but, surely, the World gets healthier every year?". This is true to an extent, for as each year goes by Man advances his standards of hygiene and his understanding of disease. He has researched into microbes and bacteria and today, generally speaking, the contagious diseases are known and can be controlled. Nevertheless, if you were to examine Western Man today closely you would be surprised at how unhealthy he really is. If you were to compare Man today with Man two hundred years ago you would have little doubt as to who was the healthier — and it would not be twentieth-century Man. Of course the doctors are not to blame for this: the way that Man lives today is largely responsible for his present physical condition. Man cannot treat his body as he does, with the wrong food he eats, the wrong fluids he drinks, the wrong hours he keeps, the polluted atmosphere which he breathes, without causing disease.

What really harms the human body are the drugs that Man introduces into it, the effects of which he does not fully understand. A doctor uses a drug to achieve a particular result — to relax a person, to relieve pain, to increase blood flow — but what else does that drug do? Many of the drugs that the Western World uses today are unnecessary, but Man is so pampered that any symptom or pain which is caused by his misuse of his body is accepted as being undesirable and must be got rid of immediately. You have a headache, so you take a pill. You have any ache, so you take a pill. For every illness of Man there is a pill. No matter whether that pill works or not you still take it for the mental comfort that it gives you. Many people are, of course, hypochondriacs. In some respects you can blame the doctors for bowing to the demands of their patients, but there are times when a doctor would like to say, "I suggest that you go away and suffer, and then next time you will learn to look after your body"! But, of course, few have the courage to do this.

Every time that your surgeons cut open a body they violate that body, and therefore I would advise anyone anticipating surgery to examine most carefully the need for it before they undergo it. I could liken a diseased body to a village in which there is a disease prevalent which you wish to destroy, and in your determination to destroy that disease and to ensure that it does not spread you burn the whole village. You may perhaps destroy the disease, but you also destroy the village with its life and purpose. This is what happens with surgery, because although a surgeon might cut out certain diseased parts of the body the very fact that those parts of the body are not present causes great disharmony within the whole body and also affects the spirituality of a person. Man today, being able to see only his physical body, would be shocked if he was to raise his vibrations just a little and see the aura, the etheric body, of a man who has undergone surgery. It is not a pleasant sight to see but, not even being aware of the etheric body, your surgeons continue to operate. Today there is almost a trend to cut rather than to cure, for it is so much easier to do so.

I am, of course, aware that there are many cases in which surgery is desirable. Some of it is good. I say this not to encourage its use but because Man, at his present state of evolution, does not know of any other way of healing. A person who has, for example, a hernia or a broken bone can benefit from minor surgery and can be relieved by the skill of the surgeon. Where surgeons should not experiment is with surgery that goes on in the brain, the heart, the liver and the other main organs of the body, for they are affecting organs that have functions other than those of which they are aware, because these organs link Man with the other parts of the Solar Body — the planets. They perform vital functions and to cut them out and destroy them severely restricts the destiny of Man while he is still incarnating in a physical body on Earth.

So I would ask you to be aware of the limitations of modern medicine and not to accept everything that it tells you as being true. Remember that medical men are not infallible: they are rarely wiser than you, and very often your own innate sense can tell you that you are right and that they are wrong. Quite often you can treat yourself better than a doctor. I am not encouraging you all to stay at home and die of your illnesses, for if you are seriously ill then obviously you must go to a doctor, but so often when you do go to a doctor or to a hospital you throw yourselves into their arms with gay abandon and submit to almost anything that they say or do to you without even questioning. This is very wrong for quite often, in some respects, you have more wisdom than they. You can feel when something is wrong for you. You know when something should not be done to your body. If they want to cut something out and you feel that it is wrong, then say so, and do not have it done. You are the master of your own destiny. Use your God-given intelligence to question what is being done to you. You would defend yourself in a court of law, you would argue with your local priest, so why not argue with your doctor or surgeon, where, after all, so much more is at stake.

In that the basic trend of medicine and surgery today is proceeding up a blind alley and in that, although it serves the modern Age, it will not serve the needs of the future Age, it will have to change. Therefore begin to look around for other means of healing. All over the World there are many small groups of people who are experimenting with great success with various forms of healing. Healing has been accomplished by the use of colour and music, by sending healing vibrations through the ether, and by the use of prayer. Miraculous cures have taken place. The medical profession is, of course, reluctant to recognise them. You have faith healers who have effected many cures as well, and yet modern medicine does not wish to know. Why is this? Perhaps it is the conscience of the profession which does not wish to be tested!

In conclusion may I say this. Modern medicine, in spite of the understanding it has gained, is not correct. It is not the way in which Man should be healed or treated. It is to change. As long as you have no other substitute to turn to you must accept it and use it. But for those of you who are intelligent enough to think about it, to ask questions, to look for other sources of treatment and, if you believe in them, to try them, then please do so, for in doing so you may be the forerunners of the New Age. If you find a successful cure, then tell your friends and advise them of what has happened to you so that they too do not follow all the other men and women of the world like lambs to the slaughter.

FREE CHOICE OR FREE WILL?

When one considers the totality of Man's spiritual life, the subject of his free choice and free will would appear on the surface to be of very little relevance. In actual fact, however, to understand completely the significance of Man's free choice and free will requires the mind of an Adept, a very highly evolved being, for if you can truly understand the limits of Man's choice, and the limits of Man's will, you will understand creation in its design and structure in the whole Universe.

Free choice and free will would appear to have very similar meanings. Very often they are misused by Man in his everyday speech, and so before we begin we must establish what it is that we mean by these words. Free choice is fairly self-evident. It means that Man is free to exercise his choice. It means that Man has a choice before him and that he is free to choose one path or the other, one way or another. Free will, on the other hand, by its very terminology — will — implies a force, a power. If you impose your will on somebody else you are directing a power, an influence, onto that person and they have no choice in the matter: they are obeying your will. Therefore will does not involve choice. It is a power directed or employed by a higher vibration, by a more evolved person, onto a less evolved person. Consequently a less evolved person cannot impose his will on a more evolved person. It has to be the more evolved person who imposes the will.

Having defined free choice and free will let us now examine whether or not Man is actually free to exercise his choice and his will. Let us begin by looking at free choice. Throughout your everyday lives you are continually faced with alternatives, some simple, some complicated. If you think about it you exercise choice at almost every minute of the day. You are forever deciding what you want to do, and by the very act of making a decision you are choosing between alternatives. This is the way in which you progress in life and learn; for the result of your choice has an effect, and depending upon the reasons or the motivations for your choice so the effect upon you will vary. Now I am not saying that you can choose rightly or wrongly for there is, in reality, no such thing as right or wrong. You will chose, and how you choose will have an effect upon you. What is it, then, that leads you to exercise that choice?

You can make a choice over many things. You can choose, for example, where you want to live and with whom you want to live. You can decide what colour to paint your house, what type of car to buy, what kind of food you want to eat, and so on. In the material world in which you live today there are many choices which have to be made and, although perhaps you would not think so, the influences that lead you to make those choices are numerous. The factors which influence your choice and impinge on your mind, for the mechanism of deciding a choice is within the mind, are very varied. It is the mind that decides your choice, and there are many sources from which that mind draws. It could be the soul, it could be the personality, it could be any one of your finer bodies reacting on your mind to influence your choice. So when you exercise choice try to establish which factors are leading you to make that choice and, as in all things, try to establish what the motivation is, what the motive force is, for that choice.

Man incarnates on the Earth with the divine gift of free choice, and it is by the exercising of that choice, properly controlled, that he will learn. If the choice is not controlled then Man will learn and evolve very slowly. Those of you who have begun to control your physical and other bodies, and to impose the discipline of your soul on your mind, will begin to make a responsible choice, and I emphasise the word responsible, in all your everyday actions, and so you will evolve more rapidly. Therefore think before you make that choice so that you make the correct one, not only for yourself but also for those around you. It is important that you think about the act of choosing for it involves the whole reason for your incarnation and existence.

Do not think that Man has always had free choice. He has not. Do not think that all the other beings in your Solar Body have free choice. They do not. Be aware that free choice is a gift to Man at this stage of the Earth's development, in its present incarnation, so that Man may advance his consciousness to perform the will of his Creator. When Man first incarnated on the planet Earth, when he dwelt in perfection with the Angels, the messengers of Infinite Spirit, he did not have and did not need free choice. For many aeons of time Man dwelt without that gift, for it was not necessary. Then the Beings of whom you know so little, your Solar Logos, and the Lords who control this Solar Body and the Earth within it, decided that in order to advance his consciousness Man himself had to learn the limitations of his being. He was therefore reincarnated on Earth with the gift of free choice from his Creator, and in that Man now had this gift he could evolve and advance his consciousness, for by his choice he would learn goodness from evil, he would recognise light from darkness, he would know life from death. Ever since this reincarnation on the Earth Man has been advancing, albeit slowly, by exercising this gift. It is only because of the way that Man has misused this gift that the Earth finds itself in its present state of consciousness.

Man has not chosen correctly. He has the choice, even today, of choosing between spirituality and materialism. He has the choice between thinking of himself and thinking of his fellow men. He has the choice of thinking about his world, the Earth, and of thinking about the other worlds, the other planets, in the Solar Body. The choice, depending upon the level of soul-evolution, is always there. For those who are incarnating on the Earth for the first or second time obviously the choice is simple and limited. For those who have evolved their consciousnesses through many lives on Earth the choice is more subtle and complicated. But every being on this Earth is here to exercise his or her choice and to learn and to evolve through that choice. As the act of exercising your choice is the prime reason for your existence it is surely worthy of your most earnest consideration. Therefore do not make a choice lightly, without thought. Remember that how you choose will have an effect not only on yourself but also on others. So choose with thought, after meditation.

Let us now examine the question of free will. Does Man have free will? This question touches on the whole concept of life within this Solar Body and, indeed, within Creation. Unevolved Man likes to think that he is supreme, that he does indeed have free will, that he can do whatever he wants, when he wants and where he wants. He believes that he can control the destiny of

Man and the destinies of the Animal, the Vegetable and the Mineral Kingdoms. He believes that he can control the destiny of the World, of its races and peoples. With the thoughtlessness of supreme egotism he believes that he is God on Earth. Unevolved Man still has a great deal to learn, for the more evolved you become the more aware you become of forces, of controls, of disciplines, of wills, of orders, of hierarchies way above the level of Man's consciousness.

If you look down at an individual being dwelling on the surface of this Earth and then withdraw into Space seeing first the street, then the town, then the country, then the hemisphere, then the Earth, then the Solar Body in which the Earth dwells, then the Galaxy in which that Solar Body dwells and then the 'Super' Galaxy in which that little Galaxy dwells, you will recognise the minuteness of Man and the complexity, the control and the organisation of Space and of life in it. It is not possible that unevolved Man living on the surface of the planet Earth could control, even if he were allowed to, such complexities of Space. When Man does not even understand how the Earth rotates and functions, when he does not even understand the influences which act on the Earth both from within and without, how could he control other, far greater, forces?

What is carried out on the surface of this Earth is the will, the power and the influence of the Beings who are responsible for this Earth and, more especially, of our God, our Solar Logos, Who stands above us all. Man might like to think that he has free will, but he does not. If he did but understand it, most things in his life are planned. Within the boundaries of his life Man has only a narrow choice to make, for he incarnates into a planned family, into a planned country, into a planned way of life. He vibrates under a certain Ray, he is born under the specific influence of certain planets. He has chosen to meet certain people in his earthly incarnation from which he will learn certain lessons. He has chosen many of the incidents that are to happen in his life: all this before he even incarnates into matter!

If I can make an analogy, I will compare the time of your incarnation on Earth to a man driving a car along a highway. In the beginning that man is placed in his car on the highway. The will of his Creator is such that he should drive along that highway from point A to point B, and as it is the will of his Creator within him he feels an urge to follow that highway. Of course he may at any time leave that highway if he so desires. He may even not return to that highway, but within him there will always be an urge, a need, to return to that highway. But where can he really go even when he is off that highway? He is in a car and therefore he can only leave the highway along the roads leading off it. He must keep to roads that have been planned, that are already laid out, for he cannot suddenly invent new roads. Let us say that God is the Being Who planned that highway, Who planned those roads. Therefore Man can travel only along the highways and the roads that God has planned. How far can he go along those roads? He has only so much petrol in his tank, and when he runs out of petrol what then happens? He is forced to stop. So as that motorist is limited by his petrol tank, so your physical life has a limit as well. The petrol tank, that limit, is already determined by your Creator. The roads are planned by your Creator. So what may you do but stay within the limitations of your Creator?

A man who is poor and dwells in a poor part of a country will not have the opportunity, unless his destiny decrees it, of travelling all over the World, of mixing with many people. He will be confined to one small part of the World as his Creator intended. A tribe dwelling in a jungle will not find itself suddenly uprooted and placed in a metropolis of one of the technologically advanced countries of the Western World. So the limitations of your Creator are there if you will but recognise them. Even you who live in the so-called civilised countries of the Western World are limited. In spite of what you might think, Man today, with all his modern material and scientific methods, still does not create, for all creation is drawn out of Infinite Mind. Infinite Mind, which is part of Infinite Spirit, releases to Man only what Man is allowed to have. Man has the choice to use what is released to him either for good or for evil, but that inspiration would not be given to Man unless his Creator intended it for him.

Modern Man has the means of destroying the Earth. He has his hydrogen and his cobalt bombs, and therefore people today think that Man could easily destroy the Earth. He has the power to do so but, of course, greater forces than Man control this Earth and he will not be allowed to do it. So all those people who fear the total destruction of this Earth through hydrogen warfare need not worry. It will not take place, for not only is the will of your Creator controlling this but also the will of all those beings more evolved than yourselves who can impose their will on you as well:

the beings on the other planets of the Solar Body, especially those from Mars, Jupiter, Venus and Saturn who are at present around the aura of the Earth influencing, guiding, helping, repairing where Man's ignorance has destroyed. Their will will be done. They will not allow the Earth to be destroyed in its entirety.

Remember that there are many beings with a greater will, a greater power, than Man. Man is an infinitesimal speck on the Earth struggling to evolve. He is like a young boy at school: he may be given a loaded gun to practise his shooting, but there is always a teacher close at hand to see that he does not shoot himself or one of his fellow pupils. The will of your Creator is that you should evolve spiritually through life in a physical body on the Earth. You are here to experience life on the Earth as well as upon the other planes of existence. This Earth is but a school onto which you incarnate to learn its lessons. The principle lesson of this Earth is one of sacrificial service, and Man has the choice of whether he wishes to sacrifice or not. Those of you who do indeed sacrifice, who do think of your fellow brothers before yourselves, who do think of the other Kingdoms before your own, who are totally aware of life on this planet, will begin to appreciate the will of your Creator, and if you understand the will of your Creator for this Earth then you will understand the Earth, the part that it plays in the whole, together with the function of those who dwell on it.

You are all born under great planetary influences, or wills. You all vibrate under one of the seven major Rays which control this planet, and you are individually restricted by that Ray under which you vibrate. These Rays bear down upon you at all times, restricting you, controlling you, and guiding you. You are restricted even more by your own evolution. So as you walk your path in life recognise that you have free choice, and that you must be responsible in that choice, but also recognise the will of your Creator in everything around you. It is not your Earth. Your brothers around you are not of your creation. The Animal, the Vegetable and the Mineral Kingdoms were all created by a greater force than you. Man creates nothing and therefore Man can control nothing. Only when you can create may you exercise the Will.

THE TRUE MEANING AND SIGNIFICANCE OF EASTER

In the same way that Man today is fascinated more by the physical act of the Nazarene's birth than by its real spiritual significance so, because of the teachings of Man's various Churches, he is concerned more with the physical acts of Easter, with the betrayal, the arrest, the trial, the crucifixion and the resurrection of the Nazarene than with the real significance of those events in spiritual terms. On Good Friday Man, persuaded by his Churches, grieves over the betrayal and death of the Master Jesus, casting blame on those who betrayed, tried and crucified him and then, on Easter Sunday, expresses joy for the resurrection of that Master, whom he calls the Son of God. I know that many of you have very firm beliefs about the meaning and significance of Easter, but I hope that in this lecture you will be able to consider a different interpretation of the Easter story.

I will begin by saying that the Nazarene came not for a single race of men but for the World. The Nazarene was born in a Jewish body for reasons of karma. He came and incarnated in matter both to fulfil his destiny and also to exemplify the Christ Principle for Humanity. The fact that he incarnated into the Jewish race does not mean that he came solely for the benefit of the Jews. He came for all Mankind, and although the Western World in particular has been attracted to his teachings, and has created the Christian religion from the events of his life, the message that he brought is for all men. Any person, of any creed, living anywhere on the Earth, through reading about the life of Jesus of Nazareth and the period when he was overshadowed by the Christ can understand how life should be lived on this Earth and the purpose for which Man incarnates. The Nazarene did not intend that the events of his life should be used as the basis for founding any sect or religion, but nevertheless the Christian religion has been created from the happenings of those times. The fundamental concepts of the Christian religion are based on the happenings of Easter, when the Master Jesus died a painful death on the cross and then, on the third day, rose again. What I wish to question, if I may, are some of the preconceived ideas which have grown up and are now regarded as fact, as dogma, about the life of the Nazarene and which have distorted the true purpose of his incarnation.

The Nazarene's destiny and life in physical matter was planned with infinite precision. The time of his birth, the duration of his life and the moment of his death were known long before he incarnated. The great Beings who control this Earth planned, with true spiritual awareness, the demonstrations that were to take place on Earth for the benefit of Mankind. Throughout his ministry Jesus of Nazareth was fully aware of the nature of his life, of what he was to do, and also of the nature and the purpose of his death. He knew that he was to die at a certain time many years before that event actually took place. That knowledge belongs to a Master such as he who has the wisdom and the consciousness to understand the spiritual factors involved. The manner and the time of his death were not, therefore, a matter of chance. He died at Easter, the time of the year when Nature all around emerges from the darkness of winter, puts on a fresh coat, a fresh body, grows and turns towards the Sun, the eternal Light, and flowers anew. Nature is, of course, the implement of Infinite Spirit, if only Man would be aware of that fact. It is through Nature that Infinite Spirit demonstrates the highest laws and spiritual facts in this Universe. The Nazarene, when he died on the cross at Easter, was symbolising this moment of rebirth in a new body.

Throughout his ministry the Nazarene was overshadowed by the Christ. Whilst the Nazarene dwelt on the Earth he was fulfilling both his own destiny as a Master and a Teacher, just as you as individual souls would do, and the Will of the Christ. You may think it strange that one being can be overshadowed by another, but it is quite possible. Throughout his whole ministry the Nazarene grounded the Christ Principle on the physical plane, the only plane which Man comprehends, but Man has tended to single out his birth and death as being the most significant parts of his life. Whilst they are of importance, they are not of supreme importance.

A little of what the Nazarene taught during his ministry is contained in the Bible. The Nazarene, inspired by the Christ, exemplified how Man should live his life on the surface of the Earth. If the Christian Churches, and Man in general, would only take the Nazarene's teachings and place them in the forefront of their doctrines they would indeed be fulfilling his aims. But they do not. They take the death of the Nazarene, exaggerate it out of all proportion to the rest of his life, and make it into a dogma. I am not saying that the Nazarene was not crucified. He was, but to one such as the Nazarene death, in any form, be it by the sword, by the gun or by crucifixion, is as nothing; a soul of his consciousness has already advanced to the level where death is of no significance whatsoever. It is only Man today who mourns the death of the Nazarene, who says that with his death a great Master was crucified, was removed from the Earth by evil people with all their fears and superstitions, and that they were to blame for what took place. What took place was planned aeons of time before it happened. The death of the Nazarene on that cross was as fixed in time as is the next coming of the Christ.

Every year the Christian Churches mourn the death of the Nazarene. On Good Friday the aura around the Earth is filled with the black clouds of wrong emotions, of wrong thoughts, of wrong beliefs, of erroneousness in every way. The Nazarene in his moment of death was passing from unreality, which is physical life, to reality, which is spiritual life. He was returning from the unreal to the real. He was throwing off the limitations of physical life, of this school of life which Man comes to experience, and was returning to his natural existence. In that crucifixion the Nazarene shed the restrictions, the sorrows, the trials and the turmoils of physical life. In that crucifixion he gave to Humanity the key which could open the doorway to its own resurrection. Death really is a birth; for as you die so you are being born again and, therefore, as you celebrate birth with joy and festivity so you should celebrate death in a like manner. By his act of death the Nazarene was demonstrating the return to a normal spiritual existence which awaits you all, and therefore all the sorrow that you express for his death is wasted energy caused by your misunderstanding of what he was doing.

From the Bible you read that the Nazarene, knowing that he was to go to Jerusalem, told his disciples that certain events were to happen, that certain plans had been made. In all the Gospels of the New Testament you may read where the Nazarene told his disciples of what was to happen, on every level of existence from the providing of a donkey to the room where the ceremony which you call the Last Supper was to take place, from his disciple Peter denying him three times to his trial and eventual death. If all these incidents were fixed in time and were destined to happen, were they not intended as demonstrations to Man of certain Principles?

Try to look behind the story of Easter and see more than that which is demonstrated by the recorded events. You can read the story of the Nazarene's death as you read any other book and can say that a man went to Jerusalem, was betrayed and falsely arrested, was given a mockery of a trial and, although innocent, was condemned to die a most painful death. But let us examine a little of the significance behind those events. The Nazarene went to Jerusalem. Even though he knew that a painful death awaited him, he still proceeded towards Jerusalem because he wished to carry out the Will of his Creator. He knew that he had to go there, not for himself, but for Humanity as a whole. He was a teacher demonstrating certain facts of existence for the benefit of his pupils. He knew who was to betray him. He knew how that man was to betray him. Remembering that a less evolved soul cannot take away the life of a more evolved soul, you can deduce that Judas Iscariot who betrayed the Nazarene must have been of equal soul evolution to him. They were, indeed, true affinities, and in that incarnation they both came into matter at the same time, the one to exemplify the Christ Principle and the other to be the cause of the Nazarene's physical death in order that Humanity could be awakened and the Christ Knowledge spread as It has spread to this day. So, by betraying the Nazarene, Judas too was performing the Will of his Creator. It was not an act of evil. No other disciple but Judas was of the evolution to betray the Nazarene, to deliver him to death for, ultimately, it was the act of Judas which resulted in the Nazarene's arrest and death. Although the soldiers who crucified him carried out the physical process of death, it is the one who is responsible who bears the ultimate responsibility.

Consider the fact that the Nazarene was convicted and sentenced to death for demonstrating and exemplifying the Christ Principle which Man has since developed into a major creed in the World today. The religious men of his time, suspicious and bound by their own dogma, would not accept his teachings, and so the mockery of his trial took place. You also have the civil leaders of the time, exemplified by Pontius Pilate, who washed their hands of the whole affair and, knowing his innocence, still allowed him to be crucified. There is symbology in that for your modern World.

The Christian religion has taken the Nazarene's crucifixion and has made it into the foremost part of its dogma. The symbol of the modern church is the cross on which he was crucified, but the true symbol of this Earth on which you dwell, the symbol which has existed since the creation of this globe, the symbol which links it not only with all the other planets in the Solar Body but also with Bodies beyond this Solar Body, is the true cross. The true cross is a cross with four balanced arms of equal proportions symbolising the number four, the number to which physical matter on the Earth vibrates. There are the four elements, the four seasons, the four points of the compass, the four major races and the four Kingdoms of Nature etc. The balanced cross is the true symbol both of the Nazarene and of the Earth. The crucifix of the Christian religion is an unbalanced cross and reflects Man's own imbalance today.

The act of crucifixion, which you read about in the Bible, symbolised the crucifying by the Nazarene of his lower aspects, the lower self that is always opposing the influence of the soul and the Will of your Creator. The Nazarene allowed himself to be crucified, placing himself upon the cross of his own free choice, and undergoing the pain of the cross so that he might advance to true spirituality. He was demonstrating that Man must place himself upon the cross of life, that Man must be willing to sacrifice, in order that not only he but all Humanity may move forward. Until Man has experienced the crucifixion of the lower elements of his being, the lower self, Humanity cannot advance.

Throughout the Nazarene's incarnation you are aware of his power as a teacher and healer. There are many recorded occurrences in the Bible of miracles that he performed. In fact, these were not miracles as such but merely demonstrations by the Nazarene of Natural Law, of Natural Power. For one of his evolution and knowledge, who had advanced to his state of consciousness in the Hierarchy, acts such as walking on the water, multiplying the loaves and fishes, healing the blind and sick, even raising the dead, were entirely natural. With the power at his command the Nazarene could have been invincible. With his great understanding and inherent ability to use the cosmic, occult, mystical and spiritual powers of the Universe, there was no one who could have touched him. If he had wanted to, he could at any time have avoided the events which took place in Jerusalem over that Easter. Even while he was on the cross he could have avoided death if he had so chosen. The ultimate temptation was for someone to say to him as he was on the cross itself, "If thou art the Son of God then take thyself off that cross". He could so easily have done that, but he did not. He underwent the process of death willingly, not only as an initiation for himself but also to demonstrate the control of the self for the Will of God.

In the Bible there is very little said about the Nazarene's resurrection. In the Gospels of the New Testament the fact that he was resurrected and came back to Earth in physical form, and that he appeared before the disciples who had witnessed his crucifixion, is mentioned only briefly. This act was, again, not a miracle but merely another demonstration of Natural Law. It is difficult for you, at your states of consciousness, to understand the act of resurrection because you do not understand the true laws of the Universe, the power of the mind or even the act of creation at your own physical level. Nevertheless great Masters such as the Nazarene can and do create and dissolve their physical bodies. It was quite possible for the Nazarene to remove his body from the tomb where it was laid and to appear in it again whenever he wished to do so, either before his disciples, or before the other people who witnessed his resurrection. A man of his evolution could appear at any time, in any form of physical body that he desired. Indeed, even today, Masters can do this.

The message of the resurrection was not that Man can resurrect his body. When you have advanced to the Nazarene's state of consciousness you too may resurrect your bodies. The Nazarene was demonstrating that even though he had risen to a higher plane of existence he was still the person that his disciples knew and remembered when he was in a physical body, and that he was continuing with the work that he had come to do. He also demonstrated through his resurrection how Man could be led into a higher occult realisation of himself. If the Nazarene had desired he could have appeared in the temple of Jerusalem itself and demonstrated his resurrection for all to see, but he did not do so for Man has to understand the nature of life on this planet and his true spiritual existence through his own awareness.

As you study the Bible try to understand its deeper symbology, for there is much symbology in it. Try to see the symbology behind the events of the Nazarene's life and you will begin to understand the true meaning and purpose of your own life, for you will see a reflection of yourself in various parts of the Nazarene's life. There is a message in the Nazarene's life for every man no matter what his state of consciousness, no matter what his colour or his creed. Remember that the story in the Bible does not belong to one religion alone.

The Nazarene demonstrated that the spiritual life which exists on the higher planes of life can, and indeed should, be present on the physical plane as well. The example of the Nazarene, and of the Christ Who overshadowed him, was one of Sacrificial Service. The whole purpose for the Nazarene's incarnation on Earth was to fulfil a plan not of his own choosing but of his Creator's. He incarnated on Earth and died on the cross to serve Mankind, to demonstrate certain Laws, so that Mankind could see in his life the true reason for its existence.

COMMUNITY LIVING

As you look around the countries of the World today, and in particular at the young people in them, you will find that one of the practices which has recently begun to be established is that of living together in a community, or a commune, as it is sometimes called. To many of the older generation, that is older in physical years, this way of life is quite abhorrent, and when what goes on in some of these so-called communities is described in the newspapers and is talked about on the radio and television it merely acts as a confirmation to them of their decision not even to investigate the nature of community living and its inner purpose and significance. There is a saying that no news is good news, and so they do not hear of the many successful communities that are in existence all over the World where people do live together happily with a common purpose, a common code, fulfilling the will of their Creator. I must begin this lecture, therefore, by asking you to forget all the falsehoods and distortions which you have read in the newspapers about these so-called 'hippy communes' and the young people who live in them, where acts of indulgence take place, to forget all that and to investigate with me the real significance and purpose of community living, especially as it applies to the Age in which you are now living.

The nature of life on this planet is that Man incarnates to fulfil the will of his Creator and to learn the lesson of this planet, which is sacrificial service through love. To live in a community requires sacrifice. It is much easier to live alone than to live with people with whom you have no family ties, and to share your everyday life with them. Man, when he first incarnates on the Earth, is happy and content to live alone. It is only after he has evolved his consciousness through many incarnations that he even begins to consider the concept of living together with other people, and when I say living together I do not mean living together in a village or small town, but living as a community. An unevolved soul will not want to live in a community because it thinks that the 'I' is far more important than the 'we'. Therefore until you have evolved to a certain level of consciousness and have realised that the 'I', the personality, is not important and that what is important is that the plan for the greater whole, the will of your Creator, is carried out, and until you are prepared to sacrifice to achieve this, you will not feel within you the desire even to try to live in a community in order to obtain the benefits that are to be had from this way of life.

It would be true to say that when you first incarnate on the Earth you are learning to become 'self' conscious. In the course of many lives on the Earth you develop the self, the individuality of the soul. When, eventually, you have fully developed and at the same time limited the self, and have imposed the necessary discipline on it, your consciousness then turns from self-development to group-development. You begin to think in terms of living and working in a group, of thinking not of the self but of the other selves in a group and of their purpose in the plan for this Earth. After you have developed this aspect of life you will, of course, then grow to become race conscious, not meaning race in terms of individual countries but rather in terms of the four major races of this Earth — the red, the yellow, the white and the black. After you have become race conscious you will then grow to become Earth conscious and think of the Earth as a whole. But all this requires many stages of development and evolution, and in this lecture I am going to look only at group living, or community living, as you call it.

The sort of people who decide that they wish to live in a community are usually those who have already begun to master the self, who have realised that the self has to be limited and controlled for the good of the whole and that it is only by controlling and disciplining the self that not only will their consciousnesses advance but also the consciousness of the Earth as a whole. They have begun to think not just of the individual consciousness but of the group consciousness, then of the Earth consciousness and eventually of the Solar consciousness. They come together to live and work in a community not only for the purpose of their own development but also for the development of the community, so that from it they may increase not only the consciousness of the community but also the consciousness of the Earth which it serves.

The physical act of establishing a community is very simple. Usually the individual souls concerned choose to work in a community even before they incarnate and, therefore, no matter how they have lived during the earlier part of their lives, as they reach an age of soul-consciousness they are drawn together to establish this community. Initially the members of the community may not be living as a community, but as individuals waiting for the correct moment of consciousness in order to come together to work in this way. Ideally there should be twelve male aspects in each community, and each of these male aspects will, of course, have its female counterpart so that the power of the male is balanced by the wisdom of the female. Each of these men will be born under a different sign of the Zodiac so that in the community there will be one of each sign bringing the power of that sign to it, thereby ensuring its correct balance. An example of this was in the Nazarene's life, for there exemplified for you was community living as it should be: the twelve men, the power aspects, who came together at the call of the Nazarene to become his disciples. Each one of them was born under a different planetary influence, and so each one had a different power, a different aspect, to present to the whole.

Obviously community living has to exist on many levels: from the physical aspects of living, eating, drinking and existing together in a community to the spiritual work of the community which involves its destiny, its consciousness, and the work which it has come together to do. When communities first start they tend to concern themselves mainly with the physical aspects of living together, for that is what they have to contend with initially. Although they might all have individual desires to be of service to their Creator, and although they are prepared to make sacrifices, it is difficult when they first come together to sacrifice to each other on the physical level. They have all lived in different environments, have had different ideas impressed upon them by their parents and teachers and, therefore, unless they are in great harmony and possess a common desire to imitate their Creator and to be of service, difficulties will arise.

The first years of community living are concerned primarily with a settling down period in which the community learns to function as a community on the physical level. It learns that the individuals in the community should live as one and yet should be separate. By this I mean that there should be an individual room, house or division, call it what you may, where a family lives as a unit as regards sleeping and experiencing the vibrations of family life, but that all the people in the community will meet in a central place where they will perform both the physical and the spiritual work for which they have come together. The community centre is the focus of the community. There should be communal dining arrangements where a rota will decide who is to prepare the food. Normal organisational methods will decide who is to grow, cultivate and provide that which is necessary for existence in a physical body. There will also be a separate centre for worship, prayer, meditation and communication with the Higher Beings who are to inspire and help the community, where marriage, birth and death will take place. This will be the spiritual temple of the community.

Problems are obviously going to arise, but these will normally be of a minor nature for the souls who have chosen to come together will soon harmonise into a unit. If by some mischance a wrong vibration, or soul, enters into the community, it will soon be discovered and will be asked to leave but, normally, souls of a certain evolution will blend together through a common desire to fulfil the exact purpose for which they incarnated. Once the physical aspects of living together have been sorted out then the spiritual work for which the community came into being can really begin in earnest. The team has been established, the power is being generated, the inspiration from Above comes down and the work of that community, in whatever field of service it may be, begins. It may be a discovery for the human race. It may be writing, painting, art, music or teaching. It may be inspiration from any of the seven major Rays which vibrate onto this Earth. Each little community all over the World will be performing its own individual function according to the Plan of Infinite Spirit.

The balance of a community is obviously important. You will have the initial balance of the twelve signs of the Zodiac under which the male aspects of the community will have been born and also, depending on the nature of the work to be done by the community, you will have other varying planetary influences. You will find that certain members of the community will be born under the strong influence of certain planets. Therefore in any one community there can be many permutations to influence the work which it will do and the direction it will take.

Let those of you who are considering living in a community

and those of you who have not yet thought of doing so but, perhaps, may be attracted to the idea, remember that to live in isolation as a family unit is basically divisive, for you tend to think only of your family. You think only of doing the best for your family, for your wife and your children, usually at the expense of everyone else around. Therefore, as the lesson of this planet is to learn to sacrifice, you must begin to think less of yourself, your family, your home, and more of other people, to act with responsibility for them as well as for yourself, and not to advance yourself at the expense of others around.

As your soul evolves, as it lives its many incarnations on the surface of the Earth, it begins to feel within it a desire to live not for one but for two, and then not for two but for four, and so the desire to build up a group is awakened. As you get to know yourself through meditation you become aware of yourself and of your limitations: you know what you can and what you cannot do. Likewise you can recognise in another man what he can do that you cannot, and you can see that to blend together would be most advantageous. If one is a writer, another a musician, a third a scientist, a fourth an agriculturist, a fifth an architect, a sixth an astrologer, and so on, how helpful it is to have all these facilities available in your family, for that is what the community is, a family, only on a larger scale. The family of the individual unit grows into a family of many people and, in the greater Plan, into the family of God. So, really, the desire to live in a community stems not only from the desire to sacrifice but also from an awareness of one's own limitations and of the attributes of others. If another man is more experienced and possesses greater knowledge than you in one particular aspect of living then is it not wise to go to him for help and advice?

So people will come together in a community each bringing their own individual talents which they will use for the good of the whole. In any community the inner band of twelve, like the Nazarene's disciples, will usually be evolved souls. They will possess great talents, great power, great influence. The inner twelve will be the foundation stones on which the community is built and people who join subsequently will attach themselves to this core group. They will live separately from the core group, perhaps in individual units, but will work with the group, will study with them and so will learn from them. They will not be allowed to participate in all the life and the ceremonies of the inner twelve, but they may share their physical life to the full. They will therefore see exemplified what they should be aspiring to attain. That is the nature of community living. Gradually the community will get bigger and bigger. Eventually those who have come to watch and learn will move off and start their own communities, and so the cycle will continue.

Community living, as you call it, was the basic way of life on Atlantis. That was how Atlantean society was structured. Taking what I have described a step further, the Atlanteans would have twelve communities living around a spiritual power-point on the Earth, a temple, which would be the equivalent of a present-day town, for people were not so numerous then as they are today. These twelve communities would combine together to create a great power centralising on a temple which would be the spiritual centre of a particular region. On the next level you would have twelve temples forming yet another group, and so the structure was built up to form the Whole.

As you can see, community living is an evolutionary process. Once you learn to sacrifice the self you then learn to sacrifice your community for the greater Plan, the greater Whole. The shift of the emphasis is from putting forward the self, from seeking benefits for the 'I', to looking at your neighbour, at the other man, of thinking not only of him but of the whole Earth on which you live, and then eventually of the planets and of the stars beyond it. It is to think not of the 'I' but of Creation. If in this incarnation you can just begin to think not of the 'I' but of the community you will have taken a great step forward in the advancement of your consciousness, for from community living and community consciousness you will begin to understand the Plan and the Purpose of Creation.

THE IMPORTANCE OF CORRECT EATING

One of the characteristics of Man's physical body is that it needs to be sustained with matter in order to replace the parts and constituents of the body which change every twenty-four hours. Every day, therefore, Man eats and drinks to sustain his body. The physical body is the vehicle of the soul. Whilst they reside in matter the spirit and the soul dwell in the left ventricle of the heart: that is where the physical body houses them whilst they are present on the Earth. It is important, therefore, that throughout its life the body is cared for and sustained according to its needs so that it in no way hinders the evolution and destiny of the soul.

As with all the other organs of the body, the stomach is controlled ultimately by the mind. When you feel hungry and you want to eat it is the mind that will control where you eat, what you eat and how you eat. An unevolved person, one who has not established the control and discipline of the mind, will not control his stomach and his eating habits. When he feels that he wants to eat, he eats. He does not particularly care when he eats, what he eats or how he eats. All he knows is that he has the desire to eat and that this desire must be satisfied. An evolved person, one who uses his mind to control his bodily functions, who is aware of his body and of what is good or bad for it, of what he should or should not eat, of when he should or should not eat, of how he should or should not eat, will exercise discipline in this respect in order to eat correctly.

You will recognise, therefore, that the way in which a person eats is really a matter of soul evolution, of wisdom. A soul that has only recently begun to incarnate on the Earth from the planet below yours in evolution will eat very crudely, whereas a great soul, a highly evolved Master, will eat very finely. You may think that all human bodies are similar, but they are not. They are all made of physical matter, but within the frequency range of matter there are many rates of vibration. All matter vibrates, and it would be true to say that the body of an unevolved soul vibrates at a lower rate than that of an evolved soul. The higher the rate of vibration the more a person can control his body and use the Natural Laws of the Universe to lead his life on Earth. You have the example of the Nazarene who, knowing the Law of Levitation, could walk upon the water.

What I am to say about correct eating will obviously not have a universal appeal and, therefore, according to your consciousnesses, you will either accept or reject it. As the basic reason for eating is to keep the physical body in a perfect condition so that it may be of service to the soul, any form of eating which does not contribute to this objective is incorrect. If you overeat, if you eat foods which are detrimental to your bodies, or even destroy parts of your bodies, that is very foolish. Many of you know that some of the foods which you eat are harmful to your bodies, yet you still continue to eat them because your jaded tastes demand that you do so. It is purely self-gratification: you like the taste, or you like the quantity, and so you eat to please that lower self. Nevertheless you should eat only to sustain your physical bodies in a perfect condition.

The vibration of your physical bodies is determined by your point of evolution. As you develop your consciousnesses within, so the vibration of your bodies will change. Remember that if you are to increase your vibratory rates, if you are to refine your physical instruments, you must first refine the matter that goes into your bodies. There are only three substances which your bodies take in: air, fluids and food. Although all three are important from the point of view of the correct functioning of your bodies, food is particularly important because the higher the vibration of the food you eat the greater its spiritual quality and its quality in matter and the more it will help you to increase the vibratory rate of your own bodies.

Those of you who seek to walk the path, who seek to advance spiritually and to be of service to Mankind, to exemplify the Christ, must be aware of the discipline necessary in this respect. If you cannot master your stomachs then you cannot master your personalities, your lower selves. You must begin with the physical aspects of your body before you can begin to control the reflection of your soul consciousness, the personality. The first rung on the ladder is to become the master of your physical body and of what you eat. In the Age in which you live, where

101

everything is mass-produced, where industry is geared to produce not what Man should eat but what industry decides is profitable, it is difficult to change your eating habits, but that is what you must do.

So far we have not discussed the question of what you should, or should not, eat. Each of you will have to decide according to your own consciousness how you should change your eating habits. What would be right for one would be wrong for another, and in this lecture I can do no more than point out a few guidelines. If you wish to raise the vibration of your bodies, you should eat only the finest foods, the foods of the highest vibrations, which are to be found mainly in the fruit kingdom — the fruits, nuts and berries which exist in profusion upon your planet. Therefore it is desirable, and note that I say only desirable, that spiritual man should become a strict vegetarian, that he should eat only the fruits of the Earth. If you are fully aware of life around you, if you have evolved to the point of consciousness when you do not wish needlessly to destroy anything, you will want to eat only of the fruits of the land, for by doing so you will be destroying nothing and will be aiding in the dispersal of the seeds of the fruits around the land.

It is not necessary, or desirable, that Man should destroy or in any way use the Animal Kingdom for food. That is not to say that Man cannot do it, for he does today, but as he is the most evolved being on this Earth he should not have to ask the Animal Kingdom to make that sacrifice. Although the Animal Kingdom does make the sacrifice for Man, for that is the nature of life on the Earth, Man does not need to eat the flesh of animals. All life is sacred. Man cannot create life and therefore he should not take it. Life is not Man's to give and take: it is his Creator's. Everything on this Earth belongs not to Man but to his Creator. Man must learn to be responsible for the Animal Kingdom, and as animals are less evolved beings he should look on them with love. He should try to help them for, truly, they look to Man for an example.

You may say that today many animals can survive only by killing each other. The weaker species are killed for food, that is true, but it happens only because the Animal Kingdom is a reflection of Man's Kingdom. Aeons of time ago, when Man dwelt in perfection on the Earth, both he and the Animal Kingdom were vegetarian. They did not kill one another for any reason. However, when Man fell from perfection, in his ignorance he misled the Animal Kingdom through his behaviour, so that now it would appear normal for members of the Animal Kingdom to kill one another in the struggle for survival. When Man examines the Animal Kingdom today it would appear to support the theory that each species interlocks with another in the struggle for survival to fulfil the plan of Nature. Because Man today is not perfect neither is the Animal Kingdom, for animals imitate Man. If you see cruelty, if you see killing in the Animal Kingdom, always remember that it is only a reflection of the Human Kingdom.

Animals feel pain just as Man does. They experience fear just as Man does, and the emotions of animals which are killed are held within their bodies. The vibration of fear is a coarsening vibration, and when Man consumes the flesh of animals he is partaking of that vibration. Furthermore, all the diseases of an animal and the polluted food it has consumed are contained within its flesh, hence when Man eats of that flesh he is partaking of those diseases and of that pollution. So, from the food aspect, the flesh of animals is the lowest of vibrations, and if Man is to walk the spiritual path he should avoid it at all costs for it will degrade his body spiritually. You are, no doubt, aware of the nutritional values that allegedly come from eating meat, but all of them can be found in other foods if Man will but look. Because when he first incarnated on Earth unevolved Man did not know any better there was some excuse for him killing animals for food, but today Man should be much more aware. He could find the correct foods to eat, and he could cultivate them if he so desired, but he does not, for much money has now been invested in the breeding and production of meat for the table.

I ask all of you who do eat meat just to consider, just to realise, what it is that you are doing. You are eating the flesh of a living being. Maybe the animal is not so advanced as a human being, but it is still linked to your Creator for it has red blood flowing through it, and anything that has red blood flowing in its veins is with soul. Look upon animals as your less evolved brothers who need your help, your guidance, your example, your love. They do not need to be slaughtered by you. As you sit at your table think of what you are eating, think of the pain that the animal went through, and consider whether its slaughter was really necessary. Remember that you are taking on its karma, its fear and its animalistic instincts, and that you are absorbing its many impurities caused by the use of Man's drugs and chemicals, which do so much harm to the physical body. Man, of course, also eats the birds of the air and the fishes of the sea. Their point of evolution varies according to the individual species, but they all have red blood flowing through them. No matter what biologists may tell you, birds and fishes do feel pain to various degrees. I repeat, all life is sacred, and Man can and should live without the sacrifice of the birds or the fishes.

You may say that it is not possible to live without eating flesh of some description. This is not true. Your 'experts' today might convince you that this is the case, that Man has been a meat-eater since time immemorial, but that again it not true. There are many people today who are vegetarians, who live quite happily, quite healthily, who produce beautiful children and thus destroy this myth. Indeed, if you are vegetarians you should be healthier, you should have healthier children, you should be more aware, you should be of a higher vibration. You should be able to enjoy every aspect of life far more than your meat-eating friends around you.

There is much that Man can eat in the Vegetable Kingdom, but today he is just becoming aware of the fact that even the Vegetable Kingdom has feelings. Tests have now been carried out the results of which cannot be ignored. These show, for example, that plants react to human emotions. If you curse a plant it does not flourish as much as one that is loved, for the elemental kingdoms responsible for growth in the Vegetable Kingdom respond to Man's thoughts. Man should, therefore, be careful with regard to what he eats in the Vegetable Kingdom, for anything which Man has to destroy entirely, such as root vegetables, should not be eaten, for within the stems of all vegetables there is white blood, or sap, flowing. The Vegetable Kingdom is on a completely different level of vibration and evolution to the Human and Animal Kingdoms, but it too is developing and evolving on the surface of the Earth. It reacts to Man's vibrations, to how Man lives his life and to how Man treats it. Obviously, if a sacrifice has to be made then far better it be something of the Vegetable Kingdom than of the Animal Kingdom, but if it is possible it is better not to have to ask for the sacrifice at all.

Man should be able to live from the fruits of the trees and bushes of the Earth. Of course I appreciate that it is not always possible to live entirely on fruit for, depending upon your position on the globe, at some times of the year fruit is just not obtainable. Moreover, because of the way in which he has abused the gift of reproduction the world is overpopulated, and Man now lives in parts of the globe where he should not be living. Originally, Man lived only in warm climes where fruit was always available.

For those of you who would like to begin the process of refining your bodies the first step is to start giving up the flesh of animals. To give up eating flesh at once and become a fruitarian would be foolish, for your bodies would not like it. Your bodies always respond best to gradual change. Just as when you are trying to cut down on the amount of food you eat you should not immediately starve yourselves for two or three days but should begin by cutting down the amount gradually, so similarly, you should become vegetarian gradually as well. You should begin by limiting yourselves to eating meat only once or twice a week and then, after a period of months, stop eating meat altogether whilst still eating fish and poultry. When you have achieved this then, as you think fit, begin to give up poultry and fish, with the whole process perhaps taking a year to eighteen months. As you gradually change so your bodies will change with you and you will find that they will become lighter, and that you will become more aware. Those of you who possess psychic powers will find yourselves becoming more psychic. Those of you who draw on inspiration for art, for science or for literature will find yourselves becoming more inspired. Those of you who are healers and wish to heal will find that you are better able to do so. You will be tuning your bodies to a finer vibration.

When you have stopped eating the flesh of animals you will then be faced with a choice of eating vegetables and fruit. So as to get the maximum benefit I must say here that it is important that whenever possible you eat only raw foods, foods which are uncooked; for when he cooks, Man destroys. Cooking may make food taste nicer. Cooking may blend various ingredients into a succulent dish to appease Man's jaded tastes but, as I said when I began this lecture, the whole purpose and importance of eating food is to sustain your bodies, not to gratify your lower selves. If you eat only raw food you will find that not only will you eat less, but you will eat better. You will have a greater supply of the necessary vitamins and nutriments for your bodies. You will find that you eat less because you need less, and you will find that your bodies become lighter and finer.

Do not condemn this way of eating if you have never tried it. If you feel that you would like to begin then make the effort, make the sacrifice, for after all, what are you doing? You are beginning to control your physical bodies in a very small way. You are beginning to say that not only will you not eat the flesh of animals, that you will not be a party to the destruction of one of God's Kingdoms and to all the suffering that goes with it, but that you will begin to control what is going into your physical bodies, the bodies that are the temples of your souls. You will begin to eat only the finest foods, the natural foods, which are the best foods for your bodies. You will begin to respond to your souls rather than to the manufacturers with their tempting advertisements for their various brands of what, for the spiritual person, is usually undesirable food.

There are many people living in the World today who are vegetarians. Every day the number increases as more and more people adopt the ways of their Creator. Today, especially amongst the young, the souls of the Aquarian Age, vegetarianism is prevalent, for some of the old souls of Atlantis are returning to the way of life that they have known before. Vegetarianism will become more universal within the next twenty to thirty years, for as the destruction of the cataclysm takes place, as much of the Animal Kingdom is destroyed, so Man will not be able to have meat and he will have to look elsewhere. If all of you have prepared yourselves by already taking that step, by already being able to live on one fifth of the food which you now consume, of being able to live only on the fruits of this Earth, you will then have taken a great step towards surviving the cataclysm to come.

MARRIAGE

In modern society the one union that nearly every man and woman will enter into at some time in their lives is that of marriage. Marriage is the basic unit of society in the World today. The spiritual reasons for marriage are very clearly laid down, but the reasons why Man enters into marriage can be very different, and one has only to examine the state of marriage in the Western World today to begin to question the very need for, even the desirability of, such a union. The reason for this, of course, is that many marriages are incorrect.

The act of spiritual marriage was established for several reasons, but primarily so that the two aspects of creation on Earth, the male and the female, the positive and the negative, the power and the wisdom, could live together in unity to fulfil a common destiny, to fulfil the will of their Creator. The prime reason for marriage should be the development of the relationship between the husband and the wife to fulfil this common destiny, and although in this destiny it may be intended that they are to have children, the having of those children, although it will occupy many years of their lives, should not be the most important part of the marriage. The husband and wife are individual souls, with their own individual destinies to follow. They also have their karma both to each other and to other people to fulfil. They have their individual tasks to perform which they chose before they incarnated into matter.

It is not essential that every married couple should have children. Today a marriage is not regarded as being complete unless there are children, but how wrong this is! Children should not be the inevitable result of marriage. They should come only to specific individuals for very specific purposes. One of the reasons why this World is so over-populated today is because Man has misused the sexual act and instead of using it for the procreation of children, and only for that act, he now uses it for pleasure. Natural Law cannot be avoided, and if Man performs the act of creation when other factors are correct then conception will take place and into his aura will come a child, not necessarily a child he should be having but merely one who is desirous of experiencing an incarnation on the surface of the Earth at that time. That child will come to him unintended, with no karmic link to him, not necessarily vibrating to him, merely because he gave it the opportunity as it waited in the aura around the Earth for a moment to incarnate.

Modern Man has created a twentieth century image around the act of marriage, so much so that it completely disguises the true facts concerning it, with the result that the young people of today are misled into seeking factors in marriage which either do not exist or else are not important. They are told that they should only marry if they fall in love but, truly, love should play very little part in the initial attraction of marriage. What should happen is that a man and a woman who, before they incarnated into matter, agreed to marry, are attracted to each other because of that common destiny, and that that mutual attraction then leads to a recognition of love. Romantic love, the infatuation between man and woman, is not real love. It is only temporary and passes with time, and those of you who marry for that sort of love will soon be disillusioned as it wears off under the strain of physical life.

There have been civilisations where a man and a women married not through their own choice but because the priests of that time, with their greater wisdom, could see that they were intended for each other and had a common destiny. Therefore they married not because they were attracted sexually, or physically, but because the priests could see from their auras that they were in harmony in other fields, on the planes which really matter; and such marriages worked very successfully. Today, because men and women do not realise what is important in a marriage, because they do not appreciate what makes a marriage work, they succumb to the pressures of society and marry at an early age before they have even thought about the meaning of marriage. The result of this is that years later, when they find that their marriage is not working out, they are faced with the problem of living with someone with whom they have little in common. Probably by this time they have had children as well, and so are no longer free agents. To go through life knowing that one has married the wrong person is a difficult path to walk.

Physical attraction should play a very small part in marriage, as should the sexual act itself. If you marry for physical attraction, what is to happen when that attraction changes or no longer exists? So what is important in marriage is that you do not marry for someone's outward appearance. You marry for a far greater attraction. You marry because you know that no matter what might happen to your partner you would always feel a common link, a common destiny, with them throughout the rest of your lives because you know that you were meant to be together, to walk a common path and, perhaps, to bring through certain destined children.

Man today generally marries far too young, and I use the term Man to mean Mankind, man and woman. Owing to the nature of the way in which Man has evolved in the Western World he reaches physical maturity at an earlier age than previous generations, but until he is twenty-one Man can still be regarded as being at school and learning, and therefore what is the point of him marrying before he has finished all his lessons, before his training for life is complete? He will change a great deal in the years from sixteen to twenty-one, far more than in ten or fifteen years of later life. Man should normally marry during his third cycle, from the ages of twenty-one to thirty, although obviously this can vary because of individual factors in the lives of the people concerned — the karma they have to pay to others, the various planetary influences under which they were born, the lessons they have to experience, etc.

In society today you are expected to marry young, and if you don't you are regarded as being abnormal and it is implied that you are wasting the most fruitful years of your life. How wrong this is. Every year of your life is fruitful, is given to you for a purpose, and should be used for the purpose for which it was given. Marriage will come when you and your intended partner are both ready for it. Both of you, of course, have free choice as you walk along your separate paths. You may deviate from them, or not walk them as fast as you should, and therefore keep your destined partner waiting. What happens in society today is that young people are not prepared to wait. They seek the pleasures of the moment, or what they think are the pleasures of the moment, and they marry the wrong person at too early an age.

In the World today because so many marriages are incorrect,

many of them lead to divorce. If there are no children involved, if both the individuals of their own free choice wish to part, then it is quite acceptable for them to do so, provided, of course, that they were not destined to marry in the first place. For if two people have come together in marriage to work out certain karmic relationships, perhaps caused by their behaviour when married in previous incarnations, then to avoid this by divorce is merely avoiding the destiny of that life. However, if one partner does not wish to divorce then a divorce should not take place. Remember that the lesson of this planet is sacrificial service in love. You are learning to sacrifice the self for another, and if in this case that other is your marriage partner who does not want a divorce, then, even if you do, you should make the sacrifice for that other half. It is far better to do that, which will lead to great soul evolution, than to divorce somebody who does not wish to be divorced, for all that happens then is that you will owe that person karma which you will have to repay in another life.

Those of you who marry and have children should not divorce, for once you have allowed children to come through you then you become totally responsible for them. It is essential that a child has the vibration of the father and the mother with it until it is past the age of twelve. A parent who does not stay with his, or her, child until that age is failing that child and will incur karma. Therefore, all those husbands and wives who have children and who realise that they have not married the right person, even if they wish to marry someone else, should not obtain a divorce. They should make the sacrifice for their children, for it is the children who are of prime importance. The fact that the parents have upset their own lives does not mean that they have the right to upset the lives of their children as well. If only parents would really consider the responsibility of having children they would not have them quite so quickly and so early in marriage, for once you have children that marriage is sealed.

It is essential that parents stay with their children until the age of twelve, when the soul is fully in the body, when they are able to fend for themselves and to understand a little more about life. Beyond that age it then becomes more acceptable for the parents to divorce if they so wish, but, in fact, children still need their parents until they reach the age of twenty-one. When they are twenty-one they are considered to have finished their period of schooling and are now regarded as adults, accountable for what they do. They no longer need, although of course they will probably still get, the support of their parents. Up to the age of twenty-one children still need the wisdom, the guidance and the example of their parents and so it is desirable that, even if they want to separate, the parents should remain together to help their children. When the children are twenty-one, then, if the parents still so wish, they can divorce. However, by that stage it is amazing how often, when given the opportunity, parents who have previously decided to divorce no longer wish to do so. Out of all the struggles, the conflicts, and the bitternesses there comes a working agreement, there comes an awareness of the other person.

There is a saying that marriages are made in heaven. How true this is. Marriages are, indeed, destined. The person you are to marry is chosen by you before you incarnate. All you have to do is to recognise the person whom you are destined to marry when he or she appears in your life! Usually, if you are not persuaded otherwise, you are not even interested in marriage until you meet the right person. Then, for the first time, you consider marriage.

Marriage, in most cases, is usually between souls of a comparable soul evolution. Remember that your soul manifestation at twenty-one is entirely different to what it will be at thirty-one, at forty-one and at fifty-one. At fifty-one you will have grown to complete spiritual fruition, and if your partner is not able to keep up with you then a great strain will be placed upon the marriage and upon your destiny. It would be true to say that an evolved soul will very rarely marry an unevolved soul, although on occasions this does happen, usually for karmic reasons or else as a sacrifice to help the less evolved soul. Therefore, one of the first things you should discover before you marry is your intended partner's basic views on life, both on a physical and a spiritual level.

I would say here, as this practice is prevalent in the World today, that to marry inter-racially is wrong. Each of the Races that incarnates on this Earth — the black, the white, the red and the yellow — has a different lesson to learn. The four Races were given to the Earth by your Creator in purity, and to mix the black and the white, or the white and the yellow, for example, is wrong. You may think that this is a harsh thing to say, but it is true. Any mixed marriage is not a destined marriage.

Remember that there is no rush to get married and that if there is any doubt time will resolve it. The young of today are hasty for the passions and the fruits of marriage, for the pleasures that it will bring, but, as any established married couple who have truly experienced marriage will tell you, all the desires, all the images, all the thoughts, about marriage are far removed from the actual reality itself and are soon destroyed. So if at any time there is doubt, then wait. Pray for inspiration and for guidance, and it will come.

When you have decided to marry, then, as marriage is a spiritual act, it is important that there is a spiritual ceremony of marriage. That is why the civil contracts which take place today are not spiritually binding. They may be legal as far as the state is concerned, but it is desirable that the spiritual ceremony of marriage is carried out in a temple of any form, of any creed, of any belief, and that the blessing of Infinite Spirit be invoked on that marriage; for if you do not ask for spiritual help in your marriage, if you do not ask for the blessings of the Higher Beings, then you will not receive them.

Remember that although you are joined together in marriage you are still individuals. You each have your own destinies to fulfil as well as your joint one in marriage. The one partner should always encourage the other to walk his or her own separate path. Although individuals, you will grow together in marriage, and for those of you who are evolved enough to marry your soul affinities, the other half of your soul expression in creation, then remember the responsibility of growing together to become the one that was destined. That is the real purpose of your marriage. Remember also that the roles in marriage are not as accurately defined as modern society would have them. Man is not always the provider. Woman is not always the housekeeper. The roles may be reversed in any way, at any time, for any reason. Marriage is a form of schooling, and in the relationship of marriage you will learn many lessons of life: control of the physical, control of the emotional, control of the tongue, control of the thought.

In any union, not only in marriage, but in friendship or any gathering together of people with a common cause, there must be balance if that union is to succeed, and so in the spiritual union of marriage it is most important that there is balance, and that that balance, once established, is maintained. If a marriage has been correctly consumated and balanced throughout its existence, with the power of the male balancing the wisdom of the female, then when eventually one of the partners dies and returns to his or her true spiritual existence the other one should be able to continue on quite happily. That is the nature of a truly balanced marriage, for there is giving and taking, the recognition by the one of the freedom and spirituality of the other at all times.

A man and a woman unite in marriage to lead their lives together. Obviously one of the first things that has to be done is the establishment of balanced physical living. However, more important than this is the spiritual balance of the marriage. You have all lived many lives in many civilisations, have created your homes, have raised your children, have seen them in turn leave and get married, and have lived according to your individual consciousnesses. Therefore, what is of prime importance is not the physical, or material, side of marriage but the spiritual, or soul, growth that comes from it, the evolution together of two consciousnesses, as was destined before they incarnated. If this spiritual growth is not taking place then the true purpose of marriage is not being fulfilled. Marriage is not just a union of two souls for the purpose of spending life together more comfortably, although many people today marry for this reason. For many, marriage is an act of company, an act of security, an act of selfishness, sometimes even an act of greed. The true purpose of marriage is to fulfil the spiritual destiny to which the two souls agreed before they incarnated into matter. If they are to fulfil this then the spiritual balance of the marriage must be correct. What is important is the balance between the spiritual consciousnesses of the individual souls. If this does not exist then there will be great conflict at all times within the marriage.

As you each individually evolve your consciousnesses it is important that your partners evolve with you. The whole purpose of the spiritual union of marriage is for the one partner to help the other as each advances along his or her path, so that if one slips behind the other may encourage, if one draws ahead the other may recognise and strive to catch up. If a husband and wife allow the gap between them to grow too great then that union is lost, and the purpose of the marriage is gone. So you see the danger. You may be married, with children whom you have conceived and created as an act of destiny, but, because your spiritual union has failed, you are condemned to a marriage on the physical or material level. You have to remain together, or you

113

should remain together, for the sake of the children who have come through you, and it is not a pleasant lesson to learn.

All evolved souls should be aware of the spirituality of life and of marriage. They should know that marriage is not just coming together, having children and running a home, for they have all done such things many times and should be able to do them as second nature. What they are here to learn is the spirituality of marriage for, ultimately, what will happen to them is that the final marriages that they will have in physical bodies on this Earth will be with their true affinities, which will result in the union of their souls into one complete balanced spark of consciousness. When they have achieved that then they may deem themselves adepts of the highest order.

All of you must strive to maintain the spiritual balance of your marriages. If you work at this balance rather than at the material balance then the latter will fall into place, for 'as above, so below'. In as much as you show consideration and love to your partners in the spiritual aspect then that will be reflected in the material and the physical aspects as well. Remember that when you surrender to your little personalities, to your emotions, your loves, your hates, your moods, you are hindering not only yourselves but your partners as well, and in that you are hindering your partners you are creating karma for yourselves. So you are affecting yourselves not only in this life, but in lives to come. Look, therefore, to this spiritual balance, for when the spirituality of the marriage is correct then other factors do not matter. If you establish that balance you have established the balance of life, and you have established the balance for eternity.

REINCARNATION

The concept of reincarnation is recognised all over the World. Many interpretations of its true meaning are to be found but, putting it simply, reincarnation means being born again, living another life again. Many people can accept that their soul, or their spirit, does indeed exist on other levels after the physical act of death takes place, but they find it hard to accept that they have actually lived physical lives before their present incarnation and that they will indeed live again in a physical body at a later stage in the evolution of the Earth.

Nothing that I am to say will convince any man of the principle of reincarnation who does not within his own consciousness already believe in it, for a belief in reincarnation is a point of consciousness. Therefore I address myself in this lecture to those people who do believe in reincarnation, although they are perhaps not aware that they have such a belief at this moment in time because they have not thought deeply about it and have not developed their consciousnesses, and to those who are already aware of the fact of reincarnation but whose knowledge could perhaps be broadened by looking at a few new aspects of it. Those of you who do not believe in reincarnation may read on and it will either confirm your views or else it will begin to make you question your attitudes towards it. To understand reincarnation you first have to understand the meaning and purpose of life, for if you do not understand that then you will not comprehend the need for, and the principle of, reincarnation. Therefore do not try to investigate reincarnation until you have thought deeply and seriously about the many aspects of life in the physical. Finally, I would ask you not to think of reincarnation according to the teachings of any organised religion which exists in the World today, but rather according to the inspiration of your own individual consciousnesses.

In your World there often occur acts of great tragedy, as you would describe them. Almost every day you can read in the newspapers of accidents in which people have been killed either in planes or cars, of murders, of tragic deaths and of thousands dying from famine or disease. Perhaps even amongst your own circle of friends you are aware of fathers or mothers who have died leaving their children to live on alone, or of children who have died leaving their parents heart-broken at the loss. Many people say, "How can God allow such suffering to take place?", and by this they imply that God, or their concept of God, is to blame for the tragedies that take place. If you lived only one life, if you had not lived before and if you were not to live again, then perhaps you might have some justification for thinking that life was cruel, that it was a pointless waste to take a man away in his prime, to remove a mother from her children, to destroy the apparent happiness of life on this Earth. But those of you who do believe in reincarnation, whilst recognising that the summit of your consciousness is still only a little pin-prick of light on a dark horizon, are perhaps beginning to see a reason for, even a justification behind, these tragic events, and to understand why families who live in great happiness suffer these tragic losses, and why 'accidents' do happen. You have recognised that nothing in this World happens by chance and that everything that exists in matter is controlled by forces greater than Man can imagine.

For Man to say that an act is cruel, and that therefore God is cruel for allowing it to happen, merely reflects his point of consciousness. If Man cannot see deeper then he will be convinced that life is cruel, that he has been hard done by, that he has suffered for no purpose. Therefore it is true to say that most of the so-called tragedies that occur in life happen to unevolved people, to the people who do not understand why these losses occur; for it is only in moments of great crisis, of great tragedy, that Man brings his finer feelings into play. When the outburst of emotion is finished, when a normal balance returns to his body, then Man begins to think, and perhaps five or ten years after the incident in his life there will slowly come from within a dawning, an understanding, as to why those events have happened.

If you accept that life on this Earth is a school to which you go like the schools which exist on Earth, you must also accept that there have to be term-times and holidays, for when one is young one cannot learn continuously, without a break. Children go to school for a fixed period of time and then have their holidays.

That is exactly what happens in life. You go to school on Earth for a fixed period of time and then you have a holiday before returning to school again. When you return to school you have within you all the knowledge that you have acquired during your previous times at school. You have within you the experience of all your relationships with your fellow pupils and teachers, the examinations you have taken, the degrees you have obtained, and you will progress onwards from that stage. If you have failed some of your examinations, then the opportunity is presented to you to take them again after more schooling. That analogy really is a much simplified description of physical life. You have been told many times that 'as above, so below'. You may take the example of going to school and raise it to the level of physical life on Earth. You may take the example of physical life on Earth and raise it to the level of life on the higher planes of existence which are present within the spiritual body which you know as the Solar System.

"Well", you may say, "I can accept that, but why do people have to die in all these tragic accidents, for they cannot possibly learn anything if they are dead?". Here, of course, you have to consider what it is that they are learning and also who is learning through the act of death. Remember that the lesson of death is learnt mainly by the people who remain alive. For a person who dies peacefully in his or her sleep the act of death is nothing. For a person who dies after a long and painful illness, death comes as a pleasant relief. The suffering occurs to the people who have watched a loved one dying, who are aware of that suffering and who feel the loss after that person has gone. However when a person dies a violent death, such as in a plane crash, through murder or in war, there is a great influence on the soul at the time of death, for sudden or violent death jars the soul, and therefore in deaths of this nature it is mainly the individual soul concerned that is learning.

It is difficult for unevolved souls to understand why people should die before the end of their 'allotted span', but what do you consider Man's allotted span to be? Should it be his three score years and ten? Is that the norm to which Man should expect to live? How often have you sometimes wished that a man were dead? How often have you expressed relief that a man has been killed? If a man has committed a murder perhaps you are relieved when he himself has been 'murdered' by the authorities as a

117

punishment for the offence he has committed? Therefore your judgement as to whether or not a person has lived his intended lifespan will be influenced by your point of evolution. However, the important factor which has to be considered in all this is that each one of your lives is planned. Not only do you choose the body into which you are to incarnate, the parents who are to conceive you, the planetary influences under which you are to be born, the country in which you are to live, your way of life and the partner you are to marry, but you also choose your moment of death and the manner in which you are to die.

As I said earlier, this Earth is a school, and you learn even when making mistakes. If you face a test and fail, you have to take it again. So if you have lessons to learn in one life which you fail to learn, then in another life you will be presented with those lessons again; for you cannot progress — and all life is an upward progression, an upward spiral — until you have learned those lessons. If, for example, you incarnated to learn the lesson of poverty, if you did not accept it gracefully and did not recognise that it is merely a condition of the mind and not a spiritual fact, then you would experience many incarnations to learn the lesson of poverty. It is quite possible for you to be born a rich man in one incarnation and a poor man in another, to be a king in one incarnation and a beggar in another. Therefore, stemming from this fact, it follows that your behaviour in one life, whether you are a king or a beggar, will greatly affect your next life.

Many of you, I know, are aware of the Law of Karma. Karma has been described as the Law of Cause and Effect. What you do will have an effect. That which you send out will come back to you, if not in this life then in another. If you consider it, this is a very just Law. Everything in the Universe, from the stars and the planets above down to Nature below, is in balance. Would it not be unjust if Man lived only one life and in that life a person could, for example, murder someone and gain by it? The Law of Creation knows no such thing as imbalance. Everything is in balance, and therefore the Lords of Karma, those high Beings who weigh the scales of justice, balance out the effect of what a person has done. These Lords of Karma judge spiritually. They are not like the judges in your courts of law on Earth. They apply the Law of the Universe, the Law of Infinite Spirit, and they judge what a person has done quite impassionately.

Let us, for example, suppose that in a fit of anger you have killed someone. Now even if you are truly repentant for what you have done and have learned from that experience, the Law of Karma decrees that you owe that person you killed an equal payment. Now that does not mean that the person you killed has to kill you. That is not payment. It means that because you have killed that person and have perhaps shortened his life, then in another incarnation you would of your own free choice perhaps sacrifice your own physical life to help in that person's development or evolution, either by demonstrating a lesson to him through your own death or else by accepting a physical injury or illness in circumstances which would constitute a test for that person. Therefore what on the surface would appear to be an unjust or a tragic death, an illness or a material loss, is not really a quirk of fate but can be the result of either your own actions in this or another life, or your offer before you came down in your present incarnation to repay certain karmic debts.

You reincarnate on the surface of this Earth for two basic reasons: firstly, to learn through your experiences in this school of life and, secondly, to repay the karmic debts that you have accumulated in other lives. Now it is very difficult at your level of consciousness to understand karma, and to understand how a certain act in one life will produce a certain effect in another. If it is at all possible for any karma caused by your actions in this life to be repaid in this life, then the Lords of Karma will act to redress the scales as quickly as possible. But sometimes, as when you have killed someone, this is not possible, and then the karma will have to be repaid in a later incarnation.

Be aware that all the incidents in your life have a significance. All those times when you think that fate is just being cruel to you have a meaning. So try to look for it. Think back in your life to what you have done. Examine the incidents that have happened to you. Try to look for the underlying meaning and you will then see and understand the greater purpose in life. There is no such thing as chance. There is no such thing as blind fate. Everything that happens on the surface of this Earth happens for a reason. In that you are all born with the divine gift of free choice, as you choose so you will have an effect not only on yourselves but also on those around you. Man has to learn to be responsible not only for himself but for his fellow-men as well. Therefore karma applies not only to individuals but to towns, to cities, to countries and, of course, to the Earth as a whole.

You may say, "Why does Man not remember his previous lives? If that were so it would be easy to accept reincarnation". The mechanism of your mind has very wisely been designed by your Creator so that you cannot remember your past incarnations. There are little shutters over certain parts of your mind which seal off the past. This means that until you have acquired a certain consciousness in an incarnation you may not draw upon the memories of your past lives. Some people do occasionally have flashes of remembrance about past lives when, just momentarily, the shutters are lifted. This is due either to a fault in the mechanism of the mind or else it is triggered off by a particular act in their present incarnation, perhaps through visiting a certain place or witnessing an experience they have undergone in a previous incarnation.

So, usually, you do not remember your past lives. You do not know of your future lives. You are aware of life only in the physical body of your present incarnation. As you develop your consciousness in your present life you will of course draw upon the wisdom, upon the examinations that you have taken in your past lives, and that will slowly come forward into your consciousness for your use. That thing which you sometimes call a conscience contains all the wisdom and knowledge which you have retained from experiences in previous lives. You will feel that it is wrong to steal, that it is wrong to kill. You will feel guilty if you do not help your fellow men when asked. You will feel these things because you have learnt all those lessons before. Therefore people who have a strong conscience have a strong soul influence.

There is really no point in knowing about your past lives. Just as the physical bodies in which you dwelt in past lives are of no significance now, so your present physical body will be of no significance in your future incarnations. Although it would be very nice to know who you had been in another life, especially if you had been someone important, most of you would be flattered and might allow it to influence the way in which you lived your present incarnation. It might prevent you from learning the lessons of this life. Very often knowledge of past lives is revealed to you only at the moment of death. Man always prefers to look back into the past rather than live in the moment, and if he knew of his past lives then he would be tempted to look back into the past even more. That is not to say that you cannot know of your past lives, for the whole content of all the lives that you have ever lived — and many of you have lived thousands of lives in a physical body — is written in a record which is known as the Akashic Record. This may be examined when you are of the consciousness to look into that record and to be aware of its contents without allowing them to influence your present life.

I ask you all to try to look into life, to see the meaning and the balance in it, to realise that your Creator, Who knows every hair on your head, is aware of everything that is done to you justly or unjustly and is aware of everything that you yourself do, justly or unjustly. Realise that as you act so you will cause an effect not only in this life but in your lives to come. You may not harm another brother without that harm coming back to you. If only Man today would be aware of that fact how pleasant life on this Earth would be! If only those countries that fought wars would realise that their karma for fighting a war to gain a piece of land or to support an ideology would, even if they were to win that war, still come back to them. The cause will have an effect. Therefore please always motivate your actions with the purest and highest spirituality.

If you think that fate has been unkind to you, if you have suffered a loss or death in the family, then try to see the reason for it. Try to understand the tragedies, as you call them, in world events and to realise that they are not really tragedies: to lose one's life is not final, and to suffer a disease is only temporary, for you live so short a time in a physical body. When you are ill try to understand that illness. Try to accept it, to transmute it and to learn from it rather than look inwards and feel sorry for yourself. Realise that nothing happens but for a reason. Realise that if you discover that reason then you will understand the principle of reincarnation and you will understand one of the greatest Laws in the Universe, a Law which controls every aspect of existence from life below you, through life at your level to even the life of your Creator above you.

121

HOW TO BE A TEACHER AND AN EXAMPLE
OF INFINITE WISDOM ON EARTH TODAY

Your World today is very imperfect. There is much evil and much ignorance. This is because the true spiritual values which should exist on the Earth, which should be taught and exemplified, are missing. Man has passed through the Dark Ages, and from them has emerged a God-less society, a society which is bent only on material advancement to the exclusion of all things spiritual. Because of this, no matter how correctly Man may have advanced along his material path, imbalance has resulted since you cannot have the one without the other.

Life in the physical body today presents many problems for those of you who are evolved enough to understand the nature of spirituality in Man and to appreciate how life should be led. If you lead the lives that you believe to be correct you are almost unique, and you stand out as one in a hundred thousand. You are the ones who are not 'normal'. It is difficult to flow against the stream, but that is what you have to do. Throughout the history of Man, as he has struggled to evolve on this planet, it has always been the case that the true disciples of the Light, of Infinite Spirit, have stood alone. If Man was leading a truly spiritual life there would be no need for Infinite Spirit to send down onto the Earth Masters and Teachers to exemplify the way in which Man should live, for Man, being aware, would already be in contact with them. He would already be listening to them, learning from them, and following his true spiritual pathway. But once this link was broken, and Man became ignorant, then it was only by these Masters incarnating into matter on Earth and exemplifying Infinite Wisdom by word and deed that it was possible to present to Man the way that life should be led.

If you intend to stand as true examples of spirituality you must become accustomed to standing alone. What you say will be different. What you think will be different. You will behave differently from the next man. Condition yourselves to the fact that you are not going to be 'one of the crowd'. This is the first lesson for anyone who seeks to walk the true path and exemplify Infinite Wisdom.

You must prepare yourselves for a solitary life. You will have your friends, but you will have few true spiritual friends. Most of your friends will be only passing ones who will come and go at frequent intervals. You will find that they have little in common with you, or you with them. No matter how you view their behaviour, their habits and their customs, you will find it difficult to accept them into your homes, for they will exemplify the very things that you have rejected. You will find that, as you evolve, your circle of friends will become smaller. You will no longer be able to relate to and communicate with the people with whom once you could, for as the path gets narrower and steeper so the numbers walking it diminish.

Having chosen to walk that path and having prepared yourselves — and by this I mean the soul-consciousness preparing the personality-consciousness for what is involved — the next lesson you have to learn is how to present what you know as Truth to the rest of Humanity. Obviously, you must always speak the Truth as you know it even if it is going to offend someone dear to you, for, after all, what is it that you are offending? Is it not purely their personality? It is certainly not their soul-consciousness, because that can never be offended by the Truth. Moreover, what is it in you that worries about giving offence to another but your own personality! You must not agree with what people say if you, in your heart of hearts, know it to be wrong, to be a falsehood. That does not mean that you deliberately go out and seek to argue and put forward your point of view. It merely means that as you meet with people and converse, as you come into contact with people in your everyday lives and as situations or problems arise, you do not for the sake of peace and quiet deny what you know to be true and remain silent. State what you know. You do not have to say how or why you know: you have to say that you know. That is all.

You have to exemplify Truth, as you know it, not only by your speech but also by your actions. You have to lead the life which you know to be correct. You will not convince anybody if you say one thing but do the opposite. It is no good saying in public, for example, that all men are brothers and should live in peace and then going home and fighting with your wife, for that convinces no man. You must demonstrate by example. That is the way you will convince people.

Because, over many lives, Man has been deceived by falsehoods he has built up within himself, within his soul, a protection against the speech of his fellow-men. Throughout his evolution unevolved Man has communicated through the means of speech. During higher phases of consciousness, when the Earth was more evolved, speech was not used, but for most of the time Man has communicated through speech and, as such, much of the wickedness and evil of Man has come through his mouth. So Man has an inbuilt resistance to speech but he cannot resist, his soul cannot deny, Truth when he sees it. If he sees Truth with his eyes his soul sees it, and there can be no denial. One deed is worth a thousand words.

If you really intend to walk the path, pay particular attention to your deeds. Every time you are going to do something get into the habit of thinking most carefully about it first, especially when it affects your fellow-men, so that your actions, when you perform them, are the result of careful judgement and not quick personality decisions. Man remembers you more by your actions than by your words.

So many of the basic principles of life in your World today are wrong that you will find yourselves in conflict with them in almost every aspect of life. You will eat differently. You will drink differently. You will live differently. You will behave differently. You will think differently. You will feel differently. In all these ways you will become different from your fellow-men. It is therefore very easy to create conflict and to antagonise people. What you must ensure, however, is that people do not antagonise you. Your actions, if they are correct, will produce different responses in people according to their soul evolution. If a man recognises the Truth in you sometimes it will annoy his personality, and he will dislike you for it. That you will have to accept. It is the reason why you are here. Eventually, as he continually sees the example before him, that man will change.

What you yourselves must guard against is that you do not become antagonistic towards your less evolved fellow-men. If you see a man kill, if you see a man steal, if you see a man tell falsehoods, even if you see a man trying to destroy the Truth which you have established, you must not feel antagonistic towards him and create evil thoughts because of what he is doing.

This is a most difficult lesson to learn. Remember that you are the evolved ones, and the first duty of evolved souls is that they are here to be of service to their less evolved brothers and that, with the power of their evolved thought, they can easily create a greater force for evil.

So be tolerant of your less evolved brothers who do not think and feel like you. It is, for many of them, merely that they are the products of the Age, of the falsehoods that have been taught and passed down from generation to generation. Remember the difficulties that you yourselves have experienced in changing your ways of life and in expanding your own consciousnesses. You, perhaps, may have had a more favourable environment and received greater help than your less evolved brothers, and therefore you are in a position to help them. You can never force a man to believe in something. You may force a man to do almost anything else: the history of your Earth has proved this, but you cannot force a man to believe in something in which he does not believe. He may pay lip service to a belief, but he will not believe if he does not want to. You cannot force his soul.

The other great lesson which you have to learn is to know how, and when, to teach. Remember that you have not been sent to convert the World! Most evolved souls incarnate for a specific reason, with important destinies and tasks to fulfil, but the one vital thing which you must learn and understand, if you are to be teachers, is to know when to teach. The sole criterion that applies to this is that you teach only those who wish to learn. By this I mean that it is no good talking to people who do not wish to hear you. It is no good going out onto the streets and trying to convert people to what you believe. You should teach only those who willingly come to you, who ask you, and who seek to listen to you through their own soul initiative.

When people have come to you, the difficulty then is to know what to teach them. Again, it takes the wisdom of your soul to decide what you should say. You have to judge the nature of their soul-evolution. Are they capable of understanding the higher or the lower teachings? How much should you tell a man at one time so that he will understand, and so on? This you will learn with practice and through experience. All teachers have to pass through this stage. Remember it is better to talk to the least evolved souls in an audience and know that they, and therefore everyone else to whom you are talking, fully understand than to pitch your talk at such a high level that only a few can understand and the rest are baffled and perhaps begin to lose a little faith in why they have come to you.

Remember that it is the people to whom you talk and teach who have to discover for themselves. We, of the Hierarchy, on our level of existence, are always saying that there is only so much that we can teach you, there is only so much that we can reveal to you until you are ready. The rest must come from within yourselves. The basic lesson which you will teach will always be: "Look within yourself, for there is the Kingdom of Heaven". You will be getting Man to look within himself, to listen to his own soul and to follow his own consciousness. Remember that what is correct for one man will be incorrect for another. All men are different. All men will think differently and will act differently. Do not judge. Do not say that one is right and another wrong. All you can do, as every Master exemplifying the Christ Principle has done when he touched the planet Earth, is to set the example and then let Man follow and imitate. That is all.

One of the greatest temptations that exists for an evolved soul who is a teacher is to succumb to the power of his own ability as a teacher. When he reflects and speaks The Truth and convinces many, and when he sees the results, it creates a deep feeling of power and majesty for what he does. Some of the greatest teachers of Infinite Spirit have forgotten that they are only instruments, that they are not the source of the wisdom, and that they too are souls learning and fulfilling a destiny. You must, of course, resist the adulation of the people who will cling to you, of the people who will even worship you for what you say and do. That, again, is a difficult temptation to resist. You must always be saying that you are merely an instrument through which the Wisdom flows from Above, and that it is not you that people should look to and thank, but their Creator.

Finally, do not look for immediate results. Do not be hurt, or surprised, if you speak to an audience and at the end of your lecture not one person smiles, or seems to understand, and they all appear to go away looking confused. Although they may not understand at the time, the seed will have been sown and later on what you said will begin to germinate in their own thought processes. They may not even remember that it was you that sowed that seed. It does not matter. Do not worry if even in your lifetime you can see no tangible results for your efforts.

126

Remember the life of the Nazarene.

To stand in the role of a spiritual teacher, to exemplify Infinite Wisdom, is a testing incarnation. It requires that you watch your every action, your every word, so that you are an example to others. It requires that you in no way mislead a less evolved brother. If you establish yourself as a teacher be sure that you walk the path, for if by example or intent you mislead or harm a less evolved brother then great karma is involved. So before you begin to teach, before you begin to say, "I believe, I know and I will demonstrate", look within yourself and ensure that there is a true reflection of Infinite Spirit.

MAN'S RELATIONSHIP WITH THE ANIMAL KINGDOM

There are four Kingdoms of Matter in existence on the surface of the Earth, namely, the Animal, the Vegetable, the Mineral and the Human: four individual vibrations which are symbolised by the four equal arms of the true cross of this Earth. All of these Kingdoms are intended to live in balance and harmony with each other. The Human Kingdom is, of course, of a higher vibration than the other three, and Man, as he is the most evolved being, is therefore placed in a position of responsibility while he lives in matter during his incarnation on Earth; for it is only natural that souls or beings of a lesser evolution will look to the more evolved soul for an example. Just as Man looks to his spiritual teachers, be they the Nazarene, the Buddha or Mohammed, and strives to follow their example, the example of a more evolved being, so the three other Kingdoms of Matter look to Man for his example, and try to follow him. Man, therefore, bears a great responsibility in this respect.

The Vegetable and the Mineral Kingdoms are controlled by the Lords of Matter who dwell within the Earth and who, through their servants in the elemental kingdoms, rule matter on the surface of this Earth. Nevertheless the elementals do follow and imitate Man. Although Man cannot see the elementals and, except on certain occasions, they cannot see him, they do receive Man's thoughts and emotions, and imitate them. The Animal Kingdom is different from the Vegetable and the Mineral Kingdoms in that, like the Human, it was created originally by the perfect breath of your Creator. The animals do not have individualised souls as does Man, but belong to what can be called a group soul. There is one group soul for the lions, one group soul for the cows, one group soul for the dogs, and so on. Just as Man in his individualised aspect is a part of the Solar Logos, your God Whose spirit dwells in the Sun, and just as when you have evolved one day you will return that spark, that spirit now within you, to that God, so every animal that incarnates on the surface of the Earth returns to its group soul as the process of death takes place. I am pointing out this difference between the four Kingdoms only so that you may see the link between the Animal and the Human Kingdoms when compared with the other two Kingdoms which are without soul.

If I could take you back to a time on the surface of the Earth when, before he was given the divine gift of free choice, Man dwelt in perfection, you would be able to see life as a whole in perfection. You would be able to see a complete replica of life on the higher spheres reproduced on Earth. You would see the four Kingdoms of Matter living in harmony and balance. You would see the Animal Kingdom itself living in perfection because it would be imitating perfect Man. There would be no evil present. However, because of Man's disharmony life today presents a very different picture. Consequently if I put a few ideas to you about how the Animal Kingdom should really live, as it did aeons of time ago, perhaps it will help you to appreciate how you should treat the Animal Kingdom today.

When Man dwelt in perfection, so did the Animal Kingdom. The animals lived in harmony with each other. They did not fight, attack and prey upon each other, for they were all vegetarians: they all lived off the herbs and the fruits of the land. Of course they died, as did Man, but they died at their appointed time depending on the group soul from which they came and on the purpose and destiny of their species. They were free to walk the Earth wheresoever they desired, and they played their part in the balance of the structure of matter on this Earth in perfection. They carried the herbs and the seeds around the Earth. They were responsible for the growth of the vegetation and, at the same time, they limited its growth. In fact they were the husbandmen for Man, for they carried and planted the seed for him, they manured it and they helped in its growth. They were of service to Man, as was intended by their Creator.

In return, Man, living in perfection, did not own or control the animals. They were free to roam where they wished. If Man needed the company or the service of an animal then the thought sent out, and transmitted from a perfect mind, was all the attraction that was needed for the required animal to come and be of service to him. If at any time the animal did not want to stay, then Man allowed that animal to go when it desired. The attraction was mutual. Man did not own or control the animals, the birds of the air or the fishes of the sea. He recognised them as sparks of creation which were not so evolved as him, and therefore he was aware of his responsibility towards them. He realised that in no way should he set an example for the Animal Kingdom which could degrade or mislead it. In no way should he harm the animals, for one does not harm a less evolved soul: one helps it at its point of consciousness. Man did not, of course, need to kill any species of the Animal Kingdom for food, for he was a fruitarian and lived entirely on the fruits of the Earth. Varying species of the Animal Kingdom, not being so evolved, did take food from the herb kingdom, the grasses, the roots and various herbs, but that was the nature of their evolution, and the herb kingdom willingly made the sacrifice for the Animal Kingdom.

You may say, "Well that sounds like a very nice fairy-tale to me, but even if I do believe it, if I do accept it, it bears very little relation to the World today where the Animal Kingdom exists in a very different environment." Certainly the wild animals do kill one another. They need to in order to survive. Man kills and controls the animals. Man breeds his own domestic animals, and by mixing the seed of the individual species he even 'invents' new breeds. The environment and the Animal Kingdom have indeed changed, but this is entirely the responsibility of Man, for, either by his example or by his own actions, Man has brought about the downfall of the Animal Kingdom. The Animal Kingdom is here to be of service to Man, but what has Man done? He has made the Animal Kingdom his slave. It is forced to obey his will, his every whim, and to sacrifice itself for the good of Man whereas, in truth, Man being the higher vibration should sacrifice himself for the Animal Kingdom.

Man should in no way take, or even demand, the sacrifice of the Animal Kingdom to feed himself. There have been times in the past when unevolved Man, because he knew no better, needed the sacrifice of the Animal Kingdom to sustain his life. When Man lived in caves, when prehistoric Man as you know him first appeared, then there was an excuse, if you could call it that, for Man to demand the sacrifice of the Animal Kingdom. But today, when Man has evolved his consciousness and lives at such a high state of civilisation, there is no need for Man to ask, or even to expect, the Animal Kingdom to sacrifice itself for him. The fact that the Animal Kingdom is 'red in tooth and claw', as one poet has described it, that animals do kill one another, is purely a reflection of Man's own behaviour. For what does Man do today but kill his fellow-men, either physically or by the erroneous thoughts which he sends out into the ether which surrounds the Earth? When Man has so little respect for the life of his fellow-men, how can he be expected to respect the life of an animal which he regards as a less evolved being? If Man steals and deceives, if he treats his fellow-men with cruelty, what else can the Animal Kingdom do but act likewise, since it copies the example of Man? If Man lives in disharmony, if he destroys the Earth and the Kingdoms of Matter, what else can the Animal Kingdom do but follow his example?

Nature, and the Animal Kingdom in particular, has not always been like it is today. Because Man has been in error for so many centuries naturally the Animal Kingdom has gradually evolved until today the state of Nature is such that only those animals who have adapted have survived. The chain of evolution, as you call it, is in truth a reflection of Man's evolution, for the animals that have survived are the ones that have done so by killing the weaker species and living on them to sustain their life. You may well look at life in the wild and see how one animal kills another for food. What this animal leaves is then eaten by another animal and the remains of the carcass is eaten by yet another animal, and so on. There is a chain of events which on the surface would appear natural but which on deeper reflection you will find to be most unnatural. The animals, like Man, should live in complete harmony and balance, each fulfilling the will and the purpose of their Creator.

It is not possible, of course, suddenly to change Man's attitude towards eating animal flesh, and even if everyone on the surface of this Earth was to refuse to eat the flesh of animals the Animal Kingdom which Man has created through mass-production and artificial methods would still need to be tended and looked after. So the situation has to change slowly. All I ask is that those of you who are aware, who consider yourselves evolved, do indeed use your consciousnesses to decide on your relationship with the Animal Kingdom.

There is a great vogue in the World today to have animals as pets. Here again there is great responsibility. You buy and sell your animals today like the men of old bought and sold slaves in the market. Civilised Man agrees that slavery is morally wrong and indefensible. It will take a little time yet before he accepts that the slavery of the Animal Kingdom is equally as wrong morally, and just as indefensible. Truly, you should not buy and sell animals at all, for they are not yours to buy and sell: you did not even create them. They are formed from the matter of this Earth and their souls belong to the group soul of their species, not to you. You do indeed risk great karma by the way you treat your animals, by your motivation for wanting them, how you buy them, how you look after them and how you sell them. If at any time you abuse the Natural Laws of this Earth, then you create karma for yourself.

Remember that if you remove an animal from its natural environment and accept it as your pet, as you call it, then you are totally and completely responsible for that animal in every respect. You should treat it just as if it were your own child. You are responsible for all its requirements, for not just physical requirements such as where it lives and sleeps and the food and drink it requires, but also for its total well-being in every aspect of life. How many of you ever think of your pet from the pet's point of view? Today Man is so selfish and thinks so much of himself that he can hardly be expected to think of what his pet wants. Do any of you who have pets ever think, ever put yourselves in their place and think not of what you want your animals to do, not of what you want them to eat, not of when you want to exercise them, not of how you want to show them, not of when you want to breed from them, not of when you want to 'put them to sleep' because they have become inconvenient, but instead put yourselves in the place of those animals and ask yourselves what they really want? Do you ever think of your animals' point of view? Do you ever consider them as being with soul, that they suffer pain just as you do and that they are evolving their consciousnesses just as you are?

Man today must begin to act more responsibly towards the Animal Kingdom. He cannot of course change things over-night, but those of you who are aware can begin to treat your animals with more respect and responsibility. Man today, because he has so little respect for the Animal Kingdom, which is just as much a creation of God as Man himself, greatly abuses it. He regards the Animal Kingdom as being unfeeling matter with which he can play to satisfy his material demands. He interbreeds animals at his whim to produce those species which he thinks are necessary for

132

his life on this Earth. In doing this he is playing with the balance of Nature, and therefore is it any wonder that today life in the countryside is breaking down, that the chain of Nature is no longer linked? A breed of animals walks the Earth that is not the creation of God but the result of Man playing with God's creation. Man does not allow his domestic animals to breed naturally, but only when he wants them to breed. He breeds not for the sake of the animals themselves but for money, for food, for pleasure, for himself and, after he has bred them, if he does not want them or if they are not profitable to him, he destroys them without even a thought for their feelings, for their emotions, for their purpose in life.

Man today, just as he is not truly aware of life as a whole, is not aware of Nature and in particular of the part that the Animal Kingdom plays in his everyday existence. Is this just because he does not think, or because he does not want to think? Every time that Man eats meat, does he stop to consider where that flesh has come from? Does he think of the pain, the suffering and the sacrifice involved? Is he aware of the cruelty involved in modern factory farming methods? Many ladies possess, or would like to possess, fur coats, but have they ever thought of the suffering involved in order to satisfy their personality gratifications? Is all the pain and slaughter really necessary? Is it really a mark of civilisation to walk around with the skins of dead animals draped around you? Has Man really advanced spiritually since he lived in caves in the days of old?

Man today derives great pleasure from the hunting and killing of animals. Sometimes he 'justifies' it by calling certain animals vermin, but more often than not he is killing just for killing's sake, to prove his own personal skill and superiority. Again, is this the mark of a civilised Man? There are many other examples which I could give of where Man is abusing or even exterminating certain species of the Animal Kingdom. I could mention the extermination of the whales and various other types of wild animal to provide Man with food or clothing which he could easily obtain elsewhere. I could also mention the cruelty inflicted on certain animals to obtain the ingredients for many of the perfumes which the modern woman uses without a thought, and the way Man mutilates his pets to conform to the fashion of the time. If Man was really aware of God, and therefore of Nature and Creation around him, he would no more destroy or abuse God's creations than he would kill or abuse himself. He cannot create the beauty of Nature and of the Animal Kingdom around him, and therefore he should not destroy it.

Man uses the Animal Kingdom in his laboratories for the most horrible experiments to fulfil his scientific aims. I would say to you that anything resulting from these experiments lacks any spiritual value for Man whatsoever, and no permanent good will ever come of it. All medical and scientific research involving the use of animals creates great karma for Man which will have to be repaid. Of course the advances obtained from this abuse of the Animal Kingdom are beneficial in that from the sacrifice of the animals Man does learn about various diseases and drugs, but all this experimentation is only necessary because medicine is so far off its true path today that it cannot find out the true nature of disease and the correct way of healing.

So please remember that from the most evolved animal down to the least evolved animal, from the cow all the way down to the worm, they all feel, they all express. According to their level of evolution and vibration they all have a purpose in the plan of things. No animal is the creation of Man. All are the creation of God and therefore should be respected as such. To destroy God's creations incurs great karma. The animals will, and indeed do, make a sacrifice for you. If they make that sacrifice, then please bless them and thank them. If they make that sacrifice, then do not misuse it, do not ignore it. Let it not be said that they have made that sacrifice in vain. Remember that all life on this Earth is sacred, and that Man with all his devices still cannot create life in the Animal Kingdom. He can take the seed from one animal and mix it with another, but he cannot create the seed, for creation does not belong to Man. Remember that the Animal Kingdom imitates the Human Kingdom, and that as Man changes so will the Animal Kingdom. Therefore you should not look at the Animal Kingdom and say that there you see cruelty, disease and death, but rather say that what you see there is a reflection of yourselves. Man must change himself, and then he will indeed be helping his brothers in the Animal Kingdom.

Those of you who are aware please begin to think very seriously about how you treat the Animal Kingdom. Treat them with the respect which is due to less evolved beings. Think of their needs before your own. Do not in any way block or hinder their evolution. Remember that in the plan of things they play an important role. Man today still does not really appreciate the role of the Animal Kingdom. Their role is not to be food for Man. Remember that, although at present they are not, the four Kingdoms of Matter should live in perfect balance. The symbol of this Earth, the true cross, is no longer a true cross, and the Vegetable Kingdom is as much out of balance with Man as is the Animal Kingdom. Events to redress this imbalance are soon to take place, but, just as you would not wish the slavery of Man to go on a day longer than is necessary, think about whether you want the slavery of animals to go on a day longer than is necessary. The choice is yours. Mankind has acted with responsibility and has largely abolished the slavery of his fellow men: may he now do the same for the Animal Kingdom.

LAW

The only true and permanent laws that exist in your Solar Body are the Natural Laws. These are the laws which govern all Spirit, all Mind and all Matter within the Solar Body, and they range from the ones which govern your individual behaviour, such as the Law of Cause and Effect, to the laws which govern matter, such as the Law of Multiplicity. Everything that exists in creation is governed by these laws, and inherent in them is the Will of your Creator, for no matter what Man might do, or might seek to do, he cannot avoid their effects. Therefore when I talk about Man's laws I am talking about regulations, or rules, which Man has drawn up according to his own consciousness and not according to God's consciousness. Man's laws are not laws in the true sense of the word.

As Man has lived and evolved on the Earth, as civilisations have come and gone, he has, of course, made his own laws. If you wish to judge the evolution of a particular civilisation you should look at its laws, its regulations for life, for in them you will see a reflection of the consciousness of that Age. As you look at your laws today you think that they are humane because you are comparing them with the laws of two hundred years ago, when a man could be hung for stealing a sheep and a hungry boy could be deported for stealing a loaf of bread. However, if you were to advance two hundred years from now and look back on the laws of today you would think how barbarous they were.

Man's laws have gradually evolved over the years to their present state and they will be changed only by the actions of Man when he truly desires a change. Some of Man's laws are evil, and oppose Natural Law, but no matter what I say Man will not change them immediately, for it is only Man's progression and evolution that will change his laws. What I am seeking to do in this lecture is to present some new aspects on Law so that you can place Man-made laws in their true perspective.

Man-made laws generally fall into two categories. Firstly there are the civil laws that stem from the need for people to live together harmoniously in society. They regulate, for example, how one drives cars, how one collects taxes, how one buys and sells, and so on. These laws are formulated by Man according to his evolution, and as his way of life changes so do his laws. They cannot be judged as being spiritual or unspiritual, right or wrong. Secondly, there are the criminal laws, and it is when we look at these that we begin to discover certain aspects of unspirituality.

So Man, whilst he lives in a physical body, is governed not only by the Natural Laws of which he is largely unaware but also by his own laws. He learns that if he breaks the laws of his society and is caught he will be punished. If Man approves of such laws, if he considers that they are just, he will obey them; but if he considers that they are unjust he will ignore them and, even if he is caught and punished, will not think that he deserves to be punished. Therefore no point is served by punishing him, and to punish any man who does not think he has broken a law is not a punishment but a crucifixion.

The laws that usually cause the most conflict today are those that refer to murder, violence, robbery and corruption. Let me begin by pointing out that the whole principle upon which your penal law is based is that of punishment for the crime. A man commits a crime: he kills or steals, and therefore the law says that he must be punished for his offence. The law does not consider that perhaps, most of all, that man needs teaching or re-educating so that he may be able to live again in society as a responsible being. It is the principle of an eye for an eye, a tooth for a tooth. Have you ever considered the fact that your Creator does not 'punish' you for your offences, and that the whole reason for Man incarnating on the Earth is to learn through his experiences and gradually to evolve his consciousness? What you do will come back to you, but never in the form of punishment. It is through your own actions that you learn to appreciate what you have done and thereby to evolve through those experiences. Any man who murders, or steals, is obviously unaware of the existence of the true spiritual laws which govern the Universe. That man should, therefore, be helped in every possible way, and you do not help him by attempting to equal the score, for whether it be in some 'primitive' country where a man found guilty of stealing has his hand cut off, or in some 'civilised' country where a man is sent to prison for so many years, the effect is the same: it is punishment.

Many countries in the World today are gradually abolishing the death penalty. The death penalty is really the ultimate in stupidity, for by the act of taking away a man's life you cannot teach him anything. No matter which one of the great Teachers you follow, be he the Nazarene, the Buddha or Mohammed, be aware that they all taught one thing — love. They taught that you should show compassion, that you should always try to help your less evolved brothers. Criminals are not helped by being executed: they are helped by counselling and re-education, by being given specialised treatment, so that they may realise the foolishness of what they have done and be returned to society as responsible members who have learnt something from their mistakes. As Man does not create life, he has no right to take it. All life is sacred and there is no justification for capital punishment whatsoever, for the greater law of the Universe will always take effect on any of Man's actions. There are many of Man's laws which are incorrect as far as Infinite Spirit is concerned, and there are many laws which Infinite Spirit commands which Man does not recognise. So you may well break a law of Infinite Spirit and, whilst not breaking one of Man's laws, still have to pay the effect.

So the definition of what is the law is not as clear-cut as you would think. If one of Man's laws conflicts with the Law of Infinite Spirit then, obviously, if you comply with the Law of Infinite Spirit and thus break Man's law, even if you are punished by a judge in a court you have in reality committed no crime. People might judge you as having done so but, truly, you have not, and the greater Record, the Record that is important, will show you as having committed no crime at all. Remember that what is important is the judgement of your Creator, not the judgement of Man, the judgement of the judges and the juries. Likewise, if you are accused of a crime and you go before a judge and a jury and are found innocent of the offence, even though you are in fact guilty you will not escape, for the Law of Infinite Spirit always has its effect. Any man who breaks the Law of Infinite Spirit, because he does not understand the real nature of his actions has to be treated like a young child and helped to understand the existence of, and the reason for, such a Law. To punish him will be of no help, for true learning cannot take place through punishment.

In the ancient civilisations the courts of law were entirely different from those of today. There was no legal profession as such. The judges were men of great spirituality, the priests of the temple, who understood the Natural Laws of the Universe. An accused person was brought before these spiritual men so that the true nature of his actions could be judged. These spiritual judges then decided on the corrective education necessary to ensure that the guilty person realised the error of his ways. These men of great spirituality could recognise the soul-evolution of an individual and also could tell from his aura whether he lied or spoke the truth. Therefore the law was administered fairly. There were no wrong judgements, and no need for a judge and jury. The judgements were spiritual judgements, and no prejudices, no clever lawyers, no bribery, no corruption, were involved as they are today.

Today far too many human factors are involved in the enforcement of the law. Modern Man, of course, is not so spiritually aware as he was in some of the civilisations of old. In certain countries the system of a judge and jury exists, and this is an advancement on the legal systems of many other countries. But even this is open to abuse, for if, because of his soul-evolution, an evolved soul carries out a particular act and is taken before a judge and jury of less evolved men, then they will perhaps find him guilty, whereas in actual fact he probably is not. For example, if you have a man who refuses to fight for his country in time of war a judge and jury will probably send him to prison, whereas in actual fact, although he is breaking the law of the land, perhaps he is obeying the Law of Infinite Spirit.

Society today is gradually becoming more and more brutal. Violence is increasing everywhere. This is the nature of the society in which you now live. It reflects Man's total lack of spirituality at all levels, from the rulers of the land to the people of the land. It also reflects the quickening of the spiral on which the Earth rotates and the events at the end of the century to which we are now proceeding.

It is hard for Man today to accept but, at the moment of conception, every child is a perfect reflection of Infinite Spirit. Most of the factors which are responsible for modern crime are to be found in childhood. Children are greatly influenced by the wrong example of their parents, by wrong education both from their parents and their school teachers and by the wrong example from the World itself. How can you expect a child today not to be violent when the whole World is violent, when every day the newspapers and the television report and show violence? A child accepts all these events as being normal. You cannot blame a child if it imitates life around it. You may find this hard to accept, but if a man commits a crime, unless he is committing that crime as an instrument of Infinite Spirit he is committing that crime against his own soul judgement and because his personality has obscured his soul wisdom.

There are, of course, always going to be certain individuals who will not learn through their own actions. They kill or steal because they do not think it is wrong. They do not desire to work because they would rather obtain money the easy way. These men will, of course, reap the effect of Natural Law, but, in that they are potentially dangerous to society, society must take action against them and must isolate them until such time as they have been re-educated. What happens today is that such people are isolated as a punishment, are not re-educated, and are then released after so many years of punishment to carry on exactly as they had done before. If you look at the crime records in the World today you will see that very often it is a few persistent offenders who continually appear before the judges; but Man does not seem to learn from this and to appreciate the need to change his present systems.

Man's whole attitude towards the law, crime and punishment, has to change. The only laws that will be respected and obeyed by an evolved soul are Natural Laws. Now I am not saying that you should ignore all of Man's laws, because many of them will reflect in some respects the greater Law. Obviously it is wrong to attack or to kill another man. It is wrong to steal, to slander or to bear false witness against another man. All these aspects, for they are only aspects, of Natural Law appear in Man's laws and should be obeyed. However there are some of Man's laws which are not correct, and these should not be obeyed. Man needs to make his laws more spiritual, more a reflection of Natural Law. He has to recognise that when a person breaks the law, not punishment but re-education is required. He must realise that most people commit crimes only because of the environment which has led them to think and behave in that way, for the sum total of Man's physical consciousness is the life he has lived, the things he has seen, the people with whom he has associated, what they have practised and done, the whole vibration of the country in which he lives.

Man must look at his forms of punishment and see if they really are having the desired effect. Remember that fear, fear of being punished, fear of being imprisoned, will in no way restrain a man who is determined to do something. Even in war, when they fear death, people will risk their lives if they believe that what they are doing is just. Man must examine his prisons and ensure that they become not punishment cells but schools of education and learning. He must ensure that the standard of life inside these prisons is of a higher standard than life outside, for here are people who need special treatment, who need a special atmosphere, who need individual attention. People who are placed in prisons need help, and help is not given by imprisoning a man within four square walls, sometimes in solitary confinement, out of sight of the sun, of nature and of life.

Finally, Man must realise that the greatest law that exists in the Universe is Natural Law. What Man does will always have an effect no matter what form of punishment Man-made laws decree. The punishment of Man in no way transmutes the effect of Natural Law, and by punishing a fellow brother Man is very often only incurring karma for himself. The greatest Law of this Universe, which has been demonstrated to Man by so many Masters when they have incarnated on the Earth, is that you do unto others as you would have others do unto you. If you break the laws of God you expect to be forgiven, you expect to be helped, you expect to be gently shown the error of your ways: you do not expect to be punished. Should not a man who breaks Man's law expect the same treatment?

Man has advanced beyond the age of an eye for an eye and a tooth for a tooth. He is slowly beginning to recognise the sanctity of life. Let him now begin to understand the purpose of God, the rule of God, and let the laws of the Universe, not the laws of Man, govern life on the Earth and then perfection, harmony and brotherhood will return to his World.

RELIGION

May I begin this lecture by saying that it is not my intention in any way to select a particular religion in the World today and to try to discredit it and prove that its dogma is wrong. What I do hope to do, however, is to present you with some fresh thoughts on various aspects of the religions of the World and to ask you to re-examine some of the views which you may have fixed in your minds about religion as a whole. It would be true to say that because of the nature of Man's physical existence almost any person living on the surface of the Earth needs, or seeks, a religion of some form, be it the worship of the Sun, the worship of fire, the worship of the Buddha or of the Christ. Man needs, and seeks, a belief in a Higher Being or God. I will not go into why Man needs to create such a belief, but will begin by pointing out some of the reasons behind the creation of the religions of the World.

Some of the great Masters who have incarnated on the Earth have had their words and their deeds recorded for posterity by one scholar or another. It would be true to say that if you closely examined the works describing the lives and the teachings of any of these great Masters, you would find that none of them ever sought to establish a religion or a Church. Not one of the great Masters who incarnated on this Earth has ever left behind a blueprint, a plan, a set of instructions, as to how Man should establish an organisation to carry on his work, to perpetuate the way of life that he had exemplified and the teachings he had taught. It is only Man, afterwards, who has deemed it necessary to create a structure of religion, which you call a Church, so as to teach and explain the wisdom of those Masters. It is inevitable when any Master incarnates and, inspired by his Creator, speaks much wisdom and performs many significant acts, that men will record and describe his words and deeds in a book of some form. It is obviously desirable that after a Master has died what he has done and taught should be made available for successive generations so that they may take from him whatever they are inspired to take. But does this require the vast religious bodies which exist today?

Before a Master departs he sometimes appoints one or two of his leading disciples to carry on his work, to teach in the way that he has taught, to repeat the wisdom that he has spoken and to tell of the deeds that he has performed. The disciples, however, never approach the vibration, the illumination, of the great Master himself, and therefore as the years go by and less inspired men receive the teachings and interpret them according to their own consciousnesses so the teachings are sometimes changed, and very often misinterpreted, and the original meanings of the Master are lost. Much of what the Nazarene taught two thousand years ago, for example, has almost been reversed by some of the Christian Churches today. They in no way reflect the truth, the wisdom and the meaning of the Nazarene's original words.

Very often it can be an advantage to learn about a religion from a book. By this I mean that if you read the Bible, the Koran or the manuscripts of the ancient religions that existed in China and Japan you can extract the wisdom of the great Masters without being influenced by the teachings and dogma of their followers today, who often misinterpret what they said. If Man today would just take the words of those Masters and ignore the dogma and the ceremony of the respective Churches how much better off he would be!

If Man was to compare the basic teachings of the Masters on which today's religions are based he would see that fundamentally they are the same. One Master might perhaps stress one particular aspect more than another, but all the great Masters taught the same basic spiritual principles. You can therefore see that it is Man himself who has created his religions. It is Man's dogma that is responsible for the division between the Buddhists and the Muslims, between the Muslims and the Christians, in spite of the fact that the Masters' teachings were the same. If you take the example of the Nazarene, and look at the number of Churches that have been created from his teachings, you will see the point which I am striving to make. The differences in interpretation of one Master's teachings, the Nazarene's, can even result in war and bloodshed. You can have two of Man's Churches which believe in the same God, which try to follow the same Master's teachings, and yet are prepared to kill each other to support their ideas, their beliefs, of what that Master said or meant. That is the nature of Man's religions today, and if all of you would only look more closely at them you would see how divisive they all are.

Looking back over the history of this World since the death of the Nazarene I would say that organised religion has been the greatest force for evil and destruction that has existed in the World. Religion has been responsible for much of Man's downfall and for Man's position today when, spiritually, he is totally lost in the World. Fortunately, the generation now incarnating, being composed of evolved and old souls, is beginning to reject and ignore Man's religions and to strike out along new paths. Thus, today, the so-called falling off in the followers of the Churches is not due to the unspirituality of Man: it is in fact due to his spirituality, for he is ignoring what is patently wrong. It is only too easy for me to ask you to look at the history of the World, as you know it, and to pick out a religion or Church that has existed throughout it, or even for more than an era, but you would not find one. Man's religions come and go as his civilisations rise and fall. The Christian Religion, for example, is comparatively recent. It has existed for only two thousand years, and yet already it is past its zenith and is beginning to decline. You can recognise the signs in the World today.

You can see, therefore, that no religion is eternal yet, surely, if a religion professes to teach the Truth of the Heavens, and the Truth of the Heavens is fixed, is eternal, should it not be so too? Religions are not eternal and will never be so because they are created by Man and not by God. God does not demand a religion: it is only Man who does. There are many religions and Churches in existence in the World today, but I can tell you that with the changes which are to come in the cataclysm at the end of this century all of them will disappear and, with the coming of the New Age, a new belief in God, a true belief in God, will appear.

You would be quite entitled to say to me, "Although what you say might be true, surely there must be some good in religion today? People are inspired by it. They do try in their own way to imitate their Creator. Surely there can be no harm in that?" To a certain extent that is true, for according to his evolution, to his spiritual consciousness, a religion, even if its teachings are false, can help in Man's spiritual progression. Man has to experience the restrictions of religion, the false teachings of the Churches, so that he may advance his evolution by overcoming them and learning to recognise that the way of God, the path to God, lies only within himself. No religion or Church can tell any man what his path, his way, to God is, for the link between every soul and its Creator is both direct and unique. No religion can tell any man, with his individualised consciousness, who or what God is.

The religions and Churches of the World today should be disseminating the teachings of their respective Masters, leaving their followers to interpret them according to their individual consciousnesses. The Churches should be striving to emulate in every way the example of their Masters. But do the Christian Churches today, for example, truly follow the example of the Nazarene? The Nazarene was a poor man, with no possessions or worldly goods. He possessed nothing but the clothes he walked in. Compare that with your Churches today. The Nazarene demonstrated a way of life and taught in parables so that Man might take from them that which his consciousness could understand, but he never told any man what to do with his life. Compare that with your Churches today. The Nazarene never advocated the use of force under any circumstances whatsoever. He was not concerned with politics in any way. Compare that with your Churches today. The Nazarene taught all men. Any man could come to him, could be healed by him, could listen to him, was welcome to follow him. He did not discriminate against any man because of his nationality, his social position or his religion. Compare that with your Churches today. The Nazarene never asked that anyone should worship him, should establish him or any other person as an idol. Compare that with your Churches today.

So you see that organised religion today is Man's creation. The dogma that has been established by the individual Churches is the result of Man's actions, not God's. As you look back over the many centuries since the Nazarene incarnated you can see how the various Christian Churches were formed. You may read in history books of the hideous crimes for which they have been responsible. You may see the evil that organised religion has wrought all over the surface of this Earth. Nations, states, towns and individuals have all been destroyed either by acts of religious persecution or by wrong demonstrations of faith. Although you might not think so, the missionaries who have been sent out all over the World by the Churches have done much harm, and the karma for that will have to be repaid.

A man of God, a priest or clergyman, whether he be a Christian, a Buddhist or a Muslim, must in every way follow and demonstrate the teachings of the Master who he professes to follow, and if in any way, at any time, he fails to do so, then he incurs great karma. One of the greatest errors that Man can make on this Earth is to mislead another brother in the name of his Creator, to misuse and abuse the power and the love of his Creator; yet this is being done all over the World today.

When one considers the organised structures of the various religions in the World today, it is obvious that they cannot be pulled down and destroyed overnight, for there are many millions of people who do indeed have faith and believe in their Churches. I can only ask those of you who do have a strong faith in a Church to examine it most closely, to see if the Church to which you belong is indeed following, in every respect, the teachings of the Master on which it was founded. If it is not, then you may well seek to question that faith further. If any priest or clergyman tells you what to do, what is right or wrong, who God is, what God wants, then do not trust him: for no man is capable of telling you that but yourself. Remember that you are all individual sparks of consciousness, not one the same, and within you as you live in a physical body on Earth you have a unique link to your Creator. You do not need to go through a third party, be it a Church or a priest. You are in direct contact with your Creator, with His ministering angels and with the Hierarchy above on the higher spheres of existence.

No matter what Man says about the spiritual events of the past, no matter what saints Man has created, no matter what holy relics Man has established, no matter what dogma Man has decreed as being infallible, no matter what ceremonies Man has established as having great spiritual power, do not rely on them: do not place your faith in them or you will be disappointed. Remember that it is Man who changes the words of God. You have only to look at the Churches over the past two hundred years to see how even during that short period of time they have changed their doctrines at the demands of their followers. If Man changes his doctrines, then those doctrines are not of God, for God is all seeing, all wise and infallible. Therefore do not place your faith in Man and his Churches. Use them for the comfort and the wisdom which they can give you according to your consciousnesses, but never let them impose their will upon you. Look directly to your Creator.

To conclude I would ask you to remember that your link with your Creator is unique and personal. That is not to say that people of similar beliefs should not come together in a place of worship, a temple, a church, to commune together with their Creator, for there is great power in the coming together of souls with similar intent and purpose, but remember that that power can be used for good or for evil. If all of you come together in your Churches to pray only for yourselves and not for the rest of the World, to pray only for those you love and not for your enemies, no matter whether they be your personal ones or those of your country, then you are not exemplifying what the great Masters have taught. If you come together and do not recognise that other souls with differing views to yours, who follow different creeds and different beliefs, have as much right and entitlement to those beliefs as you do to yours, and that you should in no way persecute them for those beliefs, then, again, you are not fulfilling the will of your Creator.

As I look around the World today, everywhere I see that the religions and the Churches are divisive: they do not unite men, they divide men. All over the World man hates man not in spite of, but because of, his religion. Many of the great problems in your World today are caused solely by religion. Those of you who stand outside these conflicts can see the falseness and the stupidity of the various religions which are prepared to sacrifice not only the lives of their followers, but even the countries of their followers, in order to support their beliefs. Yet the example of all the great Masters has always been one of tolerance, of sacrifice, even the sacrifice of their own physical lives for their fellow-men. If only the Churches of the World and their followers would similarly sacrifice, would really imitate their Creator, then peace would return to this Earth.

THE TEN COMMANDMENTS

The only source of Absolute Truth, of Absolute Wisdom, of Absolute Intellect, of Absolute Knowledge of the Plan for this Earth, is your Creator, the Lord of this planetary system, that Being Whom you call God. Therefore, as I talk to you in this lecture, I can interpret only the conditions of life on this Earth as befits my consciousness, evolution and experience of life on it. If you will accept that I have walked a little further along the path than you and, therefore, that I have a clearer picture, a clearer vision, of life and of the purpose of life on this Earth, then you may also accept and meditate on what I am to say about the Ten Commandments. You must understand that no commandment, no rule, that Man possesses, or indeed will ever possess on the Earth, can be described as absolute, as a totality, for that is not possible on this planet. An aspect of the Cosmic Whole may be beamed down upon this Earth for Man to accept and understand, but never the complete power.

As we now look at the Ten Commandments, in the form that they are reproduced in the Bible, realise that they were the guidelines for an ancient civilisation that has long since disappeared. That is not to say that they do not reflect a part of Absolute Truth, but that the reflection was intended for that ancient civilisation and will therefore not be in keeping with the Age in which you live today. You are now living at the end of the Piscean Age and at the dawning of the Aquarian Age. Mankind, through the demonstration of the Nazarene, was given the teachings of the Christ only two thousand years ago, but today, because of the environment and the changing nature of the Age, people have difficulty in seeing the relevance of the Nazarene's teachings. Obviously, therefore, it will be even more difficult for twentieth century Man to see the relevance of the Ten Commandments which were given thousands of years earlier.

Let us now examine the Commandments in detail and try to relate them not to a civilisation of thousands of years ago but to the twentieth century, to life today. Their meaning has, of course, suffered not only in translation but also as a result of changes made by various scholars who, in their desire to explain that which, because of their limited consciousnesses, they could not understand, altered not only the words but the significance as well.

The first commandment in the Bible is:

'Thou shalt have no other gods before Me'.

This stands correctly as the first law, the first commandment, and is the most important one. On the surface this commandment would appear to be fairly self-explanatory. There is indeed only one God, but He is not the kind of God you imagine, for Man cannot conceive of the true God, Whose spirit dwells within the Sun and Who controls this Solar System. That God is beyond Man's comprehension. Man can barely conceive of the Solar Lord Who dwells within this Earth, the ruler of this planet. He can only relate to the Masters and Beings who regulate and guide life on this Earth. This commandment was therefore intended to remind Man — and it is just as applicable today as it was at the time of Moses — that the intermediaries are not God and that there is only one Being, one God, of Whom all Humanity is a part.

You are, therefore, an actual infinitesimal part of that Being Whose Body is the Solar System in which you dwell, the one God, the one Being, Who exists not only for you but for all the beings on the other planets and for all forms of creation. Therefore it can be seen that all those beings within the Body, who serve that one Being, the Greater Whole, are of equal importance. Individually they advance along their own paths, but collectively, they are walking those individual paths for the good, for the advancement, to fulfil the purpose and the plan, of that one Being Whose spirit dwells within the Sun. Therefore as far as you, as far as the Martian or the Venusian is concerned, there is only one God: the supreme God of Whom you are a part. That spark that is within you now is a part of, and belongs to, that God and, ultimately, when you have evolved sufficiently, you will return your individuality to that God.

The second commandment in the Bible is:

'Thou shalt not make unto thee any graven image, or any likeness of

anything that is in heaven above, or that is in the earth beneath, or that is in the water under the earth. Thou shalt not bow down thyself to them, nor serve them: for I the Lord thy God am a jealous God, visiting the iniquity of the fathers upon the children unto the third and fourth generation of them that hate me, and showing mercy unto thousands of them that love me, and keep my commandments'.

This commandment clearly states that because you are not capable of understanding the true God, you should not create false gods, false idols. You should not elevate any idol to the position of God. You should not take any lesser beings, even though they may be more evolved than yourselves, and make them into gods as a means of satisfying your own lost egos. Living in such vastness, not only of Earth but also of space, it is so easy for Man to feel lost. Even today events in the World appear to be overtaking him. There is much evil. There is much violence. The man in the street would appear to have no control over the every-day happenings of his life. Just as the Israelites felt so many thousands of years ago, when they fled from Egypt, there appears to be no order in the World. It is in situations like these that people tend to cling to false ideologies, to false gods, to create their own substitutes on which to lean and depend, be it a religious god or be it money, power, influence, land or any other material god: they are both images created by Man as his idea of God. They in no way reflect the true greatness of your Creator, for that you cannot comprehend.

This second commandment is, then, a warning to Man not to place his faith in false gods and to be aware that, regardless of his point of consciousness, at every stage of his evolution he will create a 'God', a 'God' which he can just comprehend. To some it may be a saint, a wise man, a guru, a saviour of the people, even a Master on a higher plane of life. Have you ever stopped to consider why you need a 'God'? You may think it a harsh, an irreligious thing to say but, truly, you do not need a 'God'. Certainly you must try to be aware of the true God and you must strive to achieve His Plan for this Earth, but that is a very different thing.

In this commandment there is a reference to a God who will punish: *'for I the Lord thy God am a jealous God . . . '* The implication is that if you do not follow the wishes of that God then He will descend upon you and will punish you unto the third and fourth generation. The true God of this Earth, however, is not a God of punishment. He, and the Beings who control, guide and help this Earth, have long since progressed beyond the level of meting out punishment, for there is no point in punishing a being who does not understand. The true God of this Earth is a God of love, a God of help, a God of wisdom, a God of impartiality. You, on the Earth, have been given the divine gift of free choice to advance along your chosen paths. As you progress you will, understandably, err, but when you err the Law of this Earth is not that God will punish you but rather that you will learn through your own mistakes, for by your actions now you are sowing the seeds which will come to fruition in the future. What you are doing now — the way you treat your country, the way you treat your fellow-men, the way you treat the Kingdoms of this Earth — will affect not only you but also the beings who are to incarnate after you. You pollute this Earth not only for yourselves but also for your children and for your children's children, and the karma for this will have to be repaid in the many, many lives you have yet to live.

The third commandment in the Bible is:

'Thou shalt not take the name of the Lord thy God in vain; for the Lord will not hold him guiltless that taketh his name in vain'.

This is a fault which is just as prevalent today as it was so many thousands of years ago, for Man is still continually motivating his actions on this Earth according to his false gods. Man creates his own religions. He takes the examples of the great Masters who have incarnated on this Earth, the words they have spoken, the way of life they have demonstrated, and interprets them to justify his own actions. The Churches rephrase the words of the great Masters, invent motivations for their lives and create religions which Man then follows; and Man, believing that he is following the Will of God, obeys the commandments of the Churches and not the commandments of God.

In order to give meaning and security to his life Man needs to create a god, and he will therefore turn to any plausible god which is put before him by the priests or elders of the Age. It is so easy to lead Man astray in the name of God. Just as there was no true religion so many thousands of years ago when Moses was given these commandments, so there is no true religion in the World today. Every religion misinterprets or changes the meanings, the events, the teachings of the great Masters who have come on this Earth, and asks Man to follow not God but the

Church's idea of God.

Be aware that many men will do many manner of things in the name of their 'God'. They will say that 'God' is on their side, that 'God' helps them, that 'God' leads them, that 'God' inspires them, and in the name of their 'God' they will commit evil all over this World. They will exploit, abuse and even kill their fellow-men in the name of their 'God'. They will abuse the Kingdoms of Matter on this Earth. They will do all this for the glory of their 'God', a 'God' who, truly, does not exist except in their own minds. Beware, therefore, of any man who preaches to you of 'God' for it will be only of his idea of God. There is only one God Who is in existence at this moment in time for each of you, and that is your own consciousness.

The fourth commandment in the Bible is:

'Remember the sabbath day, to keep it holy. Six days shalt thou labour, and do all thy work, but the seventh day is the sabbath of the Lord thy God: in it thou shalt not do any work, thou, nor thy son, nor thy daughter, nor thy manservant, nor thy maidservant, nor thy cattle, nor the stranger that is within thy gates. For in six days the Lord made heaven and earth, the sea, and all that in them is, and rested the seventh day: wherefore the Lord blessed the sabbath day, and hallowed it'.

How mistranslation and misinterpretation have changed this commandment! The original statement was to remember the significance of 'The Seven', because this Earth operates on and through the wavelength and the vibration of seven. Its whole purpose and structure vibrates to seven. The Earth was created in seven days or, more literally, seven Ages. Man possesses seven spiritual centres, or chakras, which are the seeds from which Man's seven bodies spring. Man's physical body is said to change every seven years. There are seven layers to your skin. There are seven colours in your spectrum. There are seven musical notes in the scale. There are seven days in a week and four times seven days in a lunar month. The Bible refers to the life of Man as being three score years and ten, or ten times seven. The frequency of seven vibrates everywhere in life on this Earth and is most important to it. If you lived in a more spiritual society, where Man paid more attention to the spiritual sciences as opposed to the material sciences which are devoted entirely to the benefit of Man's physical needs, you would understand more of the true significance of this Earth and of its special vibration of seven. Other planets within this Solar Body vibrate to different numbers, on other wavelengths, but seven is the number of this Earth. So when this commandment says 'Remember The Seven' it is asking you to remember the number of this Earth, the structure of life on this Earth, and the purpose and significance of this Earth.

The fifth commandment in the Bible is:

'Honour thy father and thy mother that thy days may be long upon the land which the Lord thy God giveth thee'.

Here again, mistranslation has made interpretation of this commandment difficult. Let us, however, instead of mother and father substitute male and female, or positive and negative, the balance of all creation. So the fifth commandment invites you to remember creation, to remember the act of your creation, to remember what your body is composed of, the significance of its individual parts and your responsibility for it. This commandment further says that if you look after your physical frame, if you treat it and respect it as the miraculous creation given to you by your Creator which it really is, then your days will indeed be long on the surface of this Earth. You will live for more years than Man lives today. So remember the act of creation, the male and the female, the power and the wisdom, the two points of consciousness. They are the seeds through which Man evolves on this Earth, no matter whether it be the male and the positive, or the female and the negative. It is through these bodies that Man learns on the surface of this Earth, advancing his consciousness according to the choice of his destiny and the Greater Plan.

The sixth commandment in the Bible is:

'Thou shalt not kill'.

This is a very straight-forward law, but how Man wriggles to avoid it! There is no qualification. It is absolute. Thou shalt not kill anything. It means not only that one should not kill one's equals in soul evolution, but also that one should not kill one's lesser brothers be they other human beings, animals or even insects. There is a simple reason behind this law. Man does not create, he is not aware of the balance of life on this Earth, and therefore he would be most unwise to upset that balance by removing people or animals or other forms of life that have been placed there by a greater force than he to fulfil the plan and the purpose of this Earth. After all, if you think about it, Man usually kills only for his own self-interest, whether it be to win a war, to destroy an enemy, to feed his stomach or to give himself pleasure generally. He kills for personal gain or satisfaction, and what provides the motivation for that but his ego! A truly spiritually motivated person never kills anything. On this Earth there is no need for killing in any form whatsoever, and the sooner Man realises this fact the sooner peace, goodwill, perfection and harmony will return to this Earth.

The seventh commandment in the Bible is:

'Thou shalt not commit adultery'.

Man has placed a limited interpretation on this commandment to imply that he, Man, should not have sexual relations outside the bonds of marriage, and he has raised this commandment to a position of supreme importance in modern life. But this, again, is only one very small aspect of the law. I invite you to consider the wider interpretation of this commandment: that Man should not adulterate himself in thought, word or deed. He should not defile himself in any way whatsoever. This commandment means, therefore, that Man must respect his physical body. He must not eat or drink anything which will defile it. He must recognise it as being the temple of his soul. He must not use his body in any degrading act, whether it be physical or mental, sexual or otherwise. He must use the gift of creation with responsibility, and recognise that every time he commits the sexual act without intention of conception he is adulterating that act. So try to be aware of the wider implications of this commandment.

The eighth commandment in the Bible is:

'Thou shalt not steal'.

This commandment, of course, means more than the simple fact that one should not take away another person's personal possessions although, obviously, if people are to live together in society it is desirable that they should not steal from one another. The implication of steal is, however, far greater than this. It means that Man should not take that which is not his at any level, even in the World as a whole. It means that Man should not exploit his fellow-men, that one country should not exploit another country. A country that is rich and powerful should not use its position to deprive a poorer country of food or mineral resources which its people desperately need. One country should not advance at the expense of another, the rich should not exploit the poor. It means that one country should not take away another's rights to self-determination. Inherent in this is that you should treat all men as equals. You should not take away, you should not steal, any person's individual freedom in any respect whatsoever.

The ninth commandment in the Bible is:

'*Thou shalt not bear false witness against thy neighbour*'.

It is obvious that you should not tell lies about anyone, but again, there is far more to this commandment than you would see at first. To lie is to speak evil of another man, to speak evil means a thought, a thought is a creation, and that creation will remain thereafter on the invisible planes of existence around this Earth. So remember that when you tell lies you are creating evil which affects not only the person about whom you lie but also yourself and the many other people who will tap into the thoughts that you have created. Most of the wickedness and the evil on this Earth comes out of Man's mouth. If only Man would motivate his speech correctly in every respect, if he would speak only good, then life on this Earth would change in the twinkling of an eye. Every time a person speaks evil anywhere in the World, no matter whether he be a politician, a clergyman, a shopkeeper or a farmer, he is creating forces which will burden down and affect this Earth for many, many days to come.

The tenth commandment in the Bible is:

'*Thou shalt not covet thy neighbour's house, thou shalt not covet thy neighbour's wife, nor his manservant, nor his maidservant, nor his ox, nor his ass, nor anything that is thy neighbour's*'.

Another commandment put so simply yet meaning so much. Remember that all of you, as individuals, before you incarnated chose the shape and appearance of your physical body, your status in life and the manner in which you were to lead your present life: therefore be satisfied with that life. Because another person has more money, has a better car, has a larger house, goes on more holidays than you do, that does not mean that you should covet his possessions and his way of life, for he is learning different lessons to you. The fact that you covet his possessions or way of life attracts forces to you which were probably not intended for your present destiny. Also remember that the thought which you send out as you look at another person's husband or wife, at another person's car, can affect them as much as it affects you.

Recognise the force that gives matter to you. Because your personality wants a car or a house, that does not mean that you will get it, for the giver of matter, the controller of matter, on this Earth is a far greater force than Man's ego. Remember that matter belongs to no man, but at the same time respect the individuality of your fellow-men who are using that matter. They are walking their paths using the matter of this Earth just like you and, their paths being different to yours, they will require different aspects of matter. Therefore, rather than seeking to imitate your fellow-men, be yourself and walk your own path. Remember that if you seek the things of the spirit, if you seek your true path, then the matter necessary for that path will assuredly be given to you.

Man today is far removed from his true path both individually, racially and planetarily, because he continually thinks that he knows what he needs, that he knows what is best for him. He sees, he grasps, he takes, he uses, and then he discards. In all this he is motivated by greed, the desire to possess. However, once he has possessed, the desire soon goes, but the responsibility for what he has acquired has only just begun. So, as you gather possessions remember that you are also acquiring responsibilities. The least burdened Man who walks the path of life on this Earth is the man who walks alone, with few possessions, for he has few responsibilities and is free to fulfil his true purpose. The man with many riches, with many possessions, is burdened down with the responsibility for them, for even if he discards them the karma for their use remains with him.

I hope that you will now begin to look at the Ten Commandments in a new light. If you will only follow them they will change you beyond all recognition, for if you did but realise it the Ten Commandments are the keys to the doors of spiritual progression on the Earth. If you will only use those keys to unlock those doors, then one day you will stand before the majesty, the glory, the perfectness, the absoluteness, of the God of this planetary system, and when you achieve this you will have passed beyond the commandments of this Earth and will have begun to observe the commandments of the Universe.

THE SPIRITUALITY OF MAN'S PHYSICAL BODY

As you have been told on many occasions your spirit, the essence of you, dwells on many levels of existence. Man is not just a physical being; he dwells, for the most part, on other, on higher, levels of existence. Unevolved Man restricts himself by limiting his range of consciousness to the physical and so fails to realise that he is also a spiritual, a cosmic, being. As we examine the spirituality of Man's physical body we are going to have to encompass a wide range of knowledge, some of which is unknown to Man today, which I will call 'spiritual science' — scientific knowledge that is known and recognised on other levels of existence but not by Man on the Earth. Obviously, as Man does not have the kind of documented proof of spiritual science that is universally recognised, you will have to accept what I say in trust and meditate within your hearts to see if that spark within you accepts or rejects what I say in this lecture.

The spirit, the essence of you, consists of millions of vibrations. These vibrations are crystallised into seven bodies or forms. Although I have used the word body I do not want you to think of a body in the sense that you use the word when you refer to your physical body. Man does not really see his total physical body. He sees the matter of which it is made and he recognises its shape, but he does not see the aura emanating around the body, the rays of power coming in and going out of it and the magnetic fields present around it which make its shape very different from the one which he would normally recognise. So when I speak of a body I mean a collection of vibrations resulting in form. These seven bodies, sometimes known as the physical, the etheric, the astral, the emotional, the vital, the mental and the spiritual bodies, are the vehicle of your spirit while it is in existence within this Solar Body.

In this lecture we are to examine the body which vibrates at the slowest vibration, at the longest wavelength — the physical body. However, whilst we are doing so, I would ask you to remember the existence of the other six bodies which, whilst Man dwells in a physical body, are contained within or around it. The fact that Man is in a physical body should in no way limit him, for an evolved soul can and does use all its other bodies. A Master such as the Nazarene, for example, was in no way limited by living in a physical body. He could, and did, use all his bodies including his highest one: the body with the highest vibration, his spiritual body.

Man, truly, is not just a physical body. He is a being of many parts, and to limit himself to the physical is to restrict his view of Creation and of the Greater Whole, for Man's physical body is but a small cog in the larger Wheel of Life. Within Man's physical body there dwell thousands and thousands of beings with consciousnesses just like Man's. In a similar fashion the many men and women living on the surface of this Earth are part of the body that you know as the Earth. At the present time you are an actual part of that body, and when I refer to the Earth I do not mean merely the round shape of which you are aware but also the total emanation of essences finer than matter which surround it. You are an actual infinitesimal part of the body of the Being who is the Earth. The Earth in its turn is part of a greater and finer body, which you know as the Solar Body, the spirit of which resides within the Sun and the consciousness, the mind, the perfection, of which you call God.

Thus Man's physical body is but a small part in a continuous chain of creation. If you were to take an atom of the matter of Man's physical body and were to cut it in half, in it you would find a little replica of your Solar System. For within that atom there would be a central core or sun which links it to the God-head, and around that sun would be the electrons and the protons — the planets. Furthermore, if you were to magnify that sun a million times in size and then were to cut it in half you would see inside it a hundred little beings, or figures, which could best be described as 'matchstick men'. These would be characterised by a thin vertical line, or body, with two lines going out from the top (their arms), and two lines going downwards (their legs). Each of these little figures would have an individualised consciousness and that consciousness would extend through its arms and legs to tune into every vibration, or essence, of the cosmic fields around the Earth. Similarly, if I was to cut one of the protons or electrons in half you would see not hundreds but thousands of these little figures, only their consciousnesses would be linked not to the cosmic fields around the Earth, but would go right down into the Earth itself.

So you see how, as you walk this Earth, these minute beings exist within you just as you in turn are part of a greater Being, the Lord of this Earth. As above, so below: everything is a replica of the greater whole above only on a smaller scale. You may compare the hairs on your head to the trees of the Earth, the blood of your body to the water of the Earth. The essence of matter changes according to its rate of vibration, but similar functions and similar purposes can be attributed to the hair and to the tree, to the blood and to the water. Man's body, although he considers it unique, is but a replica of other bodies only on a larger or smaller scale depending on which way Man looks from his position in the scale of Creation.

Man's body is a miraculous creation. Consider that it is created from one single cell, but from this cell there grows the beautiful shape and form of the physical body with its inherent ability to allow the expression of your spirit while it exists in matter. The soul formulates the physical body that it desires taking into account many considerations, amongst them being soul memory, karma, the purpose of the life to be led and the nature of the destiny of that spark of spirit. Man today, as technologically advanced as he is, with the ability to get to the Moon, still cannot create a human body. He has in no way approached the spiritual technology, the spiritual engineering techniques, that are present in it. He can of course imitate and, according to varying degrees of skill, replace diseased parts of the body, but he cannot create parts of the body. Man lives in a magnificent piece of engineering but, because he has grown so accustomed to his physical body and uses it automatically, without thought, he fails to recognise the magnificence of that engineering.

Because Man does not belong to this Earth, because he is, truly, a cosmic being, so his physical body reflects that position. Therefore, while he is in matter his physical body not only allows him to respond to matter, to be aware of matter, but at the same time it also allows him to respond to, and to be aware of, all the influences of the Cosmos and, more particularly, of the other parts, or planets, within the Solar Body of which he is a part. He can tap into those influences, those powers, just as much as if he were in any of his higher bodies, although he is not aware of this.

Let us now examine Man's physical body. Have you ever thought, have you ever realised, what the limitations of your physical body actually are? Are they not those which you yourself have fixed? Consider a man who is blind or deaf. What does he do? He makes up a great deal for the loss of one of his senses by developing his other senses to a finer degree. For example, by touching and smelling a flower a blind person can identify both its type and its colour. All of you grossly under-use both your senses and the many other talents of your physical body. Until you really try to use your body, to exercise its many functions, you will never really know what it can do. Man must become more aware. Man must train himself to see beyond his limited range. He must train himself to hear more, to smell more, to taste more and to feel more. All the senses can and must be developed, for that is part of the purpose of Man's existence on this Earth — the physical side of his evolution. Of course hand in hand with this must go his spiritual evolution, the control and use of his six other bodies. It is only by evolving both physically and spiritually that Man will arise to ultimate perfection.

Medical science today has defined the parts of the physical body very clearly, but medical science has also limited the physical body, for people believe that the functions of its various parts are solely as defined by the medical dictionaries. This, of course, reflects the consciousness and the evolution of the Age in which you dwell, but as Man becomes more aware, and as spiritually motivated doctors and medical scientists begin to investigate and research into the true functioning of Man's physical body, so that knowledge will be increased.

To give you an idea of the true functioning of Man's physical body let us now examine just a few parts of that body. Corresponding to the seven planes of existence within the Solar Body there exist within Man's physical body seven power centres, or chakras, in different positions within the human frame. You cannot point to them, cut them out and show them as solid matter, for they are not made of the physical matter of this Earth. They are spiritual centres of high vibration tuned to the Cosmos and, basically, they reflect colour, which is vibration, for without colour Man could not exist in his physical body.

Man has more than one brain. He has four brains or four points of direct physical consciousness within his physical body. You are aware of Man's physical brain, of his reasoning, his intellect, the brain that exists in the head, which is the largest brain that Man possesses, but you should also know that Man has three other brains which he can and must use. He has a brain within his solar plexus, his emotional brain, his feeling brain. Because Man today does not use that brain that does not mean that it does not exist. It is lying dormant in many of you because Man today has based his civilisation on intellect. He does not want to feel: he wishes to reason instead. But, slowly, Man is beginning to realise that he must begin to feel again, for what use is all the reasoning, is all the intellect, without the feeling to guide and to motivate it? Man has a brain in his feet. Both his feet together form a brain. You have nerve tissue in each foot similar to that found in your physical brain and in your solar plexus. The right foot is the positive side, which registers the positive nerve energies, the left foot is the negative side, which registers the negative nerve energies, and together they form a brain. Likewise, Man has a brain situated in the palms of his hands. The right hand is the positive side and the left hand is the negative side, and together they form a brain.

The first brain in Man's head can be considered as his positive brain, the second brain in his solar plexus as his negative or receptive brain, the third brain in his feet as the brain which harnesses or grounds the emanations of the first two brains, and the fourth brain in his hands as the administrative brain, for it is through his hands that Man creates what he receives through his thought and feelings. Because Man is not only of this Earth but of the Cosmos so there are parts within the four brains which respond to and vibrate to the Solar Body. Within each of Man's four brains are to be found twelve minute cells which respond to the vibrations, the emanations, of the twelve planets of this Solar Body. Thus Man is at all times vibrating to the pulsations of the Solar Body.

I have mentioned Man's four brains in order to show you a little of the functioning, as yet undiscovered by medical science, of Man's organs. I would also mention how Man is linked to the four kingdoms of the Earth. While he resides in matter Man's spirit dwells within the left ventricle of the heart. The heart is divided into four quarters — the left and the right ventricles, the left and right atria, or the lower and upper chambers — and each of these four segments corresponds to, and vibrates to, one of the four Kingdoms of Matter. Likewise, each of Man's four toes, each of Man's four fingers, vibrates to the influence of one of the four Kingdoms. The small toe and small finger correspond to the Mineral Kingdom, the next to the Vegetable Kingdom, the next to the Animal Kingdom, the next to the Human Kingdom, with the big toe and the thumb representing the 'I am' personality controlling the lower Kingdoms.

Man must begin to learn to be aware of the spirituality of his physical body and to look beyond the limits of present medicine. Let me give you one final example. Each of the three sections of your fingers has a spiritual counterpart. The section nearest your palm represents the body, the middle section represents the soul, with the top section representing the spirit. Now you can appreciate why no two people have the same finger-prints, for just as each of you is an individual and unique spark of Infinite Spirit, each vibrating on a different wavelength, so the tops of your fingers representing your spirit reflect that individuality.

Perhaps you can now begin to see the reflection of the spiritual in the physical. They are not divided: they are one. The various parts of Man's physical body are most closely linked to, and are influenced by, the planets. The glands within his body, which control so much of his physical and spiritual existence, are most strongly influenced by the planets, yet this is a field of which Man is almost totally unaware. The planets provide power which Man uses. Man can use his physical body in many ways which he cannot now conceive. He can imitate the Nazarene. He can walk on water. He can heal the sick. He can control the Kingdoms of Matter through the use of the powers inherent in his physical body.

Man is continually attuned to forces beyond his limiting physical body. He does not walk this planet alone, uninfluenced. There are constant rays of power and energy both coming into and going out of his body. He is merely a part of a chain. The minute beings that dwell within Man's body use these influences and, therefore, how Man treats his physical body affects the lives of all those beings that dwell within him just as, similarly, how Man acts on the surface of the Earth affects the body of the Lord of this Earth — 'As above, so below'.

The body of Man is a magnificent creation. If you look at it, and think about it, you will see reflected in it the perfectness, the infiniteness, of your Creator. Surely, therefore, such a body deserves that you investigate it more closely and that you look after it more carefully: but everywhere today we see Man abusing his physical body. He does not try to purify it. He does not try to refine it. He does not try to increase its vibratory rate. He does not try to use it fully. He only limits it.

If Man is to realise his potential as a spiritual being, if he is to walk this Earth in imitation of his Creator, then he must use his physical body correctly. He must begin to understand its proper functioning. He must begin to understand its potential. He must begin to realise its significance in relation to his other bodies, and the purpose for which he dwells in it whilst he is in matter. Above all Man must realise the sacredness of his body. His body does not belong to him. It is created in God's image. He cannot create or replace its parts. He cannot create outside of it. It is given to him in a sacred trust, and for those who abuse that trust there is great karma to be paid.

Man has been given a body which reflects the magnificence of his Creator in every way. He has within it the potential of spirit and matter to rise to imitate that perfection, but he must respect that which he has been given, he must use that which he has been given. If Man begins to do so he will gradually become aware not only of life on this Earth but of life within the Solar Body and of life within the Cosmos. That is his birthright.

THE MOON

Within the Solar Body there is only one true star, only one that gives illumination and power, that sustains all life within its System: that is the Sun. The Being Whom you call God, the Solar Logos of this System, Whose spirit resides within the Sun, displays the degree of His evolution and vibration by the brightness of His illumination: hence it is impossible for Man on the Earth to look at the Sun. It is only when the Moon intervenes to cause an eclipse that Man can direct his gaze at the Sun.

Every planet and every satellite within this Solar Body is illuminated by the light of the Solar Logos, and each, according to its evolution and purpose in Creation, reflects that light. The Moon, being a satellite of the Earth and in close proximity to it, reflects the Sun's light most strongly onto the Earth and gives Man the visible moonlight of which he is aware. Because Man is limited by the range of his physical senses he does not notice, he is not aware of, the light reflected by the other planets within the Solar Body but, truly, an aware person can see and recognise venuslight, marslight, jupiterlight and saturnlight just as easily as he recognises moonlight.

One of the primary purposes of the Moon is to lead Man into a greater understanding of the Cosmos, for within the spiritual relationship between the Moon and the Earth lies the key to the Heavens. If Man was to study and examine closely the relationship between these two heavenly bodies he would, to a great extent, understand creation in the Universe. The Moon, its purpose and power, is the key not only to Man's development on the Earth but also to his development beyond it. Displayed before Man's eyes every Moon-cycle is the key to the Cosmos, but is Man fully aware of this?

It is not my intention in any way to reveal the spiritual significance and powers of the Moon, for that is not allowed by cosmic law. Unevolved Man may not be given the secrets of the cosmos until he has awakened his consciousness to the nature and purpose of those higher beings around him, and of his and their purpose on the evolutionary spiral. It is for unevolved Man to reach upward, to search diligently, using his own inspiration, and to look for the answers that he seeks. But so few seek those answers. Such is the nature of life on the Earth today that the Moon might just as well not exist!

To understand the relationship between the Moon and the Earth we have to go back to the time of their creation. Man today is busily examining the pieces of moonrock brought back by the American astronauts hoping that he will discover how the Moon came into being and, perhaps, understand a little of its environment. What Man is forgetting, however, is that although technologically he has reached the Moon through the use of his God-given intellect, in every other aspect of consciousness he is still a long way from it. He has to advance in many other fields before he may truly appreciate the purpose of the Moon and discover the true nature of its being.

Spiritual science, that is the science of Spirit as opposed to the science of Man, states that the Solar Body of which you are a part was created by the Solar Logos, that Being Whom you call God, Whose spirit resides within the Sun. Just as a child born on the Earth comes from its mother's womb, so the Sun gave birth to the Solar System. One by one the Solar Logos threw off particles of Himself until the planetary system as you know it today was formed. In the same way that a child leaves its mother's womb so the Sun gave birth to these particles, or planets. They were perfect in essence, but were molten masses that had to solidify before they could bring forth the true potential of Spirit. Over aeons of time these molten masses cooled and solidified and, aided by the angelic hosts, were helped to find their correct frequency.

Ten planets were created in this way and had been in existence for many Ages before your Creator, to fulfil His divine plan, gave birth to His last particle, His last planet. After this planet had left the Sun, the angelic hosts responsible for its development took their places on the different levels of vibration and watched and guided it as it cooled and crystallised. But before the mineral substances of the planet had completely crystallised it split into three, and from that one particle there came the Earth, its satellite the Moon and another planet which Man still has to discover behind the Moon. This undiscovered planet is the least evolved, the twelfth, planet of the Solar Body, for the Moon is not a planet but is a satellite of the Earth and its destiny is linked to the Earth's. The Moon has a vital part to play in the spiritual destiny of the Earth.

The Earth and the Moon were, then, created at the same time. The angelic hosts, the planetary and inter-planetary Masters, took their places on these orbs and, through their understanding of frequency and vibration, over centuries of time helped the elements within each globe to find their frequencies and to merge with the frequencies within the Solar System. Because of the cosmic purpose which the Moon has to fulfil it did not crystallise in the same way as the Earth. That is why Man, when he looks geologically at the samples of moonrock and analyses the data taken of the Moon's atmosphere, draws the conclusion that there is no common link between the Moon and the Earth, for although the Moon and the Earth came from the same seed they are as different as a brother and a sister can be in personality.

The Moon was created and placed precisely in orbit around the Earth so as to exert certain important influences upon it. Man today is slowly beginning to become aware of the mathematics known as the sacred geometry of the Earth. The same mathematics can be applied, only on a higher level, to the geometry of the heavenly spheres, for each of the planets is placed in orbit around the Sun and rotates along a set path according to a precise and definite cosmic formula. In the Ages gone by Man has recognised and used this formula, and it will be discovered again in the New Age. The distance of the Earth from the Moon is most critical, and it is vitally important that Man does not disturb this balance.

Although Man has reached the Moon in his spaceships, his motivation for going there was not correct. Moreover, the use that Man has made of the Moon with his experiments and his behaviour on it has in no way helped to preserve that critical balance, and by exploding his rocket heads and by his experiments on the surface of the Moon he has endangered this delicate balance. This balance is effected and preserved by the jewels which are present both within the Moon and within the Earth. The function of the jewels on which these two orbs rotate and balance can be likened to the function of the jewels within a watch. If you give a watch a shock and jerk the mechanism then it becomes unbalanced and fails: it is the same with the balancing mechanism between the Earth and the Moon. Of course the many beings on the Moon, together with their brothers from the other planets, have helped to counteract the effect of Man's naive experiments. But Man should be aware that in these experiments he risks not only the Moon but the Earth as well, for if he was to explode a bomb of any considerable size on the Moon then the finely balanced relationship between the Earth and the Moon would be destroyed. When you swing a ball on a piece of string around your finger, and then let go, the ball flies away. In a similar fashion, if Man was to upset the relationship between the Moon and the Earth the two orbs would fly apart and the delicate balance of life both on the Earth and the Moon would be destroyed, never to appear again.

Because Man is largely unaware of the invisible influences of the Earth, how can he be expected to be aware of the influences of the Moon? Just as Man, for the most part, is unaware of the presence of the elementals, the fairies and the spirits, the angels and the many beings who appear on the astral plane, just as he is unaware of life on any of the other planets within the Solar Body, so he cannot conceive of life on the Moon. But there *is* life on the Moon. A whole civilisation of beings dwells within it. Although they are similar in creation to Man, you would not recognise them as human beings because their bodies are shaped differently and they are much smaller in stature. But they do exist, with a high degree of civilisation, under the surface of the Moon.

Remember that every soul that incarnates onto a planet builds a body for itself according to the nature of the planet on which it incarnates. You, who dwell on the Earth, build yourselves a physical body which is most suited for life on the Earth. You use the matter of this Earth to build your physical body, and the mechanisms within it are those which can use the oxygen of the air, the water, the fruits of the land. Your body is designed to live in the temperature range that is prevalent on the Earth. In like manner the beings who dwell on the Moon build their bodies according to the nature of the Moon. A little concerning the conditions on the Moon is now known to Man, and if he were to sit down and consider what sort of body would be needed for life on the Moon he would perhaps conceive of the form and way of life of the Moon beings before such facts are discovered by other means. The Moon was put in orbit around the Earth to help in the Earth's evolution. The Moon beings are the servants of the Earth.

The nature of their evolution is different to yours. They do not possess that gift of free choice which your Creator has given to you so that you can advance your consciousnesses. They are directed by other forces. They fulfil the role of the Moon, helping the Earth at all times. Their power is given to you continually, regularly, according to the cycles of the Moon.

The spiritual number to which matter vibrates on the Earth is four. You are aware of the four Kingdoms of Matter, the four Races, the four points of the compass, the four seasons and so on. The Moon, vibrating to that number, in your service, has four phases, or four quarters. Each of the Moon's quarters corresponds to one of the four Kingdoms of Matter on the Earth and, during each of the quarters, the Kingdom associated with that quarter uses the power that the Moon gives according to the nature of the Kingdom and its cosmic purpose on Earth. Man can accept that the Moon moves the waters of the Earth because he is aware of the tides and has proved that its influence is responsible for them. Is it not strange how Man, having realised that the Moon can affect the tides, looks no further, for, surely, if the Moon can do this there is much else that it can do as well. In the present Age Man's physical body is composed of ninety per cent water. Can the Moon not affect that? Of course it can! Its influence is not only on the waters of the seas and the human body but on every aspect of creation on the Earth.

Anyone who looks at the Moon, especially at the full Moon, would, I think, accept that beauty is displayed there. The Moon is soft, is feminine, is wisdom. You would associate nothing harsh with the Moon. That is the nature of its influence: for as the Earth is positive, is power, is outward expression, so the Moon is feminine, is wisdom, is receptivity, is love. Therefore the female of the species on the Earth, being the wisdom and the creativity aspect, vibrates especially to the Moon's influence. It therefore controls birth to a great extent. Every woman experiences the cycles of her body which, when medical science does not interfere, correspond to the cycles of the Moon. Therefore, conception can, and should, be planned according to its phases. The Moon influences birth not only in the Human Kingdom but in the other Kingdoms of the Earth as well.

I do not wish to go too deeply into Man's spiritual bodies in this lecture, but for every influence on the physical level of which Man is aware the Moon's influence is tenfold on the higher levels.

In particular, it influences the pineal gland within Man, the receptivity, the wisdom, the learning gland of Man, and therefore knowledge and inspiration is obtained under its influence. Consciousness, also, can be increased under the Moon's influence. If you have not already tried it, carry out the experiment of trying to learn, of seeking to increase your consciousness, at the full phase of the Moon, for its powers given to the Earth at that time have great significance. Ancient Man was a little aware of this and established some of his religious ceremonies to take place during the full phase of the Moon. Some of the great Masters who have been on this Earth have incarnated, died, or performed significant spiritual acts, both on the physical and on the higher levels of life, according to the phases and the influences of the Moon.

The Moon also influences the astral body of Man while he is in the physical, and therefore it can also be a great aid to the use of this body, with all that is involved, especially in the field of psychic phenomena. So for those who seek to develop this particular aspect, this particular spiritual talent, the invocation and use of the Moon's power is, again of paramount importance. If you were to sit in meditation under the light of the full Moon you would feel increased awareness, with the power flowing through your pineal gland and spreading throughout your whole being. You would feel that greater consciousness, Infinite Consciousness, linking up with yours.

The mind and the brain are also influenced by the Moon. How you think, how you receive inspiration, how you behave, how you use your intellect and reasoning, are to a great extent influenced and controlled by it. The use of its powers can lift those little shutters on the brain, the little valves which, consciously or sub-consciously, allow in the vibrations of the cosmos, the experiences of the soul on other levels. These valves are responsive to the influences of the Moon. You have heard of the expression 'moon madness'. There are not many who suffer from this affliction but, occasionally, due to faults in the mechanism of the brain, under the influence of the full moon these shutters open and pictures, or images, of other levels of life come into the minds of some people, thus confusing them and destroying the harmony of physical life.

This is the effect of the Moon's power if it is not controlled. But for those who sit in meditation, correctly linking their consciousnesses to that of their Creator and using the power that the Moon gives, there will be moments of awareness which are both great and sudden. If the Moon shone upon the Earth continuously Man could not stand its influence and so, wisely, it appears in phases. These phases are important for they cause cycles on the Earth. The theory of the four phases of the Moon in relation to the Earth is a treatise in itself, but if Man was only to experiment a little with the four Kingdoms of Matter, to see which Kingdom responded most during which quarter, he would greatly improve the quality, the harmony and the understanding of his life on the Earth. In the past, ancient Man, although less advanced technologically, was more spiritually in balance. He understood the use and the purpose of the Moon and so could lead a more fulfilled, if not such a technologically advanced, life. If modern Man was to discover and use the Moon's influence and power no one would starve. There would be no droughts. There would be no earthquakes. There would be few natural disasters except for those which Man himself caused.

The Moon is always ready to serve the Earth. Why does Man look at it, why is he aware of its presence, without using it? Is it because in his intellect, in his ego, he considers that the key to himself, the key to evolution, the key to spiritual and material awareness, is locked within this Earth and could not be beyond it? Perhaps so. But for those of you who can cast your minds outwards, who can look at the Moon, who can vibrate towards that orb of beauty which reflects so much, including the nature of life on this Earth, you will find the key not only to Man's earthly progression but to his spiritual progression as well, and even to the progression of the Solar Body in which he lives.

THE POINT OF CONSCIOUSNESS
OF THE WORLD TODAY

All over the Earth at this time there reigns an air of disharmony, of uncertainty, of concern for the future, not only for the individual but for the World as a whole. No matter whether Man lives in the technologically advanced and rich countries or the under-developed and poor countries of the World, in those that have plenty to eat or in those that have little, everywhere he is uncertain of his purpose, of the present and of the future.

This feeling of uncertainty has, of course, existed before. In other Ages Man has had to contend with major wars, but with the advent of hydrogen bombs, germ and mental warfare, and of political, financial and mineral pressures, he truly poses a greater threat to the peace of the World than at any other time in its history. Hand in hand with this feeling of uncertainty today there is also a general disbelief in orthodox religion, with a falling off in the followers of the Churches. Man is turning away from organised religion and from God, or rather from his concept of God, to stand alone and to base his life on his own ideals, his own beliefs and creations.

Nothing in Creation belongs to Man. Being an instrument of Infinite Spirit, Man, through his mind, taps into Infinite Mind and brings down onto the physical level inspiration, or knowledge, which he then uses. He has the mental ability to do this, and even if he does not have the wisdom to motivate himself correctly he can still bring down these discoveries, for such is the nature of the divine gift of free choice which his Creator has given him. So everywhere Man uses his mind, his mental capacity, to advance his life on the Earth, although he does not have the spirituality to motivate the use that he makes of that knowledge. If he is to control his thought, Man must begin to become more aware, and in order to become more aware he must develop his spirituality, his true feelings and emotions, from within.

Man today, for the most part, acts without feeling. Because he has been given dominion over the three other Kingdoms of this Earth he can use, and also abuse, those three other Kingdoms. He thinks that he can use the Animal Kingdom as he wishes — for food, for scientific experimentation — and that he has every right to limit its true purpose and to deny it its right to free expression on this Earth. Man also uses the Vegetable Kingdom for food but, of course, he makes it conform to his own ideas and produce what he wants. Consequently he has now set in motion a chain of events which requires that the soil must be fertilised artificially, that the natural way crops grow must be altered and that the nature of the food which is provided for Man by his Creator must be changed. Man uses the resources of the Mineral Kingdom to produce what he thinks is necessary for his civilisation, no matter what the cost. The result of this behaviour without thought is the pollution of the air, the land and the sea.

Those few souls who do shout out against this abuse of Nature are treated with scorn, for Man truly believes that he can control what he has created. But Man has set in motion a chain of events which he will discover he cannot control, and so I would warn you that he has some unpleasant surprises coming to him in the years that lie ahead. Man's abuse of the three other Kingdoms of Matter has upset the balance, the harmony, of life on this Earth, and he will have to reap the effect of what he has sown. Even now it is too late to change the course of events which Man has set in motion. If he truly felt for Nature, Man would not abuse it. If he attuned himself to the animals, the vegetation, the waters and the stones of this Earth, then he would respect them for the essential parts they play in the structure of creation.

Man today can look back at the history of the Earth, as he knows it, and can recognise that he is evolving, that over the many centuries civilisation has gradually advanced and that, even if his spirituality is lacking, materially and technologically he has progressed a long way. Those of you who are aware, however, can also recognise that this Earth, and life on it, is just a part of a pattern in a vast cycle of events. You can see that life exists on many levels, both above and below Man, and you can appreciate that he is just a very small part in the structure of life within this Universe.

The Earth is part of a Solar Body. The twelve planets which exist within that Body, including their respective satellites, are all evolving together. The Earth is the second lowest planet in this Solar Body, and should by now have reached a point of consciousness whereby it can move in unison with the other planets encircling the Sun as they all move onto a new spiral of evolution. But the Earth at present is in great disharmony. If you could but stand outside the Earth and see its emanations, its vibrations, its pulsations of power, you would see that it is sick, that it is ill. Moreover, no matter what help is given by the great powers which exist within this Solar Body, if Man will not change, if he will not alter his behaviour, his expression, towards his fellow-men, if he will not live in harmony and exemplify the lesson and the purpose of this planet, sacrificial service, then he will not restore this planet to perfect health. At the present time the Earth is not emanating the power which it should be emanating — Universal Love. Remember that the emanations of all the planets intermingle in a complex pattern as they both give and receive their respective powers and vibrations and so fulfil the purpose for which they were intended.

Those of you who are aware are perhaps beginning to feel that certain events now taking place differ from any that have occurred before. You are beginning to sense that the pace of life is quickening and that time does not seem to exist as it did before. Of course your clocks still show the twenty-four hours of the day, but does not a day seem to go faster now than it did before? Do not the days and the months merge into each other so quickly that you can hardly believe another year has passed? All over the Earth there appears to be an increase in the number of disasters happening. You are constantly reading reports of droughts, floods, earthquakes, famines and diseases. Everywhere the pace of Man's existence, the violence in life, the conflict between countries, the competition, the division, the hatred, the greed, appears to be increasing. Those of you who sense this change are correct, for the whole being of this planet, the rate at which it vibrates, is being increased.

The Lords who control this planet and your Creator Whose spirit dwells in the Sun, together with many other influences, are trying to help the Earth, but their task is made more difficult by Man's disharmony. The Earth, because of Man's behaviour, has slowed in frequency. If you could stand outside the Solar Body and see the Earth you would see that, instead of quickening in frequency in co-ordination with the other planets as they move onto a new spiral of evolution, the Earth is toppling, or swaying, almost like a spinning top which is about to stop. If it did, it would send itself into oblivion. Because of this, the great Beings who govern matter through their knowledge of Infinite Law are trying to quicken the vibration of the Earth, not to alter or interfere with Man's free choice, but to bring into operation a quicker and a higher frequency. In so doing there is what appears to Man to be confusion and disruption, for he is held between the sluggishness of his own body, caused by his past behaviour, and the attempt by the Lords of the planet to bring him into a higher frequency of consciousness. These great Beings are interfering so that Man shall not be destroyed, for within his body there is the great atomic structure of the Cosmos, and in his sluggishness, when that moment arrives, and it will, when the Earth uprights on its axis, if this outer quickening had not been put into motion then the atomic structure of which Man is built would explode, because the force of the uprighting will bring into operation a great atomic expansion of the planet.

I will not go into the molecular structure and describe the behaviour of the atoms at that moment of change, but due to changes in pressure there will be a great transformation of the Earth's structure. There will be great devastation all over the Earth. It has, of course, happened before. You may read in the literature of ancient Man, and in the Bible, of similar occurrences. The cataclysm, which you would call a catastrophe, is really not a catastrophe: it is a step forward in the evolution of the Earth. Remember that to die is not a finality, and that those who die in the cataclysm to come will experience an increase in their consciousnesses, for in that moment of death they will learn. Leading up to this event there will be much disharmony and destruction as the vibratory rate of the Earth is quickened. This will occur before the great uprighting of the Earth on its axis which will take place around the end of this century. There are not many years to go.

Whether you believe me or not, whether you believe in the cataclysm which is to come, or not, does not matter. It is to come. It is to happen. The Earth is to change, and the Earth that will appear in the twenty-first century will be a very different one from the one you know now. Much of the water that exists on this Earth at present will have gone. Man will be living in an Air Age. His body will be composed mostly of air not, as now, mostly of water. He will be aware of his true spiritual existence, for he will be communicating with, and he will be aware of, beings on other planets. He will be aware that his total life is not spent solely in a limiting physical body of matter and that he can and, as his birthright, should dwell on levels beyond the physical even whilst in a physical body. He will travel to these other levels of existence. He will meet the other kingdoms, at present unseen: the Devic and the Angelic Realms. He will learn to recognise their influences, and truly give of the Earth's influence. All this is to happen to Mankind in the next century, the next Age. The Christ Principle which last came almost two thousand years ago is to come again, for at the commencement of any Age Man is given a sign, a demonstration, an example, of the way in which he should lead his life.

Many of you will not believe this, for it requires a certain level of consciousness to appreciate and understand the reason for, indeed the need for, what is to happen. But, whether you accept it or not, it is your responsibility to try and change Man's present behaviour. You have only to look around to see that Man must change, that Man has got to change, for his present way of life is so motivated that he is destroying this World in every respect. Man must begin to motivate his actions correctly. He must begin to think less of the self and more of the greater whole. He must remember that as he has the divine gift of free choice which no other being on this Earth possesses he must use that gift with responsibility.

The basic purpose of this planet is to demonstrate Universal Love, and Universal Love is exemplified through sacrificial service. Therefore Man should strive always to think of others before himself, of his family before himself, of his friends before his family, of the World before his country, of other planets before his own Earth. He must learn always to put others before himself. He must think not only with his brain, and work things out logically, but he must also feel with his heart, and determine whether what he is doing is indeed correct. Is it correct to pollute the waters and the air to achieve material gains? Is it correct to send rockets to other planets which neither ask for them nor desire them? Is it correct to abuse the Animal Kingdom? Is it correct for Man to abuse his own body? Is it correct to divide the nations of the World into those that have and those that have not? Is it correct to judge a man by the colour of his skin or by his religion? Is it correct to think of the self before everyone else that

175

exists on this Earth, when the example of every great Master who has incarnated on it has always been to put the self last and creation, in any form, first?

Man must begin to motivate himself correctly. The motivation of every act, of every thought, must be selfless. It must not be harmful to another. Man must begin to 'think' more with his heart and less with his brain, for his brain will not bring about the change that he has to make. It will be through his heart, his link with his Creator, using the inspiration of his Creator, that he will bring about this change. Man has the choice of doing good or evil. Goodness may be defined as love expressed in sacrificial service. Evil may be defined as thinking, saying or doing anything which in any way, by example or intent, can be degrading or harmful to another brother, to another being who lives on this Earth.

Remember that God works through people. Your Creator is not the God of those false religions which say that He will descend out of the clouds to redeem Mankind and put everything right. That God does not exist. It is only Man, using the powers that he has been given, who can change this World, and in as much as one of you changes then this Earth will have progressed on its upward spiral. For where there is one, there will be two, and where there are two, there will soon be four, and the great tide of evil which is now present on this Earth will begin to diminish. Then the consciousness of this Earth will begin to change.

THE PSYCHIC LAW

The Psychic Law, or the Soul Law as it is sometimes called, governs Man on all levels of his existence. In the Age in which you live today little is known about this Law. Little is understood about the powers and the influences which those spiritual beings who exist beyond the frequency range of physical matter can, and do, wield. However, as Man is entering the Aquarian Age when, due to the nature of his evolution and to the changes in his physical body, he is to become a more psychic and a more spiritual being, and is to live his life more in harmony with this power, in this lecture I am going to discuss a few aspects of the Psychic Law.

Many people who accept in faith the existence of beings such as elementals, fairies and spirits would like to see them and have their beliefs confirmed. They would like to see devas and angels. They would like to see an astral form and to travel in their astral bodies and be able to remember what they saw and experienced whilst they travelled in them. They would like to see, to hear, to smell, to feel, to taste beyond the limits of the physical body. They say, "I try. I pray that I could experience any one of these influences, and yet I see, I feel, I receive, nothing. Why is this? Moreover, I consider that I lead a harmonious and balanced life, and yet people who I know to be psychic appear to me to be living in disharmony and making great mistakes in their lives. Why should they have this gift and not me?".

Let us therefore begin to examine the Psychic Law. Firstly, remember that there is no division between spiritual and physical Man. It is Man who creates, even demands, this division. Man has limited himself to his physical body and to his physical Earth. It is Man who has said that he cannot see, hear, smell, taste or touch beyond the limiting frequency range of physical matter. Man accepts these limitations, is content with them, and seeks to investigate no further. Sometimes I think that Man deliberately buries his head in the sand, for he is ignoring the many people on this Earth who do possess and use extra-sensory perception, who can see, feel, taste, touch and hear beyond the range of most people.

As Man investigates the Animal Kingdom he becomes aware of the fact that animals can and do hear, see, smell and communicate outside his own frequency range. On another level, Man is aware of the power of electricity and of the presence of radio waves which he cannot see but which he knows do exist. There is, therefore, much that Man uses without actually being directly aware of through his five senses, but when the concept of extra-sensory perception is suggested to him Man usually cannot, or will not, consider such a 'ridiculous' proposition. Only a few, therefore, experiment with, and investigate, the Psychic Law.

Maybe you do not know of anyone who is psychic, but that does not mean that this ability does not exist, for many of those who possess psychic ability, recognising it as a spiritual talent, do not seek to profit from it in any way and use it only for the purpose of their own inner development, and to fulfil the Greater Plan. Therefore the few so-called psychic people that you do meet and hear about are not necessarily the only, or the most evolved, psychic people in this World.

To use the Psychic Law, to have extra-sensory perception, is Man's spiritual birthright. It was not intended that just a few people should have this ability. Every evolved person, and I stress the word evolved, who incarnates on the Earth should possess this ability. This was one of the demonstrations of the Nazarene when he incarnated on the Earth, for many of his miracles which are described in the Bible are merely extensions of the Psychic Law: the ability to walk on the water, to multiply the loaves and fishes in order to feed many people, to turn water into wine, to heal, to raise from the dead, to appear in a physical body after death. In such demonstrations the Nazarene was showing Mankind that for those who can advance to the consciousness to recognise, to understand and to wield such power, the Psychic Law is a reality.

Many people on the Earth today do not possess psychic ability because inherent in the structure of Man's physical body is the limitation, wisely placed there by their Creator, which ensures that they are restricted to the physical plane. If unevolved Man were able to use the Psychic Law, to wield psychic power, to any great extent, he would not be able to cope with all the extensions of his senses, and would be confused. Many of the people who today are considered to be insane, who have hallucinations, are people who are suffering from a fault in the mechanism of their brains which permits psychic influences to enter. Medical science today has not yet discovered that in the brain there are little shutters, little doors, or minute valves, which control the entry of these psychic influences into Man's brain. While Man is awake these little doors are closed, unless opened through the development of the spiritual centres, but while he sleeps the doors are opened and psychic influences can come in. However, while he is asleep Man's consciousness is dimmed and he is not aware of what his super-consciousness sees. Even so, Man can still experience dreams or nightmares, visions of confusion, which register on his conscious brain. These are caused by the astral body returning to its physical shell after travelling on other levels of existence whilst Man is asleep, when the little doors into the brain are partially open. This permits a distorted vision of other realms to be momentarily recorded on Man's physical brain.

A similar thing also happens when a person is kept awake for many, many hours and is not allowed to sleep. The etheric body, the energy producing body, which is the body which generates the life force within Man, has to withdraw from the physical body every twenty-four hours in order to regenerate itself with cosmic forces. Therefore it withdraws through the little doors I have previously mentioned whilst Man sleeps. But if Man is kept awake, when the etheric body withdraws and the shutters open Man will see what would normally have been concealed. These visions he calls hallucinations.

Similarly, many of the young today are taking drugs and are removing the natural control of their bodies so as to experience 'trips', to be able to experience visions and influences which they would not normally be able to experience. This is most wrong because they are defying the Law of Nature and are artificially experiencing something which they are spiritually not yet ready to receive.

So, you see, the psychic experience is available, and can be had, but only by overcoming the protective mechanism of your Creator. Your Creator has wisely decided that until you have evolved to a certain level, when you can fully understand the Psychic Law, you may not use it. Therefore you would be most unwise to experiment with psychic powers until such time as you can achieve them naturally through the evolution of your own consciousnesses.

The reason why Man incarnates on this Earth is to advance his consciousness, through the exercising of his own choice, along the path which he and his Creator have chosen. If Man wishes to be aware of, and to use, the Psychic Law he has to earn that right. It is not to be given to him as a gift from above. Like everything else on this Earth it has to be earned the hard way: through experience, through sacrifice, through personal achievement, through hard work. If you desire to develop your psychic abilities you must be aware that it is something which you yourselves have to achieve. It is not something which will descend upon you like rain from the clouds. I would also point out to those who do desire to develop their psychic talents that any spiritual achievement carries with it great responsibility, for as you evolve up the ladder of spiritual progression, as you advance from class to class in this school of life and evolve your consciousnesses, so hand in hand with that goes the responsibility to use those consciousnesses wisely. So if you do develop psychic ability, then you should always use it with responsibility.

There are, of course, many manifestations of the Psychic Law. The ones of which Man is perhaps most aware are those of physical and mental mediumship. Physical mediumship is mediumship which takes place outside the realm of the medium. The most common demonstrations of this are Levitation, Materialisation and Apportation. Mental mediumship is mediumship which takes place within the realm of the medium. The most common demonstrations of this are Clairvoyance, Clairaudience, Psychometry, Automatic Writing and Drawing, and Trance Mediumship. Many psychic experiences are to be had by those who do possess psychic ability, but to possess this ability requires that your soul-consciousness has practised and used these talents in other lives. As I have said before, psychic talents have to be earned, and therefore it is true to say that anyone who possesses them is an old soul. They have practised and used those talents many times, for they are not talents that can be picked up and learnt easily. Therefore, because it is only old souls who possess psychic talents, one can expect a psychic person to have a strong personality. That is why there are people who say that they know of mediums who possess strong personalities, whom they consider to be unpleasant, even unspiritual, people. Nevertheless, people who possess psychic ability have earned the right to possess it through their actions in other lives.

If you would truly seek to be psychic then you must practise your particular psychic talents and you must harmonise yourselves, for until you as individuals are in harmony, consciously or even sub-consciously, you will not become psychic. To harmonise yourselves with your surroundings is therefore your first objective, and you will discover that as you begin to achieve this, as you begin to become aware of your fellow-men, your physical bodies, Nature, the individual petals in a rose, the water flowing in a stream, the new-born lamb in spring, then that psychic ability will reveal itself to you without you even knowing it. Suddenly, in the twinkling of an eye, as you sit beside a flower one day, you will look down and there you will see a little elemental. It may be for only a brief second, but that will be enough. To see an elemental requires little conscious effort. All that happens is that you lower your rate of vibration with the correct motivation and with love, and that the elemental raises its vibration so that you meet on a common plane of matter below the normal physical range. Someone along-side you would not see it.

It is your birthright to see the fairies and the elementals below you, to see the Masters and the Teachers above you, to see the beings from the other planets, to see the Interplanetary Planes, to see the colour and to hear the sound that exists in this Universe. Man hears a piece of music played by one of the great musicians on this Earth and he thinks that the ultimate in sound has been achieved, but he has not yet begun to hear the music of the spheres. Man sees a beautiful painting by a famous artist and he thinks that he sees perfection, but he has not yet begun to understand the true meaning of colour and to recognise the true colours of the Cosmos. This right, this ability, is Man's birthright. He can, he must, be aware of it. He can, he must, use it. But it is not a toy given to a child to play with. It is a responsible part of Creation and Man will not develop his psychic ability until such time as he reaches a certain level of consciousness.

The way to become psychic is, therefore, to advance your consciousness and to place yourself in harmony with matter around you. There are many short cuts which you can try to take. It is your choice whether or not you do so. I will say no more than this: that to use this Law, this power, before you are ready for it incurs great risk. You can tap into forces, you can see visions, you can see life as it exists way beyond your consciousness, but if you cannot comprehend it and grasp it, if you cannot understand it, it will unbalance you, it will confuse you even to the point of madness. Your Creator has protected you: do not pull down that protection.

It is very easy to want to possess the ability to use the Psychic Law, to wield psychic power, but I would ask you to examine why you want to use it, what your motivation is. Remember that you can influence many people with that power. Recognise that just as you are influenced by the demonstrations of psychic power by the great Masters and Teachers so you too can influence less evolved souls, and that the moment you begin to use the psychic power to try and help your fellow-men you risk incurring great karma, for you can easily mislead them. Therefore use the Psychic Law, the Soul Law, with responsibility. If you possess this power, then remember to use it with discrimination. Do not cast pearls before time. It is a personal talent to be used according to your own spiritual motivation. It does not have to be shared with anyone, and in most cases should not be shared.

Man must motivate himself and the use that he makes of psychic power. It is a power far greater than any atomic device that Man has ever exploded. The true degree of the Psychic Law and psychic power is not that which you see demonstrated by the every-day man or medium in the street. It rises far higher. Remember the demonstrations of the Nazarene. So, once you have had your first psychic experience, once you have begun to understand the elementary principles of this Law, realise that you still have a long path ahead of you before you truly understand the all-embracing, all-important, Psychic Law.

THE PARABLE OF THE CHRISTMAS STORY

The way in which this Earth has evolved since its creation aeons of time ago is so complex that unevolved Man cannot conceive of it. Much of the Ancient Wisdom, the true knowledge of this Earth, remains unknown today, but there are a few people who are aware of some of its content and significance. They have recognised that just as creation around them is planned, just as the stars and the planets revolve in their fixed orbits in space, so life on this Earth is similarly regulated, and that the manner and the period of the evolution of this Earth is fixed just as precisely as is the revolution of the Earth around the Sun.

This Earth passes through many cycles, or patterns, of evolution, and these cycles are tied in with the rise and fall of civilisations, with the rise and fall of the four Races which inhabit this Earth, and with the coming and going of the great Masters who are sent to show the way to Man. Because of the nature of Man's evolution, at the beginning of every cycle in the Earth's development, each of which lasts about two thousand years, a great Master is sent down so that the people of the Age may have demonstrated to them the aspect of the Christ Principle applicable to that cycle and to their point of evolution and to the consciousness of the Earth at that time.

Almost two thousand years ago Jesus of Nazareth incarnated to exemplify the Christ Principle to Man who was to incarnate on the Earth under the influences of the Piscean Age. Although he was a great Master in his own right he was overshadowed, inspired and empowered by that Christ expression from the Lord of us all. There was nothing unique about the Nazarene's incarnation. Many other Masters have incarnated at the beginning of other cycles in the Earth's development and have similarly reflected aspects of the Christ Principle.

Although legends must, and will, be dispelled if they are not true, my purpose in talking to you in this lecture is not to destroy the legend which Man has created around the Christmas story but to help you to understand the true significance of that story so that, in your own time and in your own meditations, you yourselves may commune with your consciousnesses and reach your own interpretations of the meaning of Christmas.

Although the Christian Churches today would have you believe so, Christmas does not belong only to the Christians. The Christian religion may have been founded by one small group of men based on their ideas of what the Nazarene taught and did, but the Nazarene demonstrated the Christ Principle for all Mankind, for all the races of the World, for all the peoples, for all the countries. The Christ Principle belongs not only to the Christian but to the Jew, the Buddhist, the atheist or even the witch-doctor living in the jungle.

The Nazarene incarnated and exemplified the Christ Principle for the Piscean Age and, as was the case with all the other Masters who have exemplified the Christ Principle, the story of his life was written down for the souls who would incarnate many, many years after his death. So, today, the Christmas story is described in the Bible. Those of you who are beginning to develop your consciousnesses are aware that the Bible, though not being untrue, contains much that cannot be taken literally. Much of the New Testament is written in parable form. Just as the Nazarene himself taught in parables and left it to the individual to see in them the wisdom that he expressed, so the Christmas story itself is of a similar nature. Unevolved Man can believe that a woman who was a virgin gave birth to a child in a stable amongst the animals, that three wise men came from the East with gifts to pay homage to that child, and that they followed a star which eventually hovered over the place where that child was born. He can believe that an angel of the Lord appeared to some shepherds keeping watch over their flocks in a field near Bethlehem and told them of the birth of Jesus of Nazareth and that they then went to see the child. He can believe that the angels sang and heralded his coming. If you have a limited consciousness, the consciousness of a child — and that is said meaning no disrespect — then you will accept that story as it is, but in this lecture I am going to ask you to consider another interpretation of the Christmas story.

The Nazarene, as is the case with any soul who incarnates on this Earth, was born within Natural Law. That is The Law. There-

184

fore the virgin birth which is alluded to in the Bible does not refer to the birth of the Nazarene, for he was conceived and born of man and woman. The virgin birth refers to the Christ Principle which was created by the perfect breath of your Creator, and therefore because the Nazarene was overshadowed by the Christ it could be interpreted that a part of him was of virgin birth. Very little has been recorded in the Bible concerning the Nazarene's parents, but they were evolved souls, specifically chosen by the Nazarene. They were a normal husband and wife within the bonds of a true spiritual marriage, living the life which you would expect any normal married couple to live. They were not gods. They were not saints. They had their trials and tribulations like any other married couple. They were learning the lessons of life just as you are today. They had to pay their taxes just like you do. Any man who incarnates on this Earth is of the Earth: he must answer to the Earth and must live the life of the Earth.

It is said in the Bible that the Nazarene was born in a stable amongst the animals, but I would like you to consider another interpretation of this aspect of the Christmas story. If you consider that the Nazarene, overshadowed by the pure virgin light of the Christ, was incarnating into the world of Man with all its evil, its wickedness, the creations of Man's lower nature, then you will see that the story of the Nazarene being born in a stable was intended to represent the Christ Principle descending amongst the lower instincts of Man which were represented by the animals. It symbolised the pure, virgin, crystalline light of your Creator descending onto the Earth to illuminate the darkness, the lower aspects of Man, and to show him the way back to perfection.

It is said in the Bible that the angels sang and heralded the birth of the Nazarene. It is true that anywhere in the Universe at the moment of birth forces unseen by Man herald the arrival of creation. The angels did indeed sing at the birth of the Nazarene, just as they sing at the birth of any soul who incarnates into matter. The Nazarene was not getting special treatment because of his purpose in that incarnation. At the moment of his physical creation, of his birth, he was receiving the heralding of the angels just as aeons of time earlier the sending down onto the Earth of the Christ Principle also was heralded by the angels. This event serves as a reminder to Man that the invisible forces of life which he cannot see with his physical eyes, which he is not aware of with his physical senses, are always present, controlling, guiding, helping, answering the call of Man. The angels did sing at the Nazarene's birth, but only those who had eyes to see, who had ears to hear, would have received their message.

It is said in the Bible that three wise men travelled a long way following a star, and that this star led them to the place where Jesus lay in Bethlehem. They came to worship him and to bring him gifts. It is a lovely story, but I would ask you to consider a new interpretation. The Earth was the last but one of the planets in the Solar Body to be created, and at its birth all the other planets, which had already been in existence for aeons of time, helped by sending their vibrations and their respective powers onto the seed of the Earth to aid in its formation. Together with the Lord of this Solar System they helped in the creation of the Earth.

The powers of the planets are still being sent down onto this Earth, and the three wise men who travelled from afar had indeed come from afar, for they had travelled across the vastness of space. They had not come from this Earth but from other planets within your Solar Body, and that star which hovered above the stable was not a star but rather their means of transport. They came bringing gifts, so the Bible says, of gold, frankincense and myrrh. These symbolised the powers which these three great planetary leaders brought to the Earth: truth, love and harmony, the gifts of the three major planets within this Solar Body. These gifts were given not only at the birth of the Earth but also at every time that the Christ Principle has been grounded on the Earth.

The significance of the three wise men is to let Man know that he is not alone, that he is not supreme, that he is not the only being in creation. It is to let Man know that forces that have been in existence long before he was created, and will perhaps be there long after he has gone, are always present, helping and guiding him with the powers that they possess. It is to let Man know that he is part of a greater body, of a greater purpose, of the Solar System, and that as the other planets help him so he, to the best of his ability, should help them.

It is said in the Bible that some shepherds tending their flocks in the fields around Bethlehem were told of the birth of Jesus by an angel, that they went to Bethlehem to find this child, and that they then went out and broadcast all that they had witnessed. Here again, unevolved Man can believe that some shepherds were inspired to come to witness a birth, but I would ask you to consider another interpretation: that the flocks of sheep symbolised the men and women of this Earth and that the shepherds were the spiritual leaders, the Masters, the Guides, the Beings as yet unknown to Man, who are responsible for and help Man in every way as he lives his physical incarnation. So these unseen forces, these unseen influences, representing every aspect of life that exists beyond the physical, were called to witness the rebirth of the Christ Principle for the Piscean Age. They were to be made aware of the purpose of that Age, the purpose of the Nazarene, and the significance of his grounding of the Christ Principle.

Remember that life exists on many levels beyond the physical, that life in the physical is only transitory and, whilst important, is only a small part of Man's existence, and that for every being who incarnates on the surface of this Earth in a physical body there are ten in discarnate form watching over him from above. Man may consider the Earth to be overpopulated, but the Spiritual World contains numbers beyond his comprehension. It contains forces and powers which one day he will understand and meet.

You may not accept what I have just said. Some people regard the Christmas story with great reverence but, if one cannot verify its source or understand its meaning, there is no reason to revere a story written in a book almost two thousand years ago. You laugh at the tribes in the jungle as they perform their strange rituals which have been handed down from generation to generation, and you call them primitive. Yet, as he passes down his interpretation of the Christmas story, 'civilised' Man acts in just the same way. Man's present interpretation of the Christmas story belongs to the Piscean Age, but you have come to the end of that Age. The next cycle, the next two thousand years, the Aquarian Age, is upon you, and for that Age there will be another grounding of that Christ Principle. Although the Christ Principle is always with you in spirit, there is to be another physical demonstration for those of this New Age. Old beliefs, old ideologies, are to be swept aside and destroyed. On the physical level, much else is to be destroyed as well in the cataclysm that is to come within the next thirty years. There is to be a rebirth of the Earth, a rebirth not only of the surface of the Earth but also of Man, of his attitude towards life and towards the purpose of both his own destiny and that of the Earth.

Man today is tentatively moving into the 'space age'. Through technological advances he has invented a crude means of travelling through space, but he travels in the wrong manner, for the wrong reasons and at the wrong time. This he is allowed to do because he has the divine gift of free choice. Man will learn by his mistakes just as much as he will learn by his achievements. Although he travels into space Man does not understand or recognise the true nature of space. Limited by his physical viewpoint Man looks upon space as being hostile. He believes that he has the right to go where and when he pleases. But that belief is soon to be shattered, for contact with beings on other planets within this Solar Body is imminent and Man will soon be made aware that life does exist on the other planets and, what is more, that the beings who dwell on those planets are in fact more evolved than Man, and that they regard the inhabitants of this Earth as unevolved children.

Man will soon realise that he is not where he thinks he is, in the top class, but rather in one of the lowest, and that he has much to learn. He will discover that many of the beliefs, tenets and ideologies that he has created to support his narrow limiting view of life, both on the Earth and in the Universe, are incorrect. They will be destroyed at a stroke. He will learn that much of what is written in his holy scriptures describes not the visitations of a God but, truly, the visitations of beings from the other planets. He will realise just how much they have influenced and helped the course of Man's history, and he will learn to accept them as his brothers. Man will begin to seek for and to understand the true God, the real God of this planetary system, Whose spirit dwells within the Sun. At the moment he cannot conceive of this God. All he possesses is a personalised view of God created either by the Churches or his own conditioned thought.

A new realisation is dawning. It is coming whether Man likes it or not. He will be forced to accept reality. Man has only to examine the state of the World today, to examine how Christmas is actually celebrated on this Earth, to realise that the Earth needs a re-birth, that the old body must pass away and that a new child must be born with all the hopes of a new, a fresh, incarnation. Do not be afraid of the death that is to come for, as the Nazarene demonstrated to you, death is as nothing. It is not to be feared. It is part of the cycle of Man's continuing evolution, and just as Man incarnates and evolves so this planet Earth on which he dwells also incarnates and evolves.

The Christmas story, then, must be seen in a new light, in the light of the Aquarian Age, rather than in the light of the happenings of the World today where Man can celebrate Christmas, the birth of the Christ, on one day and then go out and destroy his fellow-men on the next, where Man can sit down and overfeed himself, can reduce himself to an alcoholic stupour, can waste his time and energy in a meaningless exchange of presents and yet can still feel that he is fulfilling the purpose of Christmas.

If you look at the situation and the interpretation of Christmas as it exists today you will welcome the rebirth that is to come, just as the angels welcomed the rebirth of the Christ almost two thousand years ago. You will join with the angels and sing as the moment arrives when out of the darkness there comes light, when out of the darkness there comes truth, when out of the darkness there comes harmony and goodwill, when out of the darkness there comes the realisation of the true meaning and significance of Christmas.

PROPHECY

One of the many talents which Man possesses, and one which is part of his inherent birthright, is the gift of prophecy. Although few people possess this gift today and, indeed, few have done in the past, it is nevertheless the birthright of all Mankind to be able to understand the meaning of time and, therefore, to know of the future. If you look back at the history of ancient civilisations you will discover that a prophet has always been regarded with honour. In the days of old the court prophet was an influential person, but although there were many true prophets naturally there were also many charlatans who abused the trust people placed in them, who claimed powers for themselves which they did not possess. Today, as in the past, there are amongst you prophets or seers, men of vision, who can foretell what is to come.

There is much evidence of Man's ability to prophesy, not only in the Bible but also in many other writings. These testify as to how Man has accurately predicted future events. In the Old Testament the prophets foretold that the walls of Jericho were to fall down, that disease, death, the destruction of a city, the fall of a country, were to take place. In the New Testament the Nazarene predicted his own death and could even foretell that his disciple Peter would betray him three times before the cock crowed. The disciple John foretells of the events that were, and still are, to occur to the World as described in the last book of the Bible — Revelation. Looking at one of your modern novelists, H.G. Wells predicted with amazing accuracy, long before it took place, a journey of Man to the Moon and the other planets. For any of these people to receive such inspiration there had to be a source which corresponded to the evolution of the soul that received it. For them to recognise the future, the future had to be present in some form.

Your recognition of prophecy, of its significance and purpose, and, closely associated with that, your recognition of the true function of time, will vary according to your point of consciousness. Man regards time as being a constant determined by the revolution of the Earth around the Sun. However, some scientists, amongst them Einstein, have begun to throw a new light on the dimension of time and have begun to suggest that, truly, time is not as fixed as Man would have it. To recognise the true nature of time requires an extremely evolved soul. Indeed, even a soul such as the Nazarene would only just be beginning to comprehend the true nature of time, and even he would apply his understanding of time only as far as his consciousness would allow. Only a soul more evolved than the Nazarene, one of the Inner Twelve who dwell on the Sun, would have a true understanding of time and, therefore, a greater vision of Creation.

From what I have said you could perhaps assume that the future is as planned and as fixed as the past, that Man has no influence on it whatsoever, that Man is like a puppet placed on the Earth with the strings being controlled by a greater Power solely for that Power's amusement, and that truly Man is a small, infinitesimal speck of no consequence whatsoever surrounded by greater forces over which he has no control. That assumption would be wrong. You were created in imitation of your Creator, and therefore within your physical body, as you dwell in matter today, you have the potential of your Creator. If you seek to limit yourselves it is your own limitations that you impose, not the limitations of your Creator. Man was placed on this Earth for the sole purpose of evolving his consciousness and, thereby, the consciousness of the planet Earth as a whole. Man's purpose is therefore twofold: the evolution of himself and the evolution of this planet, and from these will come the evolution of the Solar Body, thus forming a trinity.

For Man to evolve his consciousness he had to be given the divine gift of free choice, for how would he be able to learn if he could not choose, if he could not choose light from darkness, if he could not learn through the Law of Opposites, through experiencing joy and sorrow, love and hate, health and disease? So when, at a stage in the Earth's development aeons of time ago, Man was reincarnated, he was given free choice. By the exercising of this choice he can influence what is to come. When the prophets of old predicted what was to happen, although they were tapping into Higher Forces they were also using their divine knowledge of Mankind to enable them to predict the future with accuracy. They understood that the way Man thought, that the way in which he behaved, that the patterns and the auras of creation around him as he lived on the Earth, would ultimately lead to the events that they predicted. Man, of course, could change and therefore upset their predictions, for he had free choice, but, recognising his weaknesses, those prophets could see that he would not change, and that the events predicted would indeed take place.

The Plan for this Earth is more complex than Man can dream of. I can only liken it to the programme of an intricate computer in which provision is made for the free choice of all Mankind. If we bring this vast Plan down to an individual level and look at your individual lives on Earth, they too are planned: the people you meet, the major occurrences in your lives, your marriages, your children, your careers and the times of your deaths. All that is planned, but within that plan provision is made for the free choice which you will exercise. When a choice is put before you you always have the freedom to choose which path you will follow, but all those paths are accommodated within the complex computer programme for your life.

The great spiritual Masters, souls of an evolved consciousness who have lived on this Earth, have appreciated the structure and purpose of life on this Earth and have therefore been able, even without inspiration from Above, to foretell with accuracy how the events of life would proceed. It does not take a wise man to realise that if the peoples of the World lead their lives based on materialism, on the desire for personal wealth and possessions, sooner or later conflict will arise over the ownership of that wealth and those possessions. It does not take a wise man to realise that when certain men are elected to power in a particular country — and remember that they reflect the thoughts of that country — the power which those elected men wield will lead to certain events in the World. It is just as true today as it was five thousand years ago that the spiritually aware person will be able to prophesy that clouds of disharmonious thought will indeed bring about the wrath of Nature — for remember that Man's thoughts create on both the higher and the lower levels of existence around this Earth — and that the imbalance that Man creates will inevitably cause an imbalance in Nature. Therefore prophets can predict floods, earthquakes, famines and pestilences.

The wise men of old also understood the cyclic pattern of evolution of this Earth. They could predict the rise and fall of civilisations because they knew that as the Ages changed so the patterns of life on this Earth would change as well. They knew that at the beginning of an Age, at the dawn of a new civilisation, a great Master was sent down to demonstrate and teach the Principle for that Age, and therefore they could predict the coming of the Master Jesus as, even now, they can predict the coming of the next great Master at the end of this century.

To be a prophet — and I speak now of a true prophet — requires not only an evolved consciousness but also an appreciation of the true purpose of this Earth, the nature of its evolution, an understanding of the patterns of life that exist on all levels on and around it and an insight into Man's nature. If you possess this knowledge then, according to the level of your consciousness, you will be able to prophesy. You will be able to feel what is to happen to you, to your family or to this Earth. You will possess the ability to predict the winner of a horse-race, the death of a statesman or even the birth of a child, for these are all extensions of the same gift. Each time you are merely tapping into the vibrations around you and around this Earth.

The true prophet, as he prophesies, recognises that the element of choice is still present, and that if only Mankind itself will change then Mankind can change what is to come. The accuracy of prophecy relates only to the predictability of Man's actions, for normally he will proceed according to the patterns of his individual development and the conditioning his environment has imposed upon him. The way that Man has lived on the Earth during the past has laid down the patterns of future development. What Man has done cannot be undone or be destroyed: it can only be transmuted. Although Man finds it hard to understand, it is true to say that the sins of the fathers are visited upon their children even unto the third and the fourth generation.

You would ask me what I, from my point of consciousness, see for the future of your World at this time. I cannot reveal to you all that I see, for that is the responsibility of my consciousness, but I can give you some indications of what is to come. You live at a most critical time in the Earth's evolution. Events both within and beyond Man's control are leading to a rebirth of the Earth at the end of this century. The Beings who control this planet according to the Cosmic Laws, which they too must obey, have instituted changes for this Earth which will bring about a transformation not only of the surface of the Earth but also of life on it. This can be prophesied with certainty: but Man himself, being the unknown factor on the Earth, can influence the nature of this change. If only Man will live in harmony, if he will only learn to sacrifice, to put others before himself, then this great transformation of the Earth as it moves from one great era to another can be accomplished with a minimum of destruction, not only for Mankind on the Earth but for the Earth itself. But if Man continues on the path on which he is now set then the destruction will be great, for Man's influence will react upon the Natural Forces of this Earth and the dark clouds of destruction which Man himself has created will multiply the effect of the natural destruction. Remember that this destruction, which Man from his viewpoint regards as wasteful and having the finality of death and disaster, is in reality not really destruction but transformation, a part of the Plan for the evolution of this Earth. Remember that to destroy is not to eradicate, that to destroy is not to end, and that after every destruction there is a rebirth, a new beginning, and that something greater will very often arise from the ashes.

As I look at Man today and the path upon which he is now set, I can say to you that, unless Man changes, the next twenty-five years will see events take place which you cannot imagine. There will be great destruction. There will be earthquakes, heavy rains and floods, droughts, famines and plagues. The pattern of life on this Earth will change beyond all comprehension. Even now with the 'energy crisis', as you call it, you can begin to anticipate the collapse of Man's technological world. In any case the Earth is not to progress in the way that Man thinks. There is to be a drastic change in the balance of civilisation. The Great Powers, as the major countries of the World are sometimes called today, will no longer be Great Powers. There will be an equalisation of Man all over the Earth and little countries such as England will manifest qualities, conditions of life, intelligences and physical attributes which will be the saviour of this World. The great financial empires will collapse. The value of money, which at the present time is regarded as being of such importance all over this Earth, is to disappear and a new system of exchange will take its place. Through circumstances of life Man will be forced to trade with his enemies, to help them, and to treat all men as equals no matter what their race, colour or creed.

Because of this great transformation that is to take place many planetary beings are very close to the Earth at this time in order to help with this delicate process for, of course, the transformation of one part of the Solar Body affects the other parts. These planetary beings, at a higher point of evolution than Man, have been helping the Earth for many years now, but in the very near future they will actually be present on the Earth. Man will recognise them as the evolved beings that they are, and he will be forced to recognise that many forms of life exist in this Solar Body apart from his own. This will lead to the destruction of all organised religions on the Earth, and Man will turn to a new, to a true, awakening of knowledge of his Creator. Before this comes about, however, there will also be the establishment of a means of communication with these planetary beings, for Man could not accept their presence unless prepared beforehand.

At the present time your Earth is threatened by war. War will not be abolished on the surface of this Earth, for the conditions which lead to war are prevalent everywhere and therefore there will be wars in the future. These wars will occur at various points on the globe and will not, as Man would anticipate, necessarily be between the political divisions that now exist on this Earth. There will be much more sacrifice, much more bloodshed, before Man comes into the true realisation of the futility of war.

There is to be a great revolution in the fields of healing and medicine. The present path of medical research is to be diversified and from this there will come true inspiration. Man will discover the cure for many of the diseases for which he has no cure today. He will learn to cure cancer, multiple sclerosis and other diseases. He will learn to understand the true nature of disease, and from that he will discover the true nature of healing.

The political and social organisations of Man are to undergo a rebirth in every way. Amongst the young people of today there are souls of great evolution, souls who have incarnated on the Earth at this time for a specific purpose, and as they grow to physical maturity so they will seek to overthrow the established ways of Man. Already you can see this trend in the World today. Because, at present, they are young in physical years, they have little influence, but in the future as they grow older and wiser their influence will become paramount. Then you will see the breakdown of society as it exists today, and a new recognition of the value of Mankind. Old values will be rejected, and from the ashes of the old organisations a new brotherhood of Man will develop.

I do not intend to paint a gloomy picture for this Earth: I merely predict the great changes that are to come. There is still time for Man to avert much of the destruction that is to come, for if he will but change himself then he will more readily accept the changes that, whether he likes it or not, are to come. But, like the prophets of old, I have only to look at the way Man behaves today to know that my prophecies are to be fulfilled. I would wish that this was not so. I pray with you for the transformation of this Earth along the lines that were intended for it, but as I watch the behaviour of Man I know that the inevitable cannot be avoided. Therefore, fulfilling the true purpose of a prophet, I tell you these things only so that you may prepare yourselves for what is to come.

Any prophet can be accepted or ignored. If you cannot accept in your own consciousness the prophecy that is made to you, then you must reject it. That choice is your inherent birthright. But if you look at the World today, if you look at the past history of Man, if you accept the great future planned not only for this Earth but for the whole Solar Body in which you dwell, if you accept the existence of those Great Beings who do truly control this Earth and your Solar Body, then you will recognise that change is not only desirable but imminent. If you accept this, then you will meditate on what I have said and will, perhaps, begin to transform yourselves so that you, as individuals, can avoid the destruction which many of your fellow men will suffer. Where there is light it will be recognised in the darkness, where there is harmony disharmony will not prevail, and where there is truth there can be no evil. So prepare yourselves. Use the individual gift of prophecy which you all possess and let the wisdom of your Creator illuminate your pathway into the future.

THE SYMBOLOGY OF THE EASTER STORY

When you consider the Easter story you tend to think of it only in terms of the physical. You are aware only of its physical implications. You remember a man physically betrayed, physically tried and convicted by his earthly judges and physically put to death on a cross. If your consciousness permits, you may also accept the concept of his physical resurrection. However, the purpose of all the demonstrations of the great Masters who have incarnated on this Earth has always been to show Man not just how to lead his physical life on this Earth but also to point the way to life beyond this Earth, to life throughout the Universe. Let us, therefore, look at some of the particular incidents which took place in the Easter story and try to discover a deeper meaning behind the physical events.

The Nazarene had set his heart, his mind, his body, his physical and spiritual existence, on going to Jerusalem. Even though he was aware of the death that awaited him, with all its implications of pain and initiation, he went not just to fulfil a plan laid down aeons of time before but because he was proceeding towards a personal goal. If you see the city of Jerusalem as being a symbol of paradise, nirvana, a state of spiritual perfection, call it what you may, a target at which all spiritual people are aiming, then you will see that the Nazarene's journey to Jerusalem represents Man walking along that path to fulfil the greater Will of his Creator, to achieve spiritual 'knowingness'. The Nazarene was determined to go to Jerusalem to achieve this state of perfection even though he knew what was to happen to him. He had accepted the Will of his Creator because he knew that in the Will of his Creator lay the key to his own spiritual advancement.

Before the events of Easter the Nazarene and his twelve disciples partook of the Passover Supper, now referred to by Christians as the Last Supper, and from that Passover Supper came the words which have been seized upon by the Christian

197

Churches and have been made into a dogma which has limited the evolution of millions of souls. According to the Bible, as the Nazarene sat at supper with his disciples he broke the bread and blessed it saying, "Take, eat. This is my body which is given for you: eat this in remembrance of me". Then as he took the cup of wine he said, "This is my blood of the New Testament which is shed for you: drink this in remembrance of me". Man has drawn many interpretations from these two sayings, but I would like to present a new interpretation to you.

This Earth on which you dwell is a body. When I use the word body I do not want you to think in terms of the human physical frame, but rather in terms of a form which fulfils functions as does the physical body. This Earth is a body with a soul, just as you exist even now with your soul. This Earth is part of an even greater body, the Solar Body, of which you are aware. That Solar Body is part of a still greater body, of which you are not aware, at the centre of which is the star which you call Sirius. Within Man himself there are also bodies, millions of beings of creation, individual cells of consciousness, which have a similar purpose to Man but follow different patterns of evolution. Within Man himself there are beings with consciousnesses leading lives just as Man lives his life on the surface of this Earth. Therefore Man is not alone, he is not supreme, he is not unique: he is just an infinitesimally small cog in the gigantic eternal Wheel of Creation.

If Man wishes to understand Creation he should look at his own body, for contained within it is the plan, the pattern, the purpose, not only of the Solar Body but of Creation as a whole. Within him are living organisms fulfilling their destinies in just the same way as Man fulfils his on the surface of this Earth. Man, therefore, cannot live in isolation, cannot live just for himself, because not only is he part of a greater body, the Earth, and how he acts on the surface of this Earth affects the behaviour and well-being of the body of the Earth itself, but, likewise, how Man as an individual behaves affects the destiny, the life, the well-being of the millions of beings that live within him.

What Man does affects the levels of existence both above and below his own. So when the Nazarene, overshadowed by the Christ, spoke at the Last Supper of eating the bread in remembrance of him, and of the bread being his body, he was inviting his disciples to remember that the bread — and bread is the universal symbol of nourishment of all creation, of cosmic sustenance, the essence of life — which he was breaking and blessing symbolised the body of the Creator, or God, of your Solar System. The 'bread of life', as it is sometimes called, is the wisdom, the knowledge, the inspiration, of your Creator and it is within and through His body, His creation, that Man shelters and rests, that Man learns and advances. The Nazarene was asking his disciples to remember that the Christ who overshadowed him, that the Christ, the Son of your Creator, was offering His body, His way of life, for Man to partake of that body, to use it, to advance through it, so that Man in turn could then sacrifice his own body for all those beings who dwelt within him. It is the cosmic, eternal, progression of Creation. You are part of a larger and contain a smaller. The Nazarene was also reminding his disciples that whatever they ate, or whatever they took in — not in the form of food, although that, of course, is important — comes from their Creator and that, after using that cosmic life, they are then responsible for what goes forth from their bodies.

The Nazarene also asked his disciples to drink the wine in remembrance of him, and said that the wine was his blood. He chose red wine as a symbol of the blood, the very river of evolution, which flows in every physical body. Your physical blood contains the seeds of evolution and, as it runs through your body, besides fulfilling the functions of which medical doctors are aware it also guides you on your destined way. It contains the karma of your life, the destiny of your life and the knowledge for your life. It goes to every part of your physical body activating, working and controlling the casing of matter in which you temporarily reside. When you die and you leave your physical body that blood-stream transforms itself into an etheric form. That is to say that it becomes electrical energy, and the sum total of your being rises along with the spirit and flows back into what you would call a magnetic field that exists around this Earth, a magnetic field which contains the blood vibrations of all Humanity throughout the Ages. In this way the sum total of Man's incarnation since the beginning of time on this Earth is included in this field of magnetic energy around the Earth. There-fore the lives of all those beings more advanced than you, more evolved than you, possessing a greater consciousness than you, are there for you to tap into and use whenever you radiate that Christ expression and harmonise yourselves with that electrical frequency. This explains how individual Man can tap into and bring down inspirational achievements as well as technological or scientific discoveries. Therefore when the Nazarene talked of his blood being the blood of the New Testament, the New Future, he was inviting Man, after his physical death, through his expression and way of life to tap into that knowledge, that wisdom, which he possessed and to use it in the years and cycles to come. Your blood is your wisdom, is your consciousness, and at any time you can tap into that greater consciousness.

I would like you now to consider the implications of the Nazarene's betrayal, arrest and trial. The Nazarene, over-shadowed by the Christ, although he was a great Master, was rejected, denied, arrested, falsely tried and put to death for exemplifying the Plan and the Purpose of this Earth and for demonstrating the Truth of the Heavens for the Piscean Age. You must accept, therefore, that as you strive to follow a similar path you too will meet similar treatment. If you seek to introduce the true spirituality of life to people, to make them aware of an existence beyond that which they practise and observe, they will hate you, despise you and will seek to do you evil. Remember that it was actually the religious leaders of those days who were responsible for trying and condemning the Nazarene. Would it be different today? The courts of law of those days, although they knew that the Nazarene was innocent, submitted to political pressure and condemned him to death. Expediency! Would it be different today?

Remember that to be Christ-like raises you above the level of physical life. That is not to say that you deny physical life but rather that you are rising above the limitations of life on the Earth, that you are demonstrating the Christ Expression which will be foreign to many people. The very lesson of this Earth is sacrificial service through the expression of love, and therefore the sacrifice which you give so freely will be readily accepted by those who do not understand. At any time during his trial and crucifixion the Nazarene could have avoided the events which were destined for him, but he did not. Did the people who tried, convicted and eventually killed him appreciate to even the smallest extent his consciousness which, knowing that those events could be avoided, still let them happen while allowing his persecutors to think that they were supreme, that their way of life had won, had triumphed? Yet the reality of that demonstration lies in the Christ Expression today, for, although it has changed as civilisations have come and gone, a true belief in that Christ Expression still continues to exist all over the World, whereas what can you say of the beliefs of the Sadducees and Pharisees who killed him?

Remember that a demonstration of the Christ Expression is not for an hour, for a year, but for eternity, and that as you follow the Christ you are fulfilling not merely the plan of your own incarnation but the plan of eternity. The great Masters appreciate that they are fulfilling this greater plan, that they exist not just for the physical life on Earth but for Creation on a more universal scale. They appreciate that life in the physical body is restricting, is petty, is small, is insignificant when compared with Creation on the higher planes and with Universal and Cosmic Spirit.

So the Nazarene, falsely convicted, was crucified. Man has made the word 'crucified' into an emotive word with only a physical meaning: to be stretched on a cross, to be nailed to it, and to be left to hang on it until one is dead. But, truly, there are many forms of crucifixion more painful than the physical. The Nazarene felt the physical pain of his crucifixion as he hung on the cross far less than the mental pain, the pain of consciousness because he realised that he, overshadowed by the Son of God, who had come to save Mankind, had been rejected and crucified, whilst a robber, a murderer, had been released in preference to him. Many people in many lives have experienced pain far greater than physical pain. Indeed, for any great Master who has advanced and learnt to control his body, physical pain can be ignored. It is one of the first steps of the initiate as he walks the path: to learn to control physical pain to the extent that it is of no importance. Having achieved that, he then has to learn to control spiritual pain, and that is far more difficult.

On the third day after the Nazarene died on the cross his resurrection took place. A belief in resurrection is a point of consciousness. You do not believe in it merely by reading about it or by being told about it. Such a belief would be false. It is only through experiencing and undergoing it many times that it impinges itself upon your consciousness so that eventually you accept it as a fact and not a fantasy. What is important is not that a man lives again, not that he has avoided what unevolved Man calls the deep chasm of death, for death is merely a transition and is of no more significance than that, but that although he has

201

changed in form he is still fulfilling the greater plan of his being. If, as you now read this lecture, you were to die, you would still continue to fulfil, only on a higher level of existence, the unceasing plan for your evolution. You do not create only on the physical plane and then, when you die, lie in rest until you incarnate again.

You resurrect, therefore, not to avoid death but to fulfil a greater purpose. Although the Nazarene demonstrated the resurrection of his physical body — this a soul of his evolution and consciousness could do — and although he did appear before people in that body, it is of no significance except that it demonstrates the Natural Laws that govern this little Earth on which you live. The real significance of the Nazarene's demonstration lay in that he was continuing his work, evolution and spiritual progress on the upward spiral of life. When the Nazarene appeared and spoke to his disciples and to the other people who were privileged to witness his resurrection in physical form in no way and at no time did he blame those who had persecuted and crucified him. In no way did he criticise the high priests. In no way did he speak of revenge. He spoke only of the future, of what his disciples had to do now that he was gone, of the continuing plan for this Earth and for Creation all around it, and for the continuing evolution of the beings that dwell on this Earth.

There is much else that can be written about the Easter story, for Man today can find in the Bible only those things which certain religious men in the past have decided to include. The Nazarene continues to appear. The Nazarene continues to teach. The Christ Expression is still with you. The Plan for this Earth is as clearly defined today as it was almost two thousand years ago. Nothing has changed. Nothing has ceased. Everything is continuing according to this Greater Plan. Nothing that Man can do, nothing that the Pharisees or the Sadducees had hoped to achieve by the murder of the Nazarene, has in any way prevented that Greater Plan from going forward.

So when Easter approaches I would ask you to remember the purpose of this planet — sacrificial service. I would ask you to remember the sacrifice that is made for you by the Higher Beings, by those souls more evolved than you, and also of the sacrifice that is expected of you yourselves for those less evolved beings below you. You are not supreme. You are not alone. You

202

are part of a complex chain of spiritual progression, and at the present time you are the weak link in that chain. Mankind has to spiritually motivate itself to fulfil its purpose, which is the evolution of each and every one of you together with the evolution of the Earthly Body of which you are at present a part. Man has to begin to sacrifice on all levels of existence, from the least evolved soul to the most evolved soul, from sacrificing a minute of his time to help a fellow-traveller on the path of life to sacrificing his life for Mankind as a whole.

For those that freely sacrifice the reward is everlasting consciousness; for once you have given and have received the true blessings of your Creator then that state of joy, that road to Jerusalem, has begun. Once you have taken just one step on that road then for you there will be no turning back. No matter what the pain, no matter what the sacrifice, it will be a road which you will seek to walk sure in the confidence within you that you are fulfilling not only the Will of your Creator, the Will of the Body in which you live, but also the will of all those beings who dwell inside you. You will be advancing not only your own consciousness but also Universal Consciousness. If you will but do this the real power of your light will shine forth, and on levels beyond the physical you will achieve what the Nazarene achieved on a still higher level of expression. You will be performing a service to every level of life that exists in the Universe, and from that service will come an understanding of Creation and of the so-called Wheel of Life.

WOMANHOOD

Everywhere on the Earth today the results of Man's disharmony are to be seen. Man's imbalance has disrupted almost every aspect of life. In particular, as I look at the relationship between man and woman, the male and the female aspects of creation, while they are in their physical bodies of matter I see displayed there a great deal of disharmony. When we talk of the male and the female we are talking of the very essence of life, and if there is disharmony in this most important aspect then there will be disharmony in the creations of their union.

In this lecture I am going to look at womanhood, at its true role and purpose, so that those of you who read this lecture may reappraise yourselves of woman's true and unique status and, perhaps, establish a better balance in your marriages or in your relationships with your friends. I want all of you to try to forget the ideas which you have formed about the traditional roles of womanhood because these are based on the conditioning of your upbringing. I do not even want you to think of womanhood as being related to the female physical form.

The reason for, and the nature of, the creation of this Earth and of Humanity which, together with the three other Kingdoms of Matter, dwell upon it, can be understood only by highly evolved souls, by beings who have progressed beyond this school of life on Earth. Therefore, in this lecture, I will not delve too deeply into how, or why, this planet Earth was first created. Sufficient to say that your Creator, the God of this Solar Body, Whose Spirit dwells in the Sun, created this Earth with His mind. Aeons of time after this, after the molten mass had cooled, after the land and the waters had formed, after the Mineral, the Vegetable and the Animal Kingdoms had manifested, Man was created in the image of his Creator. At this time Man was still joined to the Godhead and knew only perfection. He walked hand in hand with the angels. He was hermaphrodite, both male and female, both positive and negative. Man was created through the perfect breath according to the will of his Creator. Then, for reasons inconceivable to you, the God of this Solar System decided that in order to further the evolution of the Earth, and of the Solar Body as a whole, it was necessary for Man to become individualised in consciousness and in creativity, to become a living soul, so that he could develop and bring into fruition in matter the power of his Creator. Man was to be able to bring forth on the Earth the secrets and the knowledge of the Cosmos, and thus evolve not only himself but the whole Solar Body.

So Man was reincarnated upon the surface of the Earth, was severed from his former perfection and was given the divine gift of free choice. From then on he operated upon the frequencies of positive and negative and was subject to the Law of Opposites. Man now became Adam and Eve, man and woman, and from this divine creation aeons of time ago have grown the male and the female physical forms of which you are aware today. In that great reincarnation of perfect Man, if I may call him that, his functions were split into two aspects reflecting his new birthright: the male, which we may regard as the power, the energy, the intellect aspect, and the female, which we may regard as the love, the receptivity, the intuitiveness, the force of God in motion, aspect. It was intended that man and woman should walk their individual paths in life striving to obtain perfection in their separate roles, but at the same time complementing each other and holding each other in balance so that after aeons of time they could unite again on a higher plane of consciousness.

Now is not the time to describe how woman, the female aspect, cohabited with some of the angels, the messengers of God, how the act of creation was abused and how Mankind fell from grace and lost its spiritual birthright, but it was this act of disharmony, this misuse of the true function of the male and the female, that has led to the state of disharmony that exists today. It is now only through womanhood regaining its original state of harmony and demonstrating its divine wisdom, its intuition, that Humanity as a whole can be led back to perfection.

I have tried to make this short description of the initial creation of man and woman as simple as possible, for it is important that you appreciate what happened aeons of time ago so that you may better understand the individual roles of man and woman today. I do not intend to blame womanhood for all the troubles that

Humanity now has to face, for man is equally to blame, but it was because of those initial actions aeons of time ago when the wisdom aspect, the divine, the virgin, the exemplifier of God, fell from grace, that man, who looks to woman for his example, also fell. Subsequently, because of this the structure of society in the World also fell into disharmony and eventually proceeded to the state it is in today where there is complete disharmony and imbalance between the male and the female. In the western civilisations, and even more so in the eastern ones, man, the power, the intellect aspect of creation, is completely in the ascendancy and dominates the woman, the wisdom aspect, and until this balance is restored harmony will not return to this Earth as a whole.

Man and woman are completely equal, yet opposite, sparks of Creation. They came from the same source and although they are opposites, together, like the two sides of a coin, they make a whole. They complement each other to perfection, for the original functions of perfect Man have been split equally between them. It follows, therefore, that a completely harmonised man and woman do indeed form a one and, from that one, perfection in every act, in every creation, will result: but where there is disharmony, then only imperfection will come forth. Man today has to harmonise himself with woman just as much as woman has to re-establish her position as the wisdom aspect of Creation. It is through woman, the wisdom aspect, that man will discover the truth of Creation, how life on this planet should be lived and the true nature of his existence on this Earth. But he will not discover this until he gives womanhood the freedom to be what its Creator intended it should be.

It is essential that women all over the World are released from the bondage in which they are at present enslaved by social societies which are controlled largely by the male, the power, the intellect aspect of creation and which, for the most part, has very little feeling for life. Very few women have political influence today or are in a position where they can influence the events of the World. If they were, then, indeed, how great would be the transformation of life on the surface of this Earth! Would a woman who has experienced the pain of childbirth, who has made the sacrifice of raising children, who has endured the trials and tribulations of motherhood, then sacrifice her children in acts of violence and destruction as willingly as a man does? Would any woman sacrifice her son, or any other woman's son, to achieve an ideological or political aim? But the voice of womanhood does not speak today. It is supressed by man and by the material world which he controls.

There are, unfortunately, certain statements in the Bible which have been seized upon by man as being divine revelations concerning the true status of womanhood. You must remember, however, that the Bible was written and compiled by men who traditionally believed in the inferior role of women and that the Old Testament is composed largely of extracts from scrolls and tablets written centuries earlier and from religious stories passed down from memory. Therefore the compilers of the Bible selected those segments which, to a large extent, reflected the prevailing attitudes and beliefs of their time. Consequently, in the Bible woman is portrayed as being subservient to man, and the western civilisations, which have taken so much from the Bible, have maintained this position throughout the centuries. It is only today that we have the situation in which woman is just beginning to re-establish her correct position in society.

Woman is in every way the equal, and yet the opposite, of man. Indeed, in divine consciousness, man, when he operates in a physical body, is the weaker aspect! In no way should the male and the female be compared, for they are not the same: they are complementary. Together they unite into a powerful force, but in disharmony they will create destruction. As you look around the World today you can see destruction everywhere. This is mostly because of the breakdown in the relationships between man and woman, for from their disharmony has come the destruction and violence of today. There have been civilisations on this Earth, at present largely unknown to Man, where the male and the female aspects did truly fulfil their correct roles, where they lived as equals. In these civilisations a man would study at the feet of a woman, a man would be governed by a woman, a man would be blessed by a woman. In these ancient civilisations women fulfilled the roles of ruler, teacher, prophet and priest. In the ancient Egyptian civilisations, of which Man is only just aware, you can see the remains of such a system with the hierarchy of the Pharaohs where, as you well know, it was quite normal for a woman to be one of them. Indeed, it was the balance of the male and the female Pharaohs that established the harmony of the power and the wisdom to rule and to govern the kingdom of Egypt.

As I look at your World today, where are women to be found in similar roles? They are almost completely excluded from the Church, and yet in this role they should exist in equal numbers, indeed, even outnumber men, for they were created to bring the wisdom of God down into manifestation on Earth. Woman was created to display that wisdom. That is why it is so important that she puts herself back onto her pedestal as the true virgin: virgin meaning the purity of thought and action. Woman has the intuitive sense to foretell the future. She has great psychic and healing powers. With all these talents she is well suited to be a priest. Where is woman in the teaching role today? There are women teachers, but they are usually to be found only in the lower, not the higher, posts. Yet woman, with her wisdom and her intuitiveness, is well suited to be a teacher. She has the patience and the humility, and she possesses that innate wisdom which will ensure that she will teach what is true of life, not what is false. Where is woman in government today? With only a few exceptions, why is she not to be found in the parliaments and the political assemblies of the World? There are just as many women as there are men in the World today, but everywhere man dominates the political scene. It is precisely because you have the male aspect, the intellect, the power, governing your nations without the balance of the female aspect, the wisdom, the receptivity, the femininity, that the World is in the state that it is today. For this we have to blame woman, for if she would only climb back onto her original pedestal, if she would display the divine, the virgin, aspect of Creation, if she would only be what her Creator intended — a living example of His wisdom — then man would once again respect and follow her.

So I invite all the women who read this lecture to remember their responsibilities that came with that act of creation aeons of time ago. It is for you to stand on your pedestals once more. It is for you to uphold that which you truly believe within you to be correct no matter how much it conflicts with the ways of man and modern society. It is for you to say that the political and financial systems of Man today are wrong, that the religious beliefs of Man today are wrong, that the values on which Man bases his life today are wrong and that the path upon which this World is now set is wrong. If only you will arise, unite and display your divine wisdom then you will yet save this World from the holocaust that is to come.

A wise man once said that behind every great man there stands a woman. This is often true, for it is when man and woman unite in harmony that they become a great power. They complement each other and together, in equal balance, they form a one. They can then be a great force for good in this World. But to establish that balance requires that each respects the other as the individual spark of creation that each is, and that each recognises in the other the facets of creation for which each is responsible.

Man and woman are, of course, both necessary to initiate conception, but it is the woman who gives birth to the child after carrying it within her womb, who feeds it, who nurtures it, who teaches it and trains it. The development and education of a child is also primarily the responsibility of the wisdom aspect. One of the reasons why society is breaking down today is because womanhood is not fulfilling its intended role in the raising of children. It is the mother, with her innate wisdom, who is primarily responsible for the education of her child. That is not to say that the father's presence is not important and necessary, for there must be the balance of the two, but the child that has chosen to come through the mother has chosen her for the very reason that it is her wisdom which it seeks as it forms and matures its physical body.

Past societies of which Man is not aware have, of course, practised more advanced methods of raising children. There have been societies where, once they had conceived a child, the parents did not work except for the preparation, the birth, the training and the education of that child. It was regarded as a full-time occupation, and neither the man nor the woman worked outside the home until the child was twelve. That is a concept which you could well consider in your society of today, where a woman has her child but then hands it over to other people, at an early age, so that she can go out to work. When a mother hands over her child to a virtual stranger, she is depriving it of the most priceless asset that she has to give. A mother should devote herself completely to her child until it reaches the age of twelve. No teacher can give to a child what its mother can give, and a mother who hands over the responsibility for her child to another risks great karma.

Most women unite with man in the act of marriage, for marriage is a status necessary in the current state of Man's evolution, but the fact that they have married does not mean that they should automatically have children. I would like to emphasise that the role of marriage is not solely to produce children. Many of the marriages that take place should not result in children, and if you cannot fulfil the role of a mother with complete responsibility to your child you should certainly not have children. If all mothers were aware of this fact before they conceived their children there would be fewer unbalanced children in the World today. It is the incorrect role of marriage and the incorrect role of womanhood that is the cause of the destruction and violence that is prevalent in the World today. Man and woman unite in marriage and through harmonising their individual powers and talents may achieve great things, not only in producing children, but in the realms of art, music, science, politics and religion. Man and woman, when in harmony, are a powerful force, not only learning from each other and demonstrating to each other but, by combining their individual talents, making a great one: becoming the true Pharaohs.

When man and woman create children they should remember their responsibility for that act of creation. Man must remember that he is equally as responsible for the children as the woman, and that the roles of mother and father as defined by modern society are not necessarily correct. It is difficult to overthrow the established ways of society, but man need not always be the provider and woman the housewife. It is the balance between the two that will create harmony in the family and harmony in the children. Woman should not always be regarded as the preparer of food, the cleaner of the home. This can be done by either partner of the marriage. Woman should not always be tied to the home, to the kitchen stove, for she has her own individual spark of expression within her just as the male. Why should the female be restricted in this way and not the male? It is the nature of her being that the woman who has a child willingly makes the sacrifice of remaining at home for it, but by the time that child is twelve, then she has completed her sacrifice and is free. Indeed, it is essential that she reasserts her individuality and establishes once more the balance of the marriage.

It is obvious that in society as it is today it is difficult for womanhood to portray its true role. It will need a great effort on the part of women to do this, but do this they must. The old souls now incarnating in female bodies at this the beginning of the Aquarian Age are already beginning to revolt against the chains of bondage which have been created by man. They will no longer accept the concept of the inequality of the sexes for, truly, there is no inequality except in man's mind. They are beginning to demand what is their birthright, equality of life with man, and in that they demand this equality and stand by what they believe, by what they know with their inner intuition, they will change the face of this Earth for the better.

So, finally, I say to all women, no matter what your age, remember the responsibility of womanhood. It is a responsibility which goes far beyond having children, being a mother and being a wife. It is the responsibility for one half of Creation, and if that one half is not in balance then Creation too will be in disharmony. Remember what I said at the beginning of the lecture: that it is the two halves in equal balance that will eventually unite into the one form to become the evolved being of this Earth. These will be the beings of the New Age, who will walk this Earth fulfilling and exemplifying life as it truly should be lived without the division that is now present all over this World.

Womanhood must try to exemplify what is its birthright: the feminine, the receptivity, the wisdom, the love, the force of God in motion. If all women will begin to do this, then they will transform this Earth. Remember that every time you fail in this task, every time you bow to the will of the male just because it is the male, just because it is the way of society, just because it has been done that way for hundreds of years, then you are betraying not only yourselves, not only womanhood throughout the World today, not only womanhood in the Ages that have gone, but you are betraying Creation itself, for you are denying the very purpose of your existence.

MAN'S PHYSICAL AND SPIRITUAL GUARDIANSHIP

Man, while he lives in physical matter, has never been left alone. It was not intended that he should have to discover his way back to Infinite Spirit unaided. As was the case with all the other aspects of Creation Man was given divine guidance to fulfil both his part in the plan for the evolution of the Earth as well as for his own individual evolution. Many unseen influences, of which Man for the most part is unaware, exist around him as he lives in his three-dimensional World, limited by his five senses. Shortly, however, he is to develop his sixth sense and move into a four-dimensional World where he will become aware of these influences.

In this lecture I am going to look at the influences which are responsible for the guardianship of Man, for guarding him while he strives to fulfil the will of his Creator and for instructing him, guiding him and teaching him in His ways. This is the responsibility of those beings who are known as Angels, Masters, Guides, Doorkeepers, Teachers or Controls. There are many names given to these beings by Man on the Earth to define the various degrees of their consciousnesses and their places in the Earth's evolution. It is through these great beings that Man is inspired, taught and corrected. They play an important part in Man's advancement. Today, however, you live in an Age when the majority of people deny their very existence and do not feel the impressions of these beings but rely entirely on their own intellects and reasoning powers. Nevertheless, as you are entering into an Age where Mankind will once again recognise and indeed physically see these beings it is time that Mankind was introduced to them.

Throughout the history of Mankind as you know it today Man has always recognised the presence of angels. The stories in the Bible, especially in the Old Testament, about the angels appearing to the great spiritual leaders of ancient times are manifold. In the New Testament, as well, it is written that angels were present at all the spiritually significant events that affected the life of the Nazarene: at his birth, at his baptism, at his transfiguration, at his crucifixion and at his resurrection. They were seen by many people. Even in modern times angels are still seen. You will recall that during the First World War many soldiers fighting on opposing sides witnessed what came to be known as the Angel of Mons. Even today young children see angels even if their parents do not believe them. These great beings do truly exist and can be seen when one can extend one's senses, either consciously or unconsciously, beyond the realm of limiting matter.

Angels have been in existence since the beginning of Creation. They were in existence before the creation of Man on this Earth. It is impossible for either you, or I, to understand Creation fully, but nevertheless I must attempt to describe Creation very broadly if you are to understand the part which the angels play in it. It is sufficient for me to say that when Infinite Spirit created the Universe of which you are aware Infinite Spirit created it through Its perfect breath. Infinite Spirit breathed and millions and millions of vibrations left the heart of Infinite Spirit to become sparks of life in the Universe. These sparks of life gradually became awakened to consciousness and, in time, took form. Each of these forms, according to the vibration on which it operated, undertook a certain work in the building of the Universe. This was carried out under the direction of Infinite Mind. These sparks of spirit formulated themselves according to the Divine Plan and the inherent consciousness of the seed into every vibratory level of existence that there is in the Universe today.

At this time the angels, too, were created. They were linked to Infinite Spirit. They vibrated to Infinite Spirit's power and to Infinite Spirit's will. They obeyed Infinite Spirit's commands and fulfilled Infinite Spirit's plan for the Universe automatically, for they did not have free choice as does Man. They pulsated to Divine Heart and thought through Divine Mind. The angels might be considered as the messengers of Infinite Spirit. They exist on all levels of Creation. Therefore, when your God, the Solar Logos Whose spirit dwells within the Sun, breathed and created this Solar System of which you are a part, it was the angels who were responsible for aiding and helping the formation of your Creator's plan for His Body. Angels were responsible for each one of the twelve planets within the Solar Body and for every level of existence that was present on those planets. There is an angelic realm for every level of Creation, for every vibration of life.

At the time of the Earth's creation angels dwelt upon it and were responsible for it. Because they were linked through their hearts to Infinite Spirit they vibrated, and lived, in perfection, and therefore harmony and perfection prevailed everywhere on the surface of this Earth. When, for reasons of which you cannot conceive, it was decided that the being known as Man should be created on the surface of the Earth, in the beginning he, too, was created through the perfect breath, not through the physical process of reproduction that you use today. Man was created a little lower than the angels. He walked hand in hand with them obeying the will of Infinite Spirit and his Creator, for at that stage Man had no brain and did not possess the divine gift of free choice. He could only obey and fulfil the will of his Creator. He was directed by the force of perfect love and governed by perfect wisdom.

For aeons of time Man dwelt in this state of perfection, and then the Spiritual Hierarchy which controls this Earth and the Solar Body decided that Man should be allowed to evolve himself, should be allowed to understand Creation, to eat of the Tree of Knowledge as the Bible says, and to understand the reason for, and the purpose of, Creation. Man was therefore reborn on the surface of the Earth, and was given the divine gift of free choice and the ability to reproduce himself. The angels do not possess these gifts. They do not understand Creation, they only fulfil it. The angels do not possess an intellect, a brain, and therefore they have no free choice. They cannot reproduce themselves like Man. So Man was released upon his way to discover the knowingness of Creation. He used his physical brain, his God-given intellect, his reasoning, to guide him along his way. However, Man chose to use his talents to obtain material wealth and personal gratification, and as he slowly lowered his way of life and densened his vibration so he slipped away from the contact with the angels. Whereas, before, Man had walked the face of this Earth hand in hand with the angels now, as he changed his frequency, they disappeared from his view. But that contact with the angels is still present, for Man is not a physical but a spiritual being.

When Man was given the gift of free choice and released upon his own way he was connected to the angelic realms through his physical body. It was decreed that every soul that incarnated upon the surface of this Earth should have two guardian angels. They would lead Man towards the fullest realisation possible of the Laws of Creation as far as this Earth was concerned. Therefore they assumed the shape of Man's physical form, and that is why angels are seen as men or women, only in much finer bodies. They are with Man from the moment of physical conception to the moment of physical death. They are responsible for guiding and helping him along his intended path to fulfil the will of his Creator. The angels are responsible for seeing that the will of God is fulfilled.

Each of you has two guardian angels. One is masculine in vibration, works on the positive radiation of spiritual power and links with Man through the region of his pituitary gland. The other is feminine in vibration, works on the negative or receptive radiation, the radiation of spiritual wisdom, and links with Man through the region of his pineal gland. These two guardian angels are with Man at all times as he walks his path. They are particularly close to him when he first incarnates into the physical body and up to the age of seven, which is the end of the first cycle of Man's earthly progression of three score years and ten. So for the first seven years whilst the soul is establishing itself in the physical body the two guardian angels are closely linked with it, and that is why so often young children do indeed see their guardian angels as they stand over them protecting and guiding them.

These guardian angels, therefore, guide Man throughout a particular incarnation. They never interfere with Man's free choice, but are always ready to aid Man on his pathway of spiritual progression if he asks for assistance and direction. They are concerned only with the fulfilling of Man's destiny and with his part in the Greater Plan. They are concerned with the Universal Force, not with the individual force. They are unemotional. They are givers and providers of Power. They are links with Infinite Spirit. Each planet has its different angelic realms which serve the planet during its various stages of evolution. There are angelic kingdoms for every vibration of life on the Earth. One angelic kingdom works within the centre of the Earth aiding the Mineral Kingdom. Another works with the Vegetable Kingdom directing the nature spirits in their work.

Another works with the Animal Kingdom governing the group souls of the animals.

Apart from his two guardian angels Man also has another being who protects and guides him as he walks his path in life. This being is usually known as a Guide or a Doorkeeper. You therefore have the trinity of the three beings watching over you: your two guardian angels and your guide. Your guide is usually a soul of considerable evolution who has himself lived many lives on the Earth and has evolved to a state of evolution comparable to yours, if not more advanced. You will therefore have a guide who is at least the equal of you in soul vibration, who will understand your point of consciousness and your destiny. He, himself, will have lived through many lives on this Earth and will understand the nature and the restrictions of physical life. He will therefore be able to help you as you try to advance in life. He is really the individual who holds the key to the door to the various planes of consciousness above and beyond the physical. He is the one who will help you onto those planes: hence his title of doorkeeper.

A guide is one who, because of his great love for Humanity and for Creation in general, is prepared to sacrifice a destiny on a higher plane of consciousness to be with Man in the physical aura of the Earth. Your guide can be attracted to you for two reasons. Firstly, he may be attracted to you because, as he too is learning on the eternal path of progression, knowing the destiny which you are to follow and which you chose at the same time that your guardian angels were appointed to you on the higher planes of life, he will recognise that he too would learn by watching you fulfilling that destiny. Secondly, your guide and yourself may be linked in some karmic obligation. Through actions in other lives he may owe you, or you may owe him, a debt, and this debt can be discharged by his offering to be your guide while you are in this physical incarnation.

Your guide is with you closely at all times whilst you are in the physical, and for those who are trying to develop psychic powers it is their guide who guides and protects them in this. Your guide, recognising the divine gift of free choice which you have, will not, and cannot, tell you what to do. He is responsible only for guiding and for protecting you as you walk your path in life. He will at all times urge you towards the destiny path that you chose before you incarnated if you have strayed from it, and he will at all times invoke you to follow the will of Infinite Spirit. Many people are aware of their guides, if not by name then by their presence, and through the psychic phenomenon of mediumship there is available to a few the means of communication whereby their guide may actually talk to them and to other people.

Many esoteric writings use the term 'Master'. What is a Master? A Master is a being, a spark of Infinite Spirit, just like you, who over aeons of time and many incarnations has progressed to the level of Mastership on the plane to which he has evolved. He has struggled to a complete understanding of the Light through discovering and obeying the Laws of the Cosmos. He has learnt to transcend the duality of light and darkness, goodness and evil, sorrow and happiness. He has reached a stage of perfection on the plane to which he has evolved at any given period of time. There are seven planes of existence within the aura of the Earth. You are aware of the physical, or the earthly plane, but above that you have the etheric, the astral, the emotional, the vital, the mental and the spiritual planes. Masters exist on each of these. After you have progressed beyond mastership of the physical there are still the other six levels to be mastered. One can, of course, achieve mastership on one of the higher levels without necessarily having achieved mastership of the physical, but before one obtains the mastership of the spiritual, the highest plane, which is the ultimate for evolution on this Earth, one must first have achieved mastership of all the other planes.

Masters, therefore, are great beings with a high degree of wisdom and consciousness. They fulfil Universal Service. They do not belong, they are not linked, to any individual soul on the Earth as are your guardian angels and your guide. They serve a far greater cause, and when they come to this Earth they come not for the individual but for Humanity as a whole. They will, however, speak through inspired channels to give messages to Humanity. When they incarnate on the Earth — and Masters are beings such as Moses, Buddha, Pythagoras and Jesus — they come to serve Humanity and to bring wisdom and knowledge to the Earth as a whole. They are not concerned with the individual, but with the Greater Plan. It is through the Masters that Knowledge for this Earth is revealed and given to Mankind, and that the Plan for this Earth is revealed and carried out.

There also exist, on a vibration lower than the Masters, a group of beings who are known as Teachers or Controls. These are evolved beings who through many incarnations on the different planes of existence have developed specialised knowledge in one particular aspect or another. If you are attracted to a particular subject then the appropriate teacher joins the band of teachers around you to deliver his message. A band is the name given to the group of servants who follow you in your physical existence, and all of you have many teachers within your band. These teachers are evolved beings who are attracted to you by your soul emanations, and they teach the particular aspect in which they are qualified. Therefore as you go through life, as you advance your consciousness, your teachers will change.

A teacher can reflect only his own point of consciousness. This explains why there are inspired channels all over the World bringing through knowledge which sometimes conflicts, for just because the teachers are on a higher plane of existence that does not mean that they have suddenly acquired absolute knowledge and absolute wisdom. They may still only reflect their own point of consciousness, that point on the scale to which they have evolved. If, for example, a teacher did not believe in reincarnation whilst on the physical plane of existence he would be of just the same opinion on a higher plane and would therefore teach that point of view. A teacher who is imbued with the concepts and principles of Christianity would teach from that aspect and would perhaps not agree with the teachings of another. In all these aspects, therefore, it is for you, the individual, to decide according to your own consciousness whether the words of the teacher are correct and are applicable to you, for there is no such thing as absolute knowledge, as absolute wisdom, on your Earth. Only a fraction of the whole is presented to you, and it is your God-given birthright to decide for yourself.

There are, of course, many false prophets, many evil forces, and especially in your World today you can hear of many instances of wrong communication, of wrong action, between forces on the higher planes of existence and Man on the physical level. It is possible for Man to attract and indeed be affected by disharmonious and even evil vibrations from beyond the physical, for all is not purity beyond the physical. Disharmony is present on the higher planes of existence as well, but you are protected, as in all things, by your Creator, for one of the great Natural Laws of this Universe is the Law of Attraction and Repulsion, which states quite simply that the lower vibration cannot attract the higher: only the higher vibration may attract the lower. Therefore, if you are more evolved than these evil forces they cannot, and may not, affect you unless through your own behaviour — your thoughts, your words and your deeds — you attract those forces unto you.

So, as you walk the face of this Earth you have many guardians. You do not walk alone. You are surrounded by many influences ranging from the trinity of your two Guardian Angels and your Guide to the thousands of Masters and Teachers who are available to you. There is continual guidance being given to you to help you to understand life on this Earth and to walk your correct path. For the last one thousand years Man has walked in darkness and, to a large extent, has ignored the guidance of these influences. It has been left to the occasional sage or seer to portray the correct usage of these influences and, when they did, they were usually persecuted by ignorant and unaware people. You are about to enter an Age when these influences will again be recognised. As in the days of old you will be able to see and to recognise the Masters, to see the Halls of Learning, to sit at the feet of great beings and to understand, as far as your consciousness permits, the true nature of life in this Universe.

BIRTHDAYS

Man is not just a being of this Earth, limited by his physical body and by the range of his five physical senses, but a cosmic being. He is linked continually to forces and powers beyond the frequency range of matter on this Earth. His physical body is attuned not only to the Earth and its four Kingdoms but also to the other parts of the Solar Body, the planets. Man is continually being influenced, helped and guided by many other unseen forces and powers. When he incarnates onto the Earth Man is but a transitory visitor. He comes for just a short period of time to experience life in his limiting physical body, and then he returns to his real existence on realms above the physical.

Man, when he incarnates into physical matter, becomes an instrument of frequency. At the moment of birth, when he is electrified by the ether which sets into motion the physical body that he has created, Man is influenced by many, many unseen influences. He is establishing himself for that particular incarnation on a definite frequency. His spirit, the individual spark of his Creator, is unique. There is no other spark similar to it in the Cosmos, and at the instant of birth, as it begins its walk in life within the physical body, it is establishing the celestial influences for its life ahead.

The influences that bear down upon this Earth are forever changing as the stars and the planets revolve around it, and the exact nature of their influences vary with their motion. Therefore the exact moment of your birth is important, for you are establishing the frequency of your life. Before it incarnates into matter the soul chooses its moment of birth most carefully so that it may be born under the influences which it desires to master during its walk in life. Bearing down upon this Earth are many forces: the power of your Creator, the seven major Rays, the influences of planetary and inter-planetary Beings and the influences of the many kingdoms of the angelic and devic realms unknown to Man. These influences help to form the vibrations of the child at the moment of birth.

You may now begin to see why it is so essential that children should be born naturally, at their appointed time, and why the moment of birth is so important. That is not to say that the time is critical to the nearest second, but certainly a soul plans its entry into physical matter to within ten minutes of your Earthly time. Therefore it is most wrong for the medical profession in any way to influence that moment of birth, and the current trends and practices of doctors and nurses in inducing or postponing the moment of birth are spiritually incorrect, for they are playing around with the destiny of the child which is incarnating into matter. There are many people walking this Earth who feel lost, who do not feel that they are fulfilling any purpose or achieving anything in their present lives. This is probably because their birth times, and hence the destinies which they chose before they incarnated into matter, have been changed by medical science.

At the moment of birth many forces herald the arrival of that spark of Infinite Spirit into matter. At the time of a soul's birth into physical matter there are literally hundreds of influences present, ranging from the angelic and devic realms to the spirit guides, the guardian angels, the masters and teachers and those who are to walk with that soul throughout its life. They are all present to witness this act of creation, and their power, their influence, their presence, are strongest at the time of birth.

It is important that you discover that moment in time when you were born, and as your birthday comes around each year you should sit in deep meditation and attune yourself to those influences which bear down upon you, for they will be present fulfilling their duties to help you as you walk your path in life. But how many people today ignore this help, either through ignorance or through laziness? Truly, many are ignoring the helping hand of their Creator which would guide them through the year to come, for if they sit in meditation at the moment of their birth they may know their destinies for the year to come, they may examine what they have been and what they are to be, as it is laid down in the Akashic Record of this World. They may assess the lives they have led so far. They may know the true nature of their destinies and what is intended for them, and they may ask their Creator for the help and the guidance that they need to fulfil those destinies. Much can be achieved at each anniversary of his birth if Man will but use it.

Most people celebrate their birthdays only on a physical level. They are aware of only the physical implications of a birthday: that they have lived another year of their physical life, that they have grown older, that they have become richer or poorer, that they are in good or bad health. They compare their earthly progress with their ideal of what they think they should have achieved for their age in terms of material possessions or material success and, again in terms of personal gratification, they consider what they would like to achieve in the years they feel are remaining to them. If you are truly limited by the physical, then such will be the nature of your birthday and you will, therefore, achieve nothing but physical results. You will obtain congratulations, cards and presents from your friends. You will perhaps over-eat and over-drink. But then that birthday will have passed, to join the many other birthdays which you have had not only in this life but in your many previous lives. It fades from memory, is gone forever, and what will you have achieved? How many of you can even remember your birthdays of ten years ago?

If you look at a birthday in materialistic terms it will not bring you lasting reward. But for those of you who have begun to advance your consciousnesses, who are aware of the link of Man with life eternal and of the planes of existence beyond the physical, the true awareness of a birthday brings great reward; for at the moment of the anniversary of your births you can assess the true spirituality of your beings. You may look back on how you have lived your last year, the last cycle of your life. You may assess where you have succeeded and where you have failed. You may assess how you have advanced your consciousnesses and how you have restricted them. You may plan what you wish to achieve in the year ahead of you, for if you do not plan, then you will not achieve. On your birthday you are being given the opportunity to plan, and to ask your Creator for that plan to be fulfilled. You have the opportunity of looking at that year which is to come and of deciding what you, as individuals, wish to do with that year. You will have the destinies of your lives displayed before you: you will be able to read them and, bearing in mind the influences of your present environment and of your lives so far, to decide what you can or cannot achieve in the years remaining to you. All this, of course, takes place on levels above that of physical consciousness. Even if you are not aware of it, it does

222

indeed take place, and much else which Man is not aware of also takes place at this time.

Those of you who have advanced your consciousnesses a little way along the path of evolution may begin to look at the deeper spiritual significance of birthdays. The birthday of your present incarnation into physical matter, while important, is not of supreme importance, for the time of your birth varies from incarnation to incarnation as you walk the planet Earth striving to learn different lessons. What is important is that you strive to look for the greater anniversary, for the birthday of your initial creation. You should strive to become aware of that actual moment in time when the seed from Infinite Spirit was created, when that seed which then split into two, to form two individual sparks of Spirit, became a reality. It is to that time, to the time of your first creation, that you should attune yourselves, and at the same time you should try to attune yourselves to your other halves, your affinities, your soul partners for eternity, for it is with them that you will eventually unite to form the one again, which you will then return to your Creator. In as much as you begin to tune into that more important birthday then you will begin to understand and to realise the significance of your birthdays in this present incarnation.

On your birthday you may travel and visit places unknown to you on the physical level. You are privileged to enter the Temples of Learning, the Halls of Wisdom, which you would not normally visit, to renew your acquaintance with those beings who guide and serve you and to read what is planned for you in your year ahead. Man stumbles blindly along his destiny path complaining either that he does not know what is to happen to him or that he cannot understand why certain events do happen to him. He blames fate, chance or even his idea of God, but he has not even tried to discover his destiny and to plan for the future. The opportunity for doing this is available to him on his birthday.

Birthdays are not only important on the spiritual level: they are important on the physical level as well. You are only too aware that as each year goes by, and you grow another year older, so many changes affect your physical body. It is only natural that physical Man should look on birthdays with a physical eye, and so I would now like to look at birthdays from a physical standpoint. Birthdays are but a reflection of the all-important Ages to which the Earth and the Solar Body are subject. These cyclic Ages which each last for about two thousand years, play a great part in the Plan for the evolution of this Earth, and as the Earth and the Solar Body pass through certain Ages or cyclic changes so, to a lesser extent, Man in his physical body reflects that progression.

Man expects to live for three score years and ten, as mentioned in the Bible. Those seventy years can be divided into seven cycles, for a cycle on the Earth lasts for ten years. The spiritual number of this Earth is seven, and the Earth operates on and through the wavelength and vibration of seven. So Man's earthly cycle is composed of seven years, corresponding to the spiritual vibration of this Earth. To these are added a further three years, which are provided for rest and rejuvenation before the next cycle begins, which astrologically represent the cusp. Therefore, every ten year there is a change in Man's cycle. Just as the greater whole, the Earth, passes through the various Ages, whether they be the Age of Pisces, the Age of Aquarius or the Age of Capricorn, so on a smaller scale Man passes through cycles in his own lifetime. Each of these cycles is of great importance in Man's development, for his Earthly development has been planned according to the cycle he is in.

Within Man's physical body there are seven spiritual centres, or chakras, as yet undiscovered by medical science, which are responsible for his continuing evolution whilst in the physical body. These seven spiritual centres are the seeds from which Man's seven bodies spring and it is through these higher bodies that Man is linked with the planes of existence beyond the physical. During each of Man's seven cycles one of his spiritual centres is being opened and developed. The appropriate chakra reaches maturity during the first seven years of a cycle, and during the last three years Man has the opportunity of demonstrating through his personality and soul growth what he has learned. Man has, therefore, a specific task to fulfil in each of his ten-year cycles.

In the first cycle, from birth to ten years, when Man is opening and developing his lowest centre, the centre at the base of the spine near the coccyx, he is concentrating on merely becoming aware of life in his present incarnation. He is familiarising himself with matter around him and with the five senses of his physical body. He is becoming aware of life, of energy and of nature all around him. He develops and establishes his personality and becomes aware of himself as an individual. He also brings forth his instinctive feeling for self-preservation.

During the second cycle, from eleven to twenty years, the second spiritual centre, the one located in the region of the spleen, comes to maturity. Man is enlarging his outlook, and is using the skills which he has developed during his first cycle to acquire knowledge both of the Universe and his environment. It is a period of self-realisation. He learns how to put his powers and physical senses to beneficial uses. He learns to mix with people, to associate with people, he goes to school, and he becomes conscious of life beyond the individual. He becomes more community-minded.

During the third cycle from twenty-one to thirty years, the third spiritual centre, the one located in the region of the solar plexus, come to maturity. Man turns his attention to the family unit. He expands his outlook and his consciousness beyond the self to take in the responsibility of family union, of marriage, of having children, of settling down and of building his own home. Therefore it is, or should be, during this particular cycle that Man seeks a partner and marries. During this period Man experiences the first real lessons of sacrifice, of placing others before himself. He is constantly learning through the Law of Opposites. He experiences emotions of great joy and happiness together with great sorrow and personal disappointment. By the age of thirty the three lower chakras should have been developed and Man should have reached physical maturity.

During the fourth cycle, from thirty-one to forty years, the fourth spiritual centre, the one located in the region of the heart, comes to maturity. Man, having passed through the cycles of establishing his individuality, his education and his family responsibilities, now turns his thoughts beyond the small group of his own family to conditions in the World as a whole, to the family of the Earth. During this cycle Man should become less self-centred and less possessive. He should physically work for the good of Humanity and see that people of the World have sufficient food and clothing and the freedom to develop according to their individual consciousnesses.

During the fifth cycle, from forty-one to fifty years, the fifth spiritual centre, the one located in the region of the thyroid gland, comes to maturity. By now Man, having mastered the physical lessons of life, is able to step out into the way of true spiritual unfoldment. He begins to practise and demonstrate a little of the wisdom which he has acquired through his past living. By his example he begins to display the harmony of life which by now he should have learned. By his example he is helping his less developed brothers to see how life in harmony should be lived. He should be able to express in his living the love of his Creator and to demonstrate the true way of life.

During the sixth cycle, from fifty-one to sixty years, the sixth spiritual centre, the one located in the region of the pineal gland, comes to maturity. Man, having previously displayed the knowledge and the wisdom which he has acquired throughout his life so far, now begins to teach it. It is in this cycle that Man becomes a teacher of the wisdom which he possesses and gives back to Mankind that which Mankind has given him during the previous fifty years. During this cycle he should be able to be of true spiritual service to Humanity. He should be able to teach the unenlightened and to show them, through his complete mastery of the self, how all creation works according to Divine Law — the Natural Law. The sixth chakra is the mental chakra and Man should attain mental maturity in this cycle.

During the seventh and last cycle, from sixty-one to seventy years, the seventh spiritual centre, the one located in the region of the pituitary gland, comes to maturity. During this cycle Man assesses, with a true understanding and spiritual wisdom, the life he has led, all that he has endured, the wisdom and knowingness which he has acquired. He prepares himself for the transition of death. He looks on life with an aware eye and appreciates the true values of life around him, his own purpose and what he has come to do. He should be able to spiritually enjoy the fruits of his labours, yet continue to serve Humanity as best he can. He should have mastery over all the other kingdoms of this Earth and should no longer be bound by matter.

Depending upon your age you can, you will now see, fit yourself into the appropriate cycle and see what you should ideally be striving for. I have described the progression of a spiritually aware person. Many of the souls who incarnate on this Earth will not get past the third cycle even though they live to be over one hundred years old, for that is the nature of their evolution. On the other hand, a very wise person, a great Master such as the Nazarene, would complete these cycles of development at a much faster rate than a normal person. He would be opening two centres in any one particular cycle, and so by the end of the third cycle, when he was thirty years of age, he would have become fully aware and would be in a position to give to Humanity. The fact that Man should have completed the opening of all his centres by the age of seventy does not necessarily mean that he is entitled to live only seventy years. Indeed, after the age of seventy he is in a position to really give to Humanity, as by then he will be a fully developed person.

Both the years that you have lived and the years that you are to live are important. The years do not just tick by endlessly, with no significance, for just as the destiny of this Earth is planned so also is your individual destiny, and just as the cycles of the Earth are planned so are the cycles of your own destiny. There is great significance in the years that you have lived. There is also great significance in the years remaining to you. A birthday is not just an opportunity for recognising that you are one year older for truly that is of no significance. Physical years lived do not equate with spiritual wisdom. You may live seventy years of your life and achieve little in spiritual knowingness, yet in your last year you may acquire wisdom that will greatly affect your consciousness in your next incarnation. So do not think of birthdays as marking the years that have passed, but regard them as they were intended by your Creator, as moments of rebirth. A birthday is, in reality, a time of reincarnation. Every year of your life there is demonstrated the principle of reincarnation, for as you commemorate your moment of birth you can reincarnate yourself.

As you look back and examine what you have done in your last year be aware that all the faults you have committed, all the errors you have made, are being weighed in the balance. All the evil that you have done is not taken into your true akashic record until that moment in time comes when you were born, when the planetary influences are correct. Then, together with great Beings on the higher levels, you go over what you have done in the year that has just ended and assess what should be entered in that record. Obviously you cannot oppose the Law of Karma, for what you have done will have its effect, but by the very act of recognising what you have done you can transmute it in the year to come. It is therefore important that you assess yourself over the past year. Look at yourself and see what you have done, what you have been, and plan what you wish to be in the future.

Every ten years is, therefore, an important birthday for you all.

Every ten years you should make a special effort to sit and to really observe your progress with regard to the cycle which you have just completed. After the age of thirty, the five year cycle in between, that is the thirty-fifth, the fourty-fifth, the fifty-fifth and the sixty-fifth birthday, is also important. Those birthdays have great significance because after your thirtieth birthday, when you have opened up your three lower chakras and have reached physical maturity, you then begin to develop the four higher chakras which will link you with the spirituality of life beyond physical consciousness.

So I ask all of you to begin to use your birthdays, and when your next birthday comes along to look at it with a fresh vision, to see it not as you have probably seen all your other birthdays but to look upon it as an opportunity given to you by your Creator for a moment of rebirth. At that time you can change, for all the power, all the love, of your Creator is bearing down upon you. At that moment the whole of the Heavens are pouring down their powers onto you to revitalise and strengthen you for your next cycle. You are surrounded by the angelic realms and what you ask for will be granted, but it will not be given to you unless you ask. Will you begin to do so?

MAN'S BROTHERS IN OUTER SPACE

The purpose of this lecture is to talk to you about the nature of your brothers in outer space, of their part in the plan of things for this Earth and of their presence even now within the aura of this Earth. What I am to say will in no way convince you one way or the other that there are beings living in outer space, for a knowledge and an understanding of those beings represents a point of consciousness. I would therefore ask only that you meditate on what I am to say, hold it within your hearts and perhaps at some time in the future that conviction will come to you in the twinkling of an eye, in a flash of intuition, as other events take place which suddenly turn the key in the door to your inner consciousness, allowing it to swing open and reveal the light beyond. As I speak to you now, I can understand life only as it exists within this Solar Body. That is the limitation of my consciousness, for I cannot understand the planes of consciousness beyond that of our Creator. It is He Who created this Solar Body in which you dwell, Who gave birth to the planets, or organs, of this Solar Body and Who created life on all those planets.

The Earth upon which you now dwell was the last but one of the twelve planets within our Solar Body to be created. Aeons of time, not Man's time but true, spiritual time, separated the birth of the first planet from the birth of the Earth, and therefore all but one of the other planets within this Solar Body, some of which you are aware of and some of which you have yet to discover, had been in existence evolving themselves for literally millions of years before Man was created. Therefore the point of consciousness, the understanding of life, of the beings dwelling on them will necessarily be greater than yours.

I will not discuss the forms of life on these other planets except to say that they are totally unlike the forms of life on the Earth. Your scientists would have you believe that life is not possible on these planets because the temperature is too hot or too cold, or because the air is too rare, and so on. That is because your scientists look through physical eyes. But within every cell of matter, whether it be on Venus, on Jupiter or on the Earth, there is the plan, there is the seed, for its potential growth in the plan of things. A seed of matter on Jupiter would be totally different from a seed of matter on Earth, and that seed would build its form according to the nature of its existence on the surface of that planet.

Man is not really a being of the Earth. He dwells only temporarily on the surface of the Earth to further his evolution. His soul first descends into the aura of the Earth at the moment of conception. After the seed has been fertilised, that seed, knowing the nature of life on this Earth, begins to create for itself a body within the mother's womb, a body suited to the conditions of life on the Earth. Your physical bodies, therefore, are designed solely for life on this Earth, and that is why Man finds it so unnatural as he proceeds in his spacecraft to other planets. He is physically designed solely for life on this Earth. If Man is to travel and to live on the other planets he must do so in a way different from that which he has conceived so far.

Life on the other planets, then, does exist, but in a form incomprehensible to Man. Just as Man on Earth cannot conceive of the elementals, of the fairies, of the devas, of the angels, just as he cannot conceive of life beyond the physical and of the true nature of his existence, so he cannot conceive of life on the other planets. But life does exist, and in a state of evolution far, far, advanced beyond that which Man has attained. Many of the beings who dwell on these planets have themselves evolved through the school of life which is called Earth and now dwell on these higher planes. Many of the great Masters who have incarnated on this Earth are indeed inhabitants of these planes. The fact that they dwelt for a short time in a limiting physical body of matter does not make them of the Earth. In just the same way you, too, are not of the Earth. Truly, you descend onto this plane of existence for but a short period of time to learn the lessons of life on the Earth.

Because of the point of evolution that they have reached, the beings who live on the other planets are able to observe life in this school of Earth. Because they understand the true nature of spiritual existence within this Solar Body, and because they have passed beyond the limitations and restrictions of life in the physical, they are aware of the way in which Man is advancing and of the lessons that he has to learn. Therefore in no way do they interfere with Man's progression, for if Man was to conceive of the idea that there are superior beings who could descend at will to help him around his difficulties, to change his path, it would remove one of the basic lessons of this Earth, which is that Man has to change himself. However, that does not mean that in the future a recognition and an understanding of these beings will be beyond Man's ability, for as Man unblinkers his eyes and sees beyond physical matter on this Earth so he will be led into a closer understanding of life on the other planets.

Many people have witnessed the phenomenon of unidentified flying objects. Some people have been privileged to observe a life form within them, but most of them have remained silent. Only a few have spoken about their encounters with their brothers from outer space. The reason for this is that Man on the Earth is not yet ready to accept the nature and the purpose of these beings because he is largely restricted by the concepts and dogmas of organised religion and science. Just as you look down on a young child and, for example, would be reluctant to destroy its belief in Father Christmas even though you knew it to be a false belief, so the Martian or the Venusian looks down on Man and his concepts of life and realises that Man must learn and discover for himself. Therefore they wait patiently for that moment when Man will discover the falseness of much of organised religion and science, will reject it and will begin to open his mind and look elsewhere for the true concept of life within this Solar Body.

That beings from other planets come to this Earth at all is not out of idle curiosity or even out of a desire to ease Man's burdens as he walks his path on the surface of this Earth. They come solely for the purpose of the preservation of the Earth, for Man with his intellect, his technology, but without the balancing emotion of love, is destroying this planet. With the space satellites that he sends up which cut the etheric web around the Earth, with the rockets that he sends to the Moon, damaging a delicate balance beyond his comprehension, with the way he pollutes his environment and abuses the other kingdoms of Matter, Man is destroying both himself and this planet. Indeed, by now, with the nuclear explosions that he has wrought all over the surface of this Earth, Man would have been extinct but for the help of his brothers in outer space. They have come and have helped Man, not to interfere with his free choice, but to preserve the Earth. They have

231

held the Earth in balance so that Man in his stupidity would not interfere with the final great move forward in the evolution of the whole of this planetary system.

Your brothers from outer space who come to you come in friendship. They come with understanding. It was their intention to make themselves known generally all over the Earth but, owing to the hostility of Man, this has not been possible. They have broken frequencies that could be dangerous to your evolution. They have showered rays from their own planets to disintegrate and also to mend certain atmospheric conditions and stratas which have been broken around your Earth. They have watched over and guided, on many occasions in the past, those who have travelled in outer space.

Many of the space objects which have been seen by Man have come from Mars and Venus. Mars supplies your Earth with much of its electrical energy. The beings from that planet have, during the past few years, dispersed some of the atomic radiation foolishly circulated by Man. If they had not done so the Earth would have been thrown from its position in space. When Man first exploded his nuclear devices he released energy in excess of that which is necessary for the harmonious working of this planetary system. The beings from Mars immediately set in motion a device to counteract this harmful energy. It was for this work that some of the space craft which Man has seen were used. As Man continued in his folly and exploded larger and more harmful nuclear weapons the radiations from these explosions began to effect the other planets within the Solar System and to disturb the whole solar pattern. The Venusians then came to the aid of Man on the Earth and sent forth objects to counteract this greater disharmony. It is these objects which Man calls U.F.O.'s.

Your brothers in outer space give their help in true Christlike fashion. They give it in true sacrifice to you, not desirous of reward or thanks but purely to serve the greater cause, the preservation of the whole. You may compare it to an illness in your physical body. If a part of your body is diseased, then all the other parts of the body unite together to help eradicate the illness within it. That is the analogy that I would make with regard to the beings who live within this Solar Body, your brothers. They help you for the good of the whole, a philosophy of which Man, for the most part, cannot yet conceive. He is totally resigned to, and blinkered by, the concept of the importance of the individual.

232

Such is the nature of Man's existence that he has yet to discover that the purpose of life on this Earth is to evolve beyond the individual and to recognise the greater whole and, indeed, to sacrifice the individual for that greater whole.

These beings from the other planets come, then, in varying forms of transport to correct imbalances on the Earth. With their greater wisdom, with their greater intellect and technology, they repair the Earth where Man has devastated it. Like the angels, who are the messengers of Infinite Spirit, they have been present at all the great spiritual happenings and awakenings on the surface of this Earth. As you look back at the history of Man as you know it, all the great occurrences which have changed the path of history have been witnessed by these beings. As you now approach another period of great change so these beings are again present, helping their brothers on Earth to prepare for that which is to come. Of course, this does not mean that they will descend in their spaceships and automatically help Man to avoid that which he has created. It means that they will help only those who send out the thoughts which attract them. Only those who think rightly, who act rightly, will be saved in the cataclysm that is to come. It is by your individual thoughts that they will know you, that they will contact you.

It is only natural that Man, for the most part, should be concerned mainly with physical living, but gradually he is beginning to widen his outlook. He is beginning to realise that life on this Earth is not bounded by his five senses. He is beginning to realise that he cannot look at the Earth as an individual, as a single unit, and think only of the Earth and of life on it. He is beginning to realise that the Earth is part of a greater whole, and that that greater whole, the Solar Body, is part of an even greater whole, for nothing that exists in creation can be taken in isolation. Everything is inter-dependent: the lower on the higher, the higher on the lower. They both give to and take from each other. The responsibility of Man is to become aware of his true self and to exercise the birthright given to him by his Creator: to become a god. You are all gods in the making. Ultimately you can all obtain the power of your Creator. You can all achieve that which has been demonstrated to you. You can all walk the paths of the great Masters who have been sent down to you from the higher planes of life to exemplify that which is possible. The Nazarene has shown Man what is possible.

The cycle of development of this Earth over the last two thousand years has not been an easy one, but that is the nature of the planetary influences which have had their effect upon it. You are now entering into a new period, a period of rapid change. Within the next thirty years there are to come developments which will uplift Man from the Piscean Age into the Aquarian Age, when Man will become aware of his true self, when he will recognise not only life beyond his five senses but life on the higher planes of existence. He will become aware of the true nature of his Creator Whom he now idly worships in a personalised form. He will discover that those beings who are constantly with him, guiding and helping him, shaping and moulding his life on Earth, have been fulfilling their part in the greater whole just as he, in turn, has been fulfilling his part for the millions of beings that dwell within him for he, too, is a god. As Man dwells within his God so there are beings dwelling within Man to whom Man appears as a god. Man is responsible to them just as he is responsible to his Creator above.

In conclusion, I would ask you to cast your consciousness inwards as much as you cast it outwards, to recognise not only your brothers of the other planets but also those millions of beings within you, who dwell within your body, who lead lives similar to you only on lesser levels of consciousness, to whom you are indeed a god.

THE TRUE NATURE OF HEALING

Aeons of time ago, after his conception through the perfect breath of his Creator, Man lived and vibrated in perfection. When, after many Ages in the Earth's development, the Hierarchy of this Solar Body decided to bestow upon Man the divine gift of free choice to enable him to progress through the many stages of evolution and to become a god himself, Man was reincarnated upon the Earth. From that moment, as Man exercised his divine birthright, imperfection became apparent. As he is the most evolved of the beings who dwell upon the many, many levels of existence on this Earth, Man also affected the other Kingdoms as well, and through his own imperfection caused imperfection in them too. Therefore there exists in the World today and, indeed, there has existed throughout the history of the World as you know it, a state of disharmony, a state of dis-ease, amongst all beings and all creatures on the surface of this Earth.

No matter how pure the motivation is for Man's thoughts and actions, as they mix with those of other men so that purity of thought and deed is adulterated. In similar fashion, harmonious Man, healthy Man, can be affected by the disharmonious people and vibrations around him. It must however be said that no disharmony, no evil, can affect you as an individual unless you permit it to come into your being. If you, as a perfect being, lived in perfect harmony then indeed you would walk this Earth in harmony, and although your perfection would itself be adulterated by all the disharmonious vibrations around, you yourself would manifest and remain in a state of harmony. You have the example of this in the great Masters, not necessarily throughout their whole lives but certainly during the periods of their ministry, when they were fulfilling the purpose of their destinies. Therefore, however perfect your thoughts, however perfect your actions, there will come a day when either through weakness in your own character, through ignorance, through risking your body in some foolish design or through your own imbalance, either temporarily or permanently, you will create a state of dis-ease and fall into ill health. You are then faced with the choice of how to restore yourself to perfect harmony and good health.

Throughout the history of Mankind there have always been healers. These healers have used various methods, and today there is a great variety of them both advocated and practised. The choices available to you are manifold, and when you become ill you are inevitably faced with making the decision of how you are going to heal yourself. Depending upon the nature of your evolution, your consciousness will guide you to follow certain paths. Unthinking, unfeeling Man, in his ignorance will usually subject himself to the popularly accepted healing methods of the day. No matter whether he thinks them to be correct or incorrect, because they are practised and recognised by other people as being the desirable healing treatment of the day, he will accept them. But this has been true of every civilisation that has existed, and every civilisation has had its own different methods of healing. Just as you look back on the healing of two hundred years ago and think it barbaric that a physician should attach a leech to the body of another human being to effect a cure, so Mankind of two hundred years hence will look back on your healing methods of today, when you cut open and violate the body, and consider them equally as barbaric. So what are the standards by which you should judge healing?

If you are to discover the true nature of healing there are only two sources available to you: firstly, the example of the great Masters who have incarnated upon this Earth for the purpose of demonstrating Infinite Truth to Man and, secondly, that consciousness within you which will intuitively tell you the path to follow to effect the correct treatment for your disease. The path that you follow will obviously vary according to your individual vibration, but remember that unless it is a being of great evolution and vibration there is no single person who can help your body to heal itself of all its diseases. There are different vibrations, different healers, for different diseases. Certainly, among the people who you are likely to meet as healers there is no one person who will be an absolute healer, who possesses the power, as for example did the Nazarene, to heal you of all your diseases at any particular time in your life. Therefore there are specialists, if I may call them that, even in spiritual healing.

Illness, or dis-ease, is one of the most important factors in Man's life. Because he has free choice, because he can choose wrong instead of right, because he will affect his body through his wrong actions, so Man will fall into disharmony. It is the path of evolution. It is a necessary path. Illness, dis-ease, is a lesson to be experienced, to be learnt and to be appreciated. It is part of your destiny as you walk your path in life. It is not something to be avoided, to be shunned, to be ignored, to be thrust aside. It is a fact of life to be faced. It is a test to be taken. But modern medicine regards all illness as unnecessary and thinks that all pain should be avoided. It is concerned more with curing an illness than with establishing the cause of that illness. Therefore remember that Man suffers dis-ease because of his own actions, and that it is through his own actions that he will learn.

Let us look briefly at how the Nazarene healed. You will observe that throughout his ministry there are as many reports of his healings as there are of his teachings. Truly he healed and taught the people of his time as part of his demonstration. Any healer, or anyone who wishes or professes to be a healer, should look to his words and deeds for their motivation in healing. He did not just heal people because they were ill. He did not heal every sick person that he met. In the Bible, of course, the accounts of some of the people that he healed are recorded, but not those of the people he did not. You must remember that the Nazarene healed only those people who believed in him: not in him as an individual, but in the Creator in him. It was a belief, an understanding of life, that led to their healing. The woman who touched the hem of his garments, even though she did not actually touch him, touched his aura, and because she believed and wanted to be healed she was healed. It was her belief in her God that healed her.

The Nazarene healed in many ways. If you read the stories of his healings in the Bible you will discover that he used many methods, from the laying on of hands and the blessing to the physical application of matter to the body, such as when he put mud upon the eyes of a blind man. There are many ways to heal and many forms of healing. The way in which you heal will be decided, firstly, by the point of evolution of the person whom you are to heal and, secondly, by the nature of their illness. The Nazarene's healing was, of course, largely performed through his hands. This in itself is not significant if you remember that the

237

hands are the administrative members of the mind and that healing through the hands is merely an extension of healing through the mind. It is the mind that is the sole, and only, source of all healing. Even your surgeons today, as they use their instruments to violate the body, are attempting their healing through their minds, not through their instruments. Therefore the laying on of hands merely symbolises the healing performed by the mind.

The Nazarene had the ability through his extra-sensory perception, which he possessed to a degree beyond that of which Man is aware today, to see the true nature of an illness. He could tell from the colours of a person's chakras, from the aura around them, not only the nature of their illness but also the cause of that illness. So when you are healing remember that healing has two parts. There is the healing of the disease and there is the healing of the cause of that disease. It is far better to attempt to cure the cause than to cure the actual disease itself. The basic fault of medicine today is that it does not seek to cure the cause, only the effect.

As you live on this Earth you are essentially a magnetic being. Your whole body is a mass of magnetic fields vibrating within the greater magnetic field of the Earth, which itself vibrates within the even greater magnetic field of the Solar Body and the planets which are a part of it. When you are in dis-ease the magnetic fields within your body are out of harmony, and the power of, shall we say, the Nazarene's healing lay in his recognition of the disharmony of those fields and his ability to harmonise them, or to polarise them, so that the healing could automatically then follow. Let us take the example of a cut on your hand. It is no good you trying to heal a cut once the physical cut is actually there. What is needed is that the healing forces of the body be directed to that cut to effect a cure. If you apply that example to all the other illnesses that can be present in Man's body you will see the point that I am trying to make. You do not necessarily cure the visible signs of illness: you activate the healing processes of the body to effect a cure. Each one of you is a unique individual, and although you all appear to have similar physical bodies, in truth not one of you is the same. Each one of you will heal in different ways. Therefore you heal someone by activating the individual's healing processes so that they can heal themselves. Perhaps you are now beginning to realise how complicated the process of diagnosis and healing really is.

There are two basic forms of healing. Either you are an inspired instrument in which you allow yourself to be a channel for the power of greater beings — and this is the form in which most healing takes place on this Earth — or else you, as an actual individual of considerable soul evolution, whilst still using the power of your Creator heal through your own ability, through your own knowledge. This, of course, is the level to which all people must eventually evolve. It is part of the evolutionary pattern of life on this Earth that you first become an inspired instrument and allow yourself to be used for healing, but then through that use and through that healing will come the desire from within you not to be just an instrument but to understand that which is happening through you. You will want to know the how, the why and the wherefore of healing, to know why some people become ill and why others do not, why you can cure some people and not others. To be a healer in one's own right falls to few people on this Earth, and then it is usually associated with souls of considerable evolution who have chosen a particular path and destiny to effect a way of healing upon this Earth. Healers in the World today are, for the most part, inspired healers: that is, they are channels for the power of greater beings above. Let no healer think that he, or she, is the source of such healing, that he or she possesses powers which others do not, for they are only instruments.

Just as the greater beings above are on different levels of vibration, reflecting their different points of consciousness and evolution, so also are their ways of healing. Various Masters, throughout their past incarnations, have evolved various ways of healing. That is why as you look around the field of healing today, especially at New Age methods, you discover that there are many approaches, many ways, to bring about healing. But the interesting point to note is that the healing of the New Age is very often diametrically opposed to the healing that has been developed by the medical profession of today. A great clash is soon to come. Established medicine is to be faced with the choice of either accepting the healing methods of so-called unmedical, 'unskilled', people or else of opposing them. There will be a battle in which only one approach will survive, and there is no doubt as to which one it will be.

In the World today there are many methods of healing which

239

are considered outlandish, unreal, beyond the realms of Man's understanding. You have the phenomenon which you know as psychic surgery. This in itself does not reflect the true nature of healing. It is, basically, a form of healing for primitive people, with the healers merely acting as channels for that greater healing power from above. The method is purely that which is best suited to the environment in which the healers work and live. What is important, however, is that healing does take place.

All of you, as individuals, if you want to be healers should not think that you have to follow the established paths of old, for you do not. If you feel within you the desire to heal, then follow that desire and allow your own inner intuition, your own consciousness, to guide you as to how you should heal, as to the manner in which you should heal and as to which people you should heal.

If you are to practise true spiritual healing it is essential that you are able to assess the vibration of the person who comes to be healed. It is important that you heal only where the lesson has been learnt, where the pain has been appreciated and where the reason for that illness has been understood. Truly, if you heal somebody only to allow them to experience the same illness a short time later, then you are incurring karma for yourself. To heal is a great responsibility, and it is only evolved souls who should take that responsibility upon themselves. I do not say this to deter anyone from healing but merely to make them aware of their responsibility in this matter.

Remember that you cannot heal everybody. You will be guided intuitively towards those people whom you can heal. If you are a channel then do not judge the results of your healing. Try to understand why some people are healed and others are not, but do not question that fact, for you are merely the channel for a greater power. As you attune yourself with the healing power that is coming through you so you will grow to understand it. You will begin to understand the nature of its power and also the reason for its use, so that eventually you will become so in harmony with that healing force that you will be at one with it and will have almost become a healer in your own right. Remember that you are schooling yourself eventually to do this. You are studying at the feet of great Masters of whose presence you are only dimly aware but whose powers you feel.

There is in the Hierarchy of this Earth a band of healing beings. These devote themselves solely to the healing of Mankind on this

Earth and all healers vibrate to their influence. Those of you who feel that you are healers will all be linked within this so-called School of Healing that exists on the higher levels of life. Nightly, in your sleep state, you return to this School to acquaint yourselves with the true nature of healing and with the particular influences of your own Masters and healers.

You are now entering the Aquarian Age, and with this Age are to come the healing methods appropriate to it. There is to be a change in the field of medicine. There is to be a change in Man's attitude towards dis-ease, in his realisation of it and in his healing of it. Man will be led into a deeper realisation of himself. He will understand that all dis-ease comes from within, not from without, and that the sole task of the healer is not to heal the without but to heal the within. You heal not the effect of the dis-ease but the cause, and if, every time a person comes to you for healing, you look for the cause and you ask for the healing of that cause, not the effect, then you will be fulfilling your true role as a healer.

To be a healer requires great sacrifice. To be a healer requires great humility. Above all, to be a healer requires one great and single attribute: love, for without love you will achieve nothing. Therefore, if you do not feel love for a person, and I use the word love in its true spiritual sense, as demonstrated by the Nazarene, do not try to heal him, for you will do more harm than good. You cannot, and may not, understand the true nature of every disease. You cannot, and may not, understand every healing method that is present in the World today. All you can do is to reflect that which you know to be true, the healing light that comes through you.

THE REAPPEARANCE OF ATLANTIS

There are many legends which exist today about the civilisation of Atlantis, but the facts are few, what evidence there is is tantalising, and unless Man is able to tap into and understand the wisdom of the ancients he may not know or recognise the existence of Atlantis. However, such a civilisation did exist. Indeed, it reached the highest evolutionary point that Man has ever known on this Earth. It far surpassed, both technologically and spiritually, Man's position today.

A greater understanding of Atlantis is soon to become a reality. Within the near future scientists will begin to discover an accurate record of Atlantis, but the purpose of the release of this knowledge is not to satisfy Man's curiosity but to prepare the World for the reappearance of Atlantis in the cataclysm that is to come around the end of this century. The reappearance of Atlantis at this time is not without significance, for in the transformation of this globe, as the waters are pushed hither and thither, as mountains rise and lands subside, as the surface of this Earth is moulded by divine intent for divine purpose, so the land, the substance and the matter that was Atlantis, will rise to the surface again for the use of Man. The New Age will usher in a new Atlantis with all the possibilities and the evolutionary concepts of the old one.

The final passing of Atlantis took place fifteen thousand years ago, although its demise had begun thirty-five thousand years earlier. It is the Age of Aquarius that now ushers in its rebirth into matter. Do not think, though, that with this rebirth will come only good, for with the rise of Atlantis to the surface there will also come the evil of Atlantis: all the disharmony and erroneousness that necessitated its destruction so many years ago. It is up to you, the Atlanteans who have reincarnated at this time, to accept and transmute that evil and so prepare the land for the Age that is to come. Many evolved souls who died in the cataclysm that destroyed Atlantis have held the balance for all these years, but with the rising of Atlantis they will relinquish that responsibility. Therefore, Man, with his increased awareness and higher consciousness gained in his many incarnations since then, will have to cope with that evil whilst at the same time accepting the gifts, the benefits and the evolutionary knowledge of Atlantis.

Whether or not you believe in Atlantis does not concern me. As with all great wisdom your point of consciousness will decide your degree of recognition. I would, however, like to point out that several great civilisations of which Man is unaware have come and gone on the surface of this Earth. Because Man's knowledge of the early stages of his development is very sketchy, because the buildings and the written evidence, the record of Mankind, disappeared long ago, so Man cannot establish through physical means the true history of this Earth.

When Man was first placed upon this Earth he was created by the Lord of the Sun in imitation of His perfection. Man was not of this Earth, and was not intended solely to live on it. When he first walked the Earth he walked in perfection, knowing no error. He lived in a civilisation known as Cordemia, the first great civilisation of Man on this Earth. If it was to be placed geographically it would be around the waters which you call the Dead Sea. It was only subsequently that Man was given the divine gift of free choice, and it was with that gift that his downfall began.

As the cyclic evolution of the zodiacal ages of this Earth was fulfilled so the civilisations of Man rose and fell, striving to achieve the heights and crashing to the depths. Great civilisations such as Lemuria came and went. Gradually Man evolved himself in consciousness to the point where he was ready to partake of the knowledge of the Cosmos. He had learnt the true meaning of physical life on this Earth, and was now ready to embark upon the learning of the knowledge of the higher planes. In preparation for this great event a land was specially prepared for him which up to that time had not been touched by Man. It had lain beneath the waters where it had been prepared by those of the spiritual hierarchy who dwell in the centre of the Earth. Thus, with the dawning of the Age of Atlantis, in the movement of the Earth in a cataclysmic rebirth the great continent of Atlantis appeared, and the Age of Atlantis began.

If I had to place Atlantis geographically on your globe, it would be centred in the Atlantic Ocean. Is it not strange how the name persists even to this day? Atlantis stretched from Iceland in

243

the north to the Falkland Islands in the south. It stretched from what is now the west coast of Africa to the east coast of America. It was a beautiful land of towering mountains, the tips of some of which remain as the Azores. All that remains of the great continent today are a few scattered points of power and vibration, some of which you are aware of, which were thrown off when Atlantis submerged beneath the waves. Great Britain possesses several of them, particularly Iona, but also including the islands of the Hebrides, the Scottish Western Islands and the West Country of England. Iceland and Greenland, the eastern coast of Canada and the eastern coast of America down to the state of Maine are also parts of old Atlantis. These are the only geographical areas that are left of what was Atlantis.

As with any great civilisation many nationalities inhabited Atlantis, and I would draw a comparison with the great Age now beginning in America. There, too, you have all the nationalities of the World gathered together in one continent. So it was in Atlantis. The most evolved, the greatest of all the Races, were directed to Atlantis to fulfil this dream of the Earth.

The Age of Atlantis lasted for thousands of years. There were several distinct periods in its history as various influences, such as the root races and the zodiacal ages, affected its destiny, but it eventually rose to become, to a great extent, a reproduction, an externalisation, of life on the higher planes. The Atlanteans came to recognise the greatest fact about life on this Earth, namely, that God, the Creator of all life, is in all life. They accepted no separation between this planet and the Solar Body in which it resides. Whilst recognising the physical, they did not accept its limitations. They realised that the power of the Sun, the cosmic energy of our Solar Logos, the Creator of all life within this Solar Body, was also the moulder of all physical matter on this Earth. They were aware that they themselves were not of this Earth and that whilst they dwelt in physical bodies of matter, for which they were responsible, they were really far higher beings than the matter of this Earth. Therefore they looked not at the individuality, at the lower aspect, of the 'I', but at the higher aspect. A community system of life existed on Atlantis. Although many individual nationalities were present, the spirit of Atlantis was the spirit of God. They recognised no difference between races, but merely the common purpose of life on this Earth.

Over the course of many civilisations the Atlanteans rose to a

244

high state of technological achievement. They tapped into and used the energy of the Sun for the creation and sustenance of their society. Man today ignores this, the greatest, factor in his life and takes the Sun's powers for granted. He knows little of the real gifts of the Sun, but the Atlanteans recognised its true power and used it. They used it not only for transportation, for building, for healing, but for every aspect of their spiritual life as well. They used it for worship. The Atlanteans recognised that because there is an aspect of the Godhead in each cell of matter, which is energised by the Sun, all matter is controlled by the Sun. They discovered the relationship between the energising factor of the Sun and life on this Earth.

There are a few examples remaining today of the immense buildings which the Atlanteans created. The great pyramids of Egypt and Stonehenge in England are examples of Atlantean architecture. There are also archaeological 'problems' in other countries which Man today cannot solve, which can all be traced back to Atlantis. Because the Atlanteans understood the structure of matter they could dissolve and recreate it. The vast blocks of stone which were used in the construction of these edifices were dematerialised, moved to the spot where they were desired and then rematerialised. This may seem impossible to you, but it is true. The matter of this Earth is held together by the energy of the Sun. If you discover the way in which matter is held together you can then dissolve it and re-create it at your will.

The government of Atlantis was, of course, run by the priests, or elders, of the Temple. These were men of great evolution, Masters who had trained and incarnated especially for that role, and they ruled and taught the country with great spirituality. Communication with the Higher Beings was an everyday occurrence. Whilst the priests could attune themselves at will to the Spiritual Hierarchy, even the ordinary people in the street could attune themselves to the higher planes of existence through the means of a magnetic device. By strapping this to themselves in times of prayer and meditation they heightened their senses, and so could communicate directly with the Higher Beings. It was also a time when Masters from the other planets walked this Earth. Communication with, and the presence of, other planetary beings was an accepted fact. The Atlanteans themselves also travelled to the other planets within this Solar Body, but not in the physical sense of using rockets and spaceships, for they had discovered the power of the mind. They had conquered the force of gravity, and could 'fly'. They could move themselves from place to place, defying the Law of Gravity.

In instances of disease or illness the Atlanteans recognised that the source of the disease lay not in the physical but in a higher body. Therefore they always cured the higher body, not the physical. If a person was ill he was taken to a place of healing, a temple, and placed in a healing room. This room was constructed of a certain type of stone, of crystal, and was so shaped and angled that the power of the Sun was diffused into beams of different coloured cosmic light and energy. The person was then placed in the middle of the room and, depending upon the nature of his illness, so the correct rays of light, and therefore colour, were directed onto him. Also, of course, the priests of that time, being evolved souls with a high degree of consciousness, could look at the akashic record of the person who was ill — for illness is not necessarily only of one's present life, but can stretch back through many previous lives — and they could cure, or attempt to cure, the true cause of the dis-ease in that person.

You would say to me, bearing in mind the picture that I have just painted, "Why, then, did Atlantis fall?". Atlantis fell for the same reason that all the other civilisations have fallen: Man's erroneousness. Although the people of Atlantis had reached a high point of evolution, although they had tapped into cosmic powers and, because of the era in which they lived, had developed their psychic abilities way, way beyond your comprehension, they did not motivate themselves correctly. They used their knowledge of the Cosmos, their point of evolution, not to fulfil the will of their Creator and His divine Plan but to fulfil their own ideas of creation. They used their knowledge for personal satisfaction and gain, to obtain power, to amass wealth, to control other beings, to further their own plans, no matter what the cost. The powers which the Atlanteans were given, and which in the initial stages they had used for construction, were eventually used for destruction, and so the downfall of Atlantis, with its eventual subsidence beneath the waves, began. This subsidence was brought about not only by the great Beings of the Spiritual Hierarchy but also by the few remaining true priests of Atlantis. These priests recognised that Atlantis must be destroyed and so they offered to sink with it to hold the evil in balance. They realised that Man must experience further cycles of evolution before he would again be in the position to accept the responsibility and the knowledge of Atlantis.

Before any great civilisation disintegrates the seeds for the next are removed to safety. Out of Atlantis came the peoples who were to be the founders of the races which exist today. Present racial characteristics can all be traced back to Atlantis. Atlantis, then, sank beneath the waves, and its evil went with it to be held in balance by great Beings. The Earth was transformed in a cataclysm, Man was reborn and the march of Man began again. Many of you were Atlanteans. Anyone who possesses psychic powers to any great degree owes it to that great Atlantean civilisation and to the use which he made of those powers then. All over the World today psychic discoveries are taking place in preparation for the new Age of Atlantis.

Many of the souls who lived in Atlantis are now incarnating in preparation for its reappearance. They are young in physical years, but old in spiritual evolution. Unfortunately, many of them are misguided at this time because they lack spiritual direction and motivation and because their higher selves, their spirits, cannot understand or accept the restrictions of the dense physical life of Earth today, for they remember only the spirituality of old Atlantis.

Atlantis is to rise again. The Christ is to come again. The seeds for the New Age are already sown, not only the physical seeds of man and woman but also the seeds of mind and matter, the seeds of creation, the seeds of the other Kingdoms of this Earth. All is prepared for this great awakening, this great step forward in the evolution of the Earth. It is the opportunity for Mankind to redeem itself and to prove that this, the next Age of Atlantis, will be the final one. Citizens of Atlantis, are you ready for that moment of redemption?

THE COSMIC MEANING OF THE CROSS

As I look upon the altars of your Churches I see there the crucifix which has been made into the symbol of the Christian religion today, but the crucifix that I see is a man-made, not a God-given, symbol, and in that Man has crucified himself he worships a crucifix. The true symbol of Easter, the true symbol of this Earth, is not the crucifix but the true cross, the cross of four equal arms. It is on the cosmic meaning of this true cross that I wish to talk now.

As with all matters of cosmic knowledge, it is difficult to choose a point in the history of the evolution of this Earth at which to begin, for so much is unknown to unseeing Man today. That is not to say that the wisdom and knowledge is not available to him, for there are various Masters of great evolution situated all over this World who hold and preserve that wisdom and knowledge for the great Age that is to come. However, I will begin by saying that originally this Earth was created in the seven Ages, the seven eras, which are described in the first book of the Bible, Genesis, as the seven days of creation. The Creator of the Earth, after He had formed its structure, after He had divided the land from the water, after He had created the Vegetable and then the Animal Kingdoms, finally on the sixth day, or in the sixth Age, He created Man and placed him upon the Earth. At that time Man was linked to the Godhead. He knew only perfection. He was not the individualised spark of consciousness which he is now. He walked hand in hand with the angels and with great beings from the other planets within this Solar Body and, indeed, from galaxies beyond this Solar Body. References to this time are to be found in the ancient literature of Mankind. It was, as the Book of Genesis says, a true Garden of Eden. This civilisation, which has the spiritual name of Cordemia, was situated roughly in the area which now lies beneath the Dead Sea, and it was in that Garden of Eden that Man first incarnated and was instructed by the angels and by great beings concerning the true purpose of this Earth.

After many Ages of dwelling in perfection in this civilisation of Cordemia it was deemed necessary that Man should be individualised as a spark of consciousness and that he should evolve himself through the exercising of his own choice on the surface of the Earth. Therefore, Man was reincarnated in that civilisation of Cordemia. He was placed on the Earth once more, but now with the divine gift of free choice, and Adam and Eve, man and woman, positive and negative, the power — the male aspect, and the wisdom — the female aspect, were created. This was the basis of Man's creation, for it was through his understanding of the Law of Opposites that he was to evolve and to acquire the knowingness of his Creator. He now had within him the ability to arise to be a perfect imitation of his Creator, the God of this Solar System. It was here that Man was taught the symbol of this Earth, the true cross. In his new-found knowledge, in his new-found expression, this cross, the symbol of matter on the Earth, presented to Man the unity of all life upon this globe.

Every planet within this Solar Body has a symbol which links it not only with the Solar Lord of the individual planet but also with the Creator of its Solar System, the God Whose spirit dwells in the Sun, and with Infinite Spirit beyond. The symbol of the Earth, as I have already mentioned, is the true cross of four equal arms. It is the symbol given to this Earth by your Creator to demonstrate the purpose and the nature of this Earth on which you dwell. Our Solar Body operates on the spiritual wavelength of twelve, and this fact is manifested by there being twelve planets and twelve planes of existence within the Solar Body. However, physical matter on the Earth operates on the wavelength of four, and this fact, symbolised by the four arms of the cross, is demonstrated by the four points of the compass, the four Kingdoms of Matter, the four basic elements and the four Races, the foundation stones from which Man today derives his heritage. Each one of the four when subdivided into a trinity makes up twelve, and so establishes the relationship with the spiritual wavelength of the Solar Body.

It is written in the Book of Genesis that out of the Garden of Eden there flowed four rivers. These four rivers refer to the four separate streams of cosmic consciousness which formed themselves into four basic types of Man on this Earth, the four Races: the White, the Yellow, the Black and the Red. Each of these four

Races further subdivided into the trinity of Spiritual Law, the trinity of Creation: the father, the mother and the son, or the power, the wisdom and the receptivity or, as it is called in the Bible, the Father, the Son and the Holy Ghost. So again you have twelve sub-divisions, referred to in the Bible as the twelve tribes of Abraham, which reflect the twelve subdivisions of the Solar Body.

The true cross, therefore, symbolises those four Races. If we regard the cross as symbolising the four points of the compass, I would place the White Race at the north, the Yellow Race at the East, the Black Race at the south and the Red Race at the west. It was through the evolution of those four Races, each according to their own cosmic pattern and design, that the World was to harmonise itself and to advance in evolution. It was recognised that the Races should evolve individually but yet should live together in unity, that they should evolve their own individual consciousnesses before uniting in one cosmic whole. You may now see why so much of the conflict on this Earth today has been caused by the mixing of the Races, by one Race overpowering another and subjugating it, by one Race making another follow its pattern of evolution. If only the Races of the World today would return to an understanding of their true cosmic consciousness they would in no small way harmonise this Earth on which they dwell.

Each of the four Races, then, in turn represents one of the four elements of matter: the White Race air, the Yellow Race water, the Black Race earth and the Red Race fire, and it is through the vibration and the understanding of those four elements that the individual cosmic evolution of the Races is to be accomplished. Although I have placed the White Race at the top of the cross that does not mean that it is the superior Race, for all the Races are equal and are incomparable. It means only that the White Race, being the Race of the air, of the mind, is at the top of the cross because it is the ascendant Race as we move into the Air Age, the Age of Aquarius.

The purpose of each of the four Races was to demonstrate and develop the individual talent which it possessed. The Yellow Race, which represented the element water, through the vibration of healing was to attune itself to the wisdom of Creation and to draw down to Earth that which was necessary for the evolution of Mankind. In its divine emotion, its philosophy, its pulsation with the cosmic heart, the Yellow Race should be bringing down the radiation of wisdom to Humanity. If you are born of the Yellow Race you have come to create perfection in the realm of wisdom.

The Black Race, which represented the element earth, was responsible for grounding Mankind to the earth. It was the conducting element to earth, and through its spiritual knowledge it should be able to bring from the centre of the Earth the power and the harmony necessary for the Earth. The Black Race vibrates to the frequency of earth. If you are born of the Black Race you have come to create perfection in the realm of earth.

The Red Race, which represented the element fire, was the Race associated with the cleansing aspect of life, for it is only by undergoing complete cleansing that Man and the Earth will harmonise themselves and survive. Through its union with the elements of the earth, and its knowledge of the plant and animal life, the Red Race should be establishing a direct and harmonious communication with all aspects of consciousness. If you are born of the Red Race you have come to create perfection in the realm of cleansing.

Finally, the White Race, which represented the element air, was to be the Race of the mind, the Race which provided the mental faculty of Man and Life, and today you may see how true this is, for the civilisation of the western world is a civilisation of mind, with little other influences to harmonise it. It was, then, through the mind that the White Race was to bring down the cosmic knowledge necessary for the education of the World and for the New Age. The White Race, in this Air Age, the creative Age of Mind, should be giving the Earth in its creativity, in its search into cosmic life, in its revelation into cosmic law, its new education. If you are born of the White Race you have come to create perfection in the realm of mind.

Since they flowed out of the Garden of Eden, and went to various parts of the World, over aeons of time those four rivers, the four Races, have gradually merged their cosmic blood-streams. As the Races have come and gone in the natural rise and fall of cyclic evolution so their original purity has been lost. As the nations have competed, as the peoples of the World have looked only to their own ends and not to those of their fellow men, so the original harmony and balance has gone. As you look at the true cross be aware, therefore, that it symbolises the purpose of this planet: the harmonising of the four Races, of the four elements, individually at first but then merging into a one, to reveal the true power and glory of this Earth. It may be compared to a windmill with four sails. As the sails begin to move in the cosmic wind and gather speed so the colours symbolising the Races blend into one to give a picture of perfection, not seen when they were stationary. The Races of the World today must, therefore, grow individually and yet unite together. They must be separate, each responding to their own cosmic consciousness, not imitating the more technologically advanced or the more intellectually advanced Races, but responding to their true inner feelings.

Man today associates Easter with death and resurrection. He thinks of it only in terms of the physical, and so for him the cross symbolises death and resurrection, although, in reality, it has a far greater meaning, for it symbolises the Laws that govern this Earth. Man is convinced that life in the physical is reality, but if he would only begin to open his eyes and look beyond the physical to the true, the cosmic, meaning of life he would then begin to understand the reality of his short transition in his physical body of matter.

THE TRUE MEANING AND SIGNIFICANCE
OF CATACLYSMS

In this lecture I am going to talk about the true meaning and significance of cataclysms. Each of you will have a different idea about the meaning of the word cataclysm, and you will probably think of it according to the way in which you have been conditioned by your earthly teachers and by the environment around you. As with the principle of reincarnation, so a belief in the principle of cataclysmic change represents a point of consciousness. Nothing that I am to say will make you believe in this principle if your own spiritual investigation and point of consciousness do not permit it. Therefore I do not expect in this lecture to convince you that cataclysms do indeed take place as a result of Natural Law: I merely invite you to meditate on what I say and to see if within your hearts there is not a response to my words.

If you examine the actual meaning of the word cataclysm you will note that it comes from the Greek language: 'cata' meaning down, away, and 'clysmos' meaning flood, deluge — thus meaning a sinking or flooding away. The reason for the choice of this term is that water does play a significant part in a cataclysm, an event which results in a great transformation of the surface of this Earth, with large tracts of land sinking beneath the seas and other parts being washed over by great waves with subsequent destruction and reshaping of the terrain. When I talk of a cataclysm I am not talking of the cataclysm which is to come or of the cataclysms that have taken place. One cataclysm has no more significance than another. Each merely represents a change of direction, a restructuring of matter to fulfil Divine Will, the Plan for this Earth.

A cataclysm is probably regarded by most of you as a tragic event. To you it signifies death, destruction, the extermination of a large part of Mankind, the disappearance of the beauty of Nature, of much of the Animal, the Vegetable and the Mineral

Kingdoms, and the reduction of Man's civilisation to rubble. However, in reality, a cataclysm is a process of evolution through extreme change rather than a meaningless act of destruction. Your World is continually in a state of flux. Mankind and the Earth are forever changing in the eternal progression of the Plan for this Earth, but because normally the change is slow and subtle Man does not see it. It is only change of a sudden nature that Man observes and feels. Therefore when I speak of a cataclysm I do not want you to think of it in terms of a tragedy.

If I say that a cataclysm is coming do not think that disaster looms nigh, that the purpose of your life is limited, that everything is to be destroyed in it and, therefore, that there is no point in pursuing the aims of your life. A cataclysm does bring change, but you are forever changing. In every hour of every day, as you live in your physical bodies of matter, you are changing, and you will continue to change and evolve until the moment of that cataclysm. For some there will be death in it but, as you know, death is only another form of change. Therefore death in a cataclysm does not mean the extermination, the ending, of life: it is, rather, a rebirth. I would therefore invite you to regard a cataclysm not as an ending, not as a finality, but truly as a beginning. I would ask you to look at the cataclysm which is to come at the end of this century not as the ending of an Age but as the birth, the dawning, of a New Age.

Cataclysms are your Creator's way of ensuring that the continuing Plan for the evolution of this Earth is carried out. They are as natural as the other changes which Man can observe on the surface of this Earth — the birth and death of Man, the birth and death of Nature, the restructuring of the elements of the Mineral Kingdom that take place all around you every year. Everything in matter is in a continuous state of change. It is up to Man's consciousness to interpret and to recognise the purpose of that change, and then evolution will take place.

You will meet many people who cannot accept the idea of cataclysmic change: that is their point of consciousness, which must be respected. Others can accept the principle of cataclysmic change whilst not comprehending the reason for it, and will therefore look upon it with incorrect motivation. The purpose of this lecture, then, is to talk to those people who do indeed believe in cataclysmic change and to invite them to motivate their thoughts correctly so that they may truly appreciate the real nature and the purpose of a cataclysm.

Because Man has created a world which knows only of material and financial controls he does not wish to envisage a state when those controls are no longer valid, and he is reluctant to enquire into the true nature of cataclysmic change. But the evidence is there for him to see. All over this globe there are signs of not one, not two, but of several cataclysmic changes which have transformed the face of this Earth. As well as the two or three cataclysms which Man can identify there have been many others which he will never discover.

In various ancient manuscripts there are descriptions of the most recent cataclysms. The Bible refers to at least two, even if the descriptions of them when translated into a modern language, are a little vague. The last cataclysm which took place almost seven thousand years ago is described in the Book of Genesis where you find the story of Noah's Ark and the flood. In that story there is symbology yet again, but nevertheless that description is directly descended from the stories of Man passed down from father to son over many generations long before they were written in the book of the Jews. You may also recognise a reference to a previous cataclysm in the description of the formation, or rather of the change, of this Earth in the first chapter of the Book of Genesis. Man will not, and cannot, know of the divine processes of Infinite Spirit's creation, and the first chapter of the Book of Genesis refers not, as most people believe, to the creation of this World, a creation which in his present state of consciousness Man will never understand, but to the reformation, to the re-establishment, of life after yet another great cataclysm.

Not only in the Bible, but also in many other religious books, in the engravings and carvings of ancient races, in the legends preserved even to this day, there is much evidence of the great cataclysmic changes that have taken place on this Earth. Through the examination of stratas of rock modern geologists have proved beyond doubt that great cataclysmic changes have indeed taken place on this Earth's surface. Forces of which Man cannot conceive, either scientifically or naturally, were employed to bring about these transformations. There are many riddles which your scientists are unable to explain: for example that of large prehistoric animals being discovered in states of preservation which defy comprehension in parts of the World where Man would not expect to find them. Man has also discovered ancient legends describing races of men which no longer exist. He has the stories of Atlantis, of Lemuria and of Mu. All this evidence lies before him if he would but look at it and examine it. For the evolved souls who desire to know of the next cataclysm the evidence is there for them if they will but seek it. I say this not to convert you to the concept of cataclysmic change but rather to arouse your curiosity, to make you look for yourselves.

Let us now briefly examine the mechanism of a cataclysm. This Earth on which you now live is not as stable a body as you would believe. By this I mean that there are many variations in the pattern of the Earth's rotation, some of which your scientists of today have discovered. The axis of the Earth varies through minute angles which can actually be measured. When greater influences are brought to bear the axis of rotation of the Earth can be, and is, changed dramatically, thus causing a cataclysm. At this point, however, I must differentiate between a natural and a Man-made cataclysm, for with the present advancement of his scientific knowledge, and without the wisdom to use it, Man can bring about a cataclysmic change of his own making. If Man proceeds on the path on which he is now set and explodes his nuclear devices on such an unstable body as the Earth, he would precipitate the natural cataclysm that is planned by his Creator for around the end of this century. If that were to happen then the death and destruction amongst Mankind would be far greater than that caused by the natural event.

Forces beyond your control acting both within and outside the realm of this planet set in motion the mechanism for initiating a cataclysm. If I was to speak of the Solar Lords, of your Creator — that Being whom you call God — and of great Beings beyond this Solar Body who control the destiny not only of your own Solar Body but of Galaxies beyond it, it would be beyond your comprehension. Therefore I will say only that the destiny of this Solar Body in which you now dwell, together with the life of your planet, the Earth, are controlled by great Forces to fulfil a plan for evolution which does not know mistake or failure. These great Beings control life within this Solar Body, as well as on your Earth, and according to the cyclic pattern of planetary and inter-planetary evolution so your Earth passes through the influences of certain vibrations. When such influences are brought to bear upon the Earth, magnetic forces within the Earth react to these vibrations and thereby trigger off a state of fluidity in the Earth's crust which allows movement of the land masses on the surface.

When these cataclysmic changes take place, large tracts of land are moved around like pieces of a jig-saw puzzle. Large portions of the Earth's surface rise and fall, appear and disappear. This is what confuses your geologists today, for they look at the surface of this Earth as they now see it and try to deduce its whole evolution from just one small portion of its present surface. That is why they fail, for the whole structure of the Earth is not visible to Mankind today. Ancient legends tell of the great civilisation of Atlantis which existed roughly where the Atlantic Ocean is today. You have also probably heard of the great civilisation of Lemuria which existed in the area which is now the Pacific Ocean, and perhaps even of Cordemia which existed in the area around the Dead Sea in the Middle East. All these civilisations have disappeared, apparently without trace — but they have existed. Your explorers today keep on discovering material which points to facets of Man's development which they cannot explain: buildings which twentieth century Man could not construct, symbols, descriptions of great space beings, conditions of life which even Man today has not achieved. Yet still Man will not see the true answer and realise that in past civilisations, now buried beneath the seas or beneath the strata of the Earth's surface, Man has risen to far greater heights than he has in his present short cycle since the Noah's Ark cataclysm seven thousand years ago.

Man has not had the time to advance. It has taken him over six thousand years to civilise himself to a degree and now, when the period for advancement is at hand, his motivation is not correct. There have been civilisations in the past which have had a further six thousand years to develop beyond the state at which Man is now in his present cycle, and therefore you can appreciate where the mind of Man could go from this point in time if he was motivated correctly. Man has achieved great heights before. He has flown in his own 'flying saucers' to the other parts of this Solar Body. He has understood conditions of life beyond Man's present comprehension. He has lived more in harmony with God's Laws than he does today, and yet just as a beautiful rose comes to full bloom and then dies so Man in those earlier civilisations has also died, for such is the Law of Change. Without change there can be no evolution, and great change on this Earth is brought about by the divine mechanism of the cataclysm.

In the not too distant future the Earth will experience another great cataclysmic rebirth to fulfil the Law of Cyclic Evolution. Man's so-called Western Civilisation is, for the most part, to be crushed into minute particles. The way of life which has been established is to disappear in seven days of great change, and at the end of that seventh day, the day of rest, when the cataclysm ceases, Man will see a new Earth before his eyes just as did the men of old. Through the act of physical death in this cataclysm many people are to leave this Earth and return to their higher bodies, for this is part of their individual destinies in this incarnation. The cataclysm is a great regulator of the Earth's population; or should I say that the misuse of the divine gift of creation by Man is corrected by the Higher Forces in this way.

After the cataclysm this Earth will have been transformed beyond your comprehension. Man, in effect, will have been returned to another Stone Age, but he will have with him those priceless few who have evolved their consciousnesses to understand, to prepare for and to survive such a cataclysm. Just as God approached the man whom you know as Noah and warned him of what was to come, so I talk to you now. Just as Noah was warned and could therefore prepare for the cataclysm that was to come, so too must you, so that when the day occurs, when suddenly the Earth moves on its axis, when the Sun appears to stand still, when darkness descends upon the face of the Earth and when destruction beyond your comprehension takes place, you will greet it with recognition, as being a sign of what is to come, as confirmation of your faith and certain trust in your Creator.

I am asking you, therefore, to understand the need for, and the purpose of, a cataclysm, to see why Man has to change, to see why Man must change. I am asking you to prepare yourselves so that after the cataclysm at the turn of the century you will have the tools to advance the Aquarian Age. You are the seeds which will have been planted in the dirt and rubble of a cataclysmic change and which will grow to fruition and herald the New Age. That is the responsibility of you old souls who are incarnating at this most difficult time in the Earth's evolution: to bring about the transformation from destruction into growth. Many are to die. They will return to their higher bodies and will wait for a long time before they again return to this Earth, for the Age of Aquarius is to be an age of great evolution. After this next cataclysm the period of time before the next one occurs is to be longer than it has been in the past. Man is to have a long cycle of evolution, but eventually that too will change. In this New Age Man will progress and evolve beyond his wildest dreams. The Earth will become what it should be: a vibration of Universal Love fulfilling its purpose in the Solar Body. It will be giving out its emanations not just to this Solar Body but to Creation beyond.

Many men have prophesied that a cataclysm is coming. Over the last one thousand years many seers and prophets have spoken of this event. Before you dismiss these prophecies as the warnings of cranks seek to establish why they were warning you. They have long since died: the warnings were not for them. The only motivation they had in making their prophecies was to foretell what was to come. They prophesied so as to warn a race of men which would be far removed from them both in its way of life and in its evolution. You may disregard the voice of God at your peril.

HEALTH AND HARMONY

You live in an Age of great technological achievement. In the space of just over fifty years Man has progressed from building the first aeroplanes to landing rockets on the moon. However, those of you who are becoming aware of the true meaning of life have begun to recognise that with this great material achievement has not come the same kind of advancement in Man's spirituality and that the disharmony and the conflict which is apparent all over this globe is due to this imbalance. This same criticism can also be levelled against Man's medical progress, and in this lecture I would like to examine this field, more particularly because in the Age which is now dawning Man's attitude to medicine and healing is to change most dramatically.

I will begin by saying that I in no way desire to pour scorn on the medical profession of today, for much of medical science is good. Medical scientists, doctors and surgeons are often over-shadowed by the Healing Hierarchy to aid them in their work. The medical profession, however, has existed for thousands of years and, as a result of the traditions which have grown up, has become somewhat hidebound in its attitudes. Today, it is only a brave doctor or surgeon who opposes the established medical practices and beliefs.

Man today possesses the state of medical art which befits his point of evolution. You may find this hard to believe, but there is no such thing as new knowledge. Knowledge is released to Man only as a result of the utterings of his soul-determination, which in turn are governed by the consciousness of the Age in which he lives. Man has just passed out of the Piscean Age, which was an Age of Darkness. This was predetermined, for it is only by know-ing darkness that Man can know light, and so that which has been experienced by Man in this Age has been an essential part of his evolution. Similarly, the medical profession also has experienced an Age of Darkness, and that which is practised today is the result of that same evolutionary process. To those of you who know the medical profession it is evident that it has devoted itself with great single-mindedness to the study of disease. It can now identify, categorise and attempt to heal almost every disease or injury known to Man today. Would that this same energy had been directed to the study of health rather than to the diagnosis of disease! Man has looked only at the symptoms of disease, and has sought to treat them alone: he has not concerned himself with the causes of disease. This state of affairs is due not only to the Age in which he has lived but also to the level of his soul evolution. You are now moving into an Age where Man will begin to investigate the true nature of health as opposed to disease, and therefore I would like to examine what the essential ingredients of health are.

Many of the teachers who give these lectures have drawn a comparison between the Solar Body in which you, and this little Earth on which you dwell, exist, and your own physical body. Whilst this is not an altogether accurate comparison, it would be true to say that the planets within this Solar Body perform similar functions to the organs within your own physical body. Indeed they are closely related, for each of the main organs within your body vibrates to the influence of the planets. That is the way in which physical Man is tied to cosmic Man. As you look up at the sky and see the way in which the planets revolve in their set orbits and observe the harmony of the Universe you truly see the Divine Plan in operation. Similarly, the organs within your own physical body should operate in harmony.

Everything that exists in the Universe vibrates on a precisely fixed frequency, and the different rates of vibration can be distinguished by their colour. Your whole physical being is a mass of colour, and if I look at a person I see not a physical shape but emanations of colour. These can also be seen by people who have the gift of clairvoyance and are referred to as auras. The colours which surround you are a result of the blending of the rays from the planets with the rays from the very essence of your being which are transmitted from your spiritual centres within. If you had eyes which were not limited to the normal range of physical vision you could look up into the skies and see similar patterns of colour blending between the planets and the Earth. Likewise, if you had ears which were not limited to the normal range of physical hearing you could hear the sounds of true celestial music:

not the music of Man, but the music of the Spheres. That is why it is said that in the New Age healing will be effected through colour and sound, but it will not be through the colour which Man now sees and it will not be through the sound which Man now hears.

Within Man's physical body, then, the organs vibrate to fulfil their individual functions. They are energised by seven centres of cosmic radiation, sometimes known as chakras. These chakras, of which you are probably already aware, are situated in a vertical line ascending from the base of the spine to the head, commencing with the lowest near the coccyx, the second in the region of the spleen, the third in the region of the solar plexus, the fourth in the region of the heart, the fifth in the region of the thyroid gland, the sixth in the region of the pineal gland and the seventh in the region of the pituitary gland. Each of these radiates a colour which corresponds to a colour in the spectrum: the first and lowest red, the second orange, the third yellow, the fourth green, the fifth blue, the sixth indigo and the seventh violet. It is these centres of colour which energise and harmonise Man's physical body.

You may now see that the way in which your organs vibrate, both individually and together, determines the health of your physical body. In the same way that, due to the lack of spirituality at the present time, the Earth is in a state of disharmony, affecting the Solar Body as a whole, so, similarly, if one of your organs is in disharmony it too affects the whole physical body. Man cannot live in isolation within his Solar Body and neither can the organs act in isolation within his physical body. They are all a part of the whole.

It should be understood that the organs of Man's physical body all vibrate at different frequencies. Each of you, being a unique spark of Spirit, has an individual vibration which will not be found anywhere else in the Cosmos. Therefore, when the medical profession seeks to classify men and women into groups and to prescribe similar courses of treatment for similar diseases they are committing a grave error, for no two people are the same. Certainly Man has similar organs which function in a similar way, but they vibrate at different frequencies. Therefore, for example, when a surgeon comes to perform operations such as transplants he should realise that he will never completely succeed, for whilst putting organs of a different vibration into another person might prolong the life of that person for a short period of time it can only bring disharmony and lead eventually to further disease. Your medical scientists are already aware that the body rejects all foreign organs, and that unless they can find a way to overcome this rejection then these transplants will not work. It is, of course, very natural for the body to reject that which is foreign to it, that which it does not want.

In this era of heart transplants, medical science thinks that it is approaching the zenith of its skill and knowledge. Indeed, in the future perhaps scientists will even create forms — I will not call them babies — in test tubes. It therefore behoves the medical profession to listen very carefully to the warnings of those who are aware of a deeper meaning to life. Situated within the heart, within the left ventricle, are the spirit and the soul of Man while he resides in a physical body. Therefore, when you remove a man's heart you also remove with it his soul and his spirit. When you take the original heart out of the recipient and replace it with a heart from a different being, all you are doing is creating a zombie. It is said in the Bible that the time will come when the Spirit of God will no longer walk upon the face of this Earth. This indeed prophesies that one day there will be a race of zombies on Earth who will not be a part of Spirit, who will not be joined to the God-head. This is also true of test-tube babies, with which medical scientists are at present experimenting.

If Man is to maintain his physical body in perfect health he must live in harmony, but besides harmonising his body he must also harmonise himself in thought, word and deed. Just as your Creator Whose spirit dwells within the Sun has harmonised His own body, in which you dwell, to provide you with the light, the power, the energy of the Sun and the love which makes your existence possible, so the millions of beings who dwell within you look to you as their 'God' to provide them with similar harmonious conditions which are their birthright. That your body is not your own is a difficult concept to grasp, but be aware that you live within your physical body through the grace of a greater force. It is given to you in a sacred trust which you must respect, otherwise karma of the highest order will be incurred. You should look after your body if not for yourself then for the millions of beings of evolution who look to you in the same way that you look to your God. It is through the harmonisation of the organs, the heart pulsating with the lungs, the liver pulsating with the gall bladder, that the harmonisation of the whole is carried out. In this there is an example to Man, for if he will but harmonise himself with life around he will harmonise the Earth on which he dwells as a whole.

How are you to harmonise yourself with life? It is simple. Many Masters have come and shown the way. They have come onto the surface of this Earth, at great sacrifice to themselves, to demonstrate the way in which Man should live in harmony so that he may further the very nature of his being. Perhaps the greatest precept of all time which the Masters have taught is that you should do unto others as you would have others do unto you. This would appear on the surface to have a simple interpretation, but the cosmic, the mystical, meaning of that saying goes far deeper, for it means that you allow every being around you, however unevolved, the degree of attunement, of harmonisation, which you yourself expect. It therefore means that you send out only the purest thoughts, the purest words, the purest deeds, for that which you send out takes form on levels above the physical and, once established, can be tapped into and used by Mankind all over the world. Therefore if you create disharmony, jealousy, hatred, greed, indolence, then these will unite with similar clouds to be tapped into by other men, for within your physical body, as I have mentioned, is the means whereby Man can tap into the many other levels of the Cosmos.

A wise man once said, "Man, know thyself". It is one of the great escapes of intellectual man to search for some great esoteric truth, to seek this outside of himself when, truly, that truth is within, within not only the murmurings of his soul-consciousness, but also within the very make-up and structure of his being. If you can truly see and recognise how the various parts of your physical body unite as a one, as a whole, how they are responsible each to the other, how they give and take, how they harmonise with each other, how they blend with all that is, then you will see in that the way of your Creator and the purpose of life on this Earth.

If you are all to live in harmony you must first respect your physical bodies as the divine birthright which they are, for when it is written that Man was created in the image of his Creator that identifies the true nature and potential of your physical bodies. You are, indeed, gods in the making. That was the demonstration of Masters such as the Nazarene who whilst in their physical bodies of matter could practise and demonstrate the knowledge of the Cosmos, those things which in his simplicity Man calls miracles. It is possible for Man to walk on the water, to heal the so-called incurable, to raise from the dead. You can do these things if you will but harmonise your bodies. In considering your bodies you must realise that they are entities in themselves which are worthy of respect and, indeed, are worthy of consultation, for they can tell you what they need. They are not dumb creatures which cannot communicate. They can tell you at any minute of the day what they want. Normally Man listens to them only in time of illness, but how much better if he were to listen to them in health and so ensure the continuation of that health.

Health is basically controlled by the mind. It is perhaps difficult for you to understand, but the mind is ultimately the major cause of all ill health, for you attract unto yourselves that which you are. If you send out hate, if you send out fear, if you send out greed, then you will attract similar forces unto you, and as they flow into your body so disharmony will result, and therefore disease and illness. Your scientists are becoming aware that many illnesses can be discovered and examined on the etheric level even before they take form and become visible on the physical level. Indeed, the healing of the future will be concerned with the etheric level, and Man will treat his illnesses before they even manifest in the physical.

If Man is to live in harmony he must understand as far as his individual soul evolution permits that which is required of him in his life in the physical. He must accept the destiny which he has chosen and his station in life. He must learn to be content with this, and to recognise that the Divine Plan knows no fault. Much of the so-called illness in Man today is caused through the dissatisfaction in his being with that which he has created for himself.

If you are to become beacons of light, if you are to prepare yourselves for the cataclysmic changes which are to come in the near future and if you are to prepare yourselves for the disease, the famine, the droughts that are to affect Mankind, as has been prophesied by many sages and seers, then you must begin now to harmonise your very beings. If you can do this, if you can preserve your health, as you define it, then you will be ready for the tests that are to come, but if you cannot live in harmony with life, then you will perish. The choice is simple.

GUIDANCE FOR A YOUNG PERSON

In this lecture I am going to outline the position in which many of the young people of today find themselves, and the kinds of choices which they have before them. Please do not think, though, that this lecture is intended solely for young people. One of the faults of society today is that it divides itself into various segments. The old think that they have no link with the young, the young think that they have nothing in common with the old, and so division is created and the interchange, the communication, between old and young which is so essential for both their developments is restricted.

When I refer to a young person I am, of course, referring to a person who is young in physical years, not young in soul evolution for, truly, at the present time there are a large number of evolved souls incarnating into young physical bodies. When I talk of a young person I am talking of a person under the age of thirty, for that is the age when full physical maturity is generally reached. It is at the end of the thirtieth year that the soul has opened and sensitised the three lower chakras of the body. In each of the first three ten-year cycles one of the three lower chakras is developed, and it is only when the third chakra, the solar plexus chakra, the emotional chakra, has been developed, that a person has fully reached physical maturity.

Because of the situation in which the World exists today, with only a short time to go before a cataclysmic change and a rebirth of the surface of this Earth occurs, it must be remembered that the souls who incarnate upon the Earth at this time do so for very specific and destined reasons. It is a difficult time in which to incarnate, with difficult lessons to learn. Indeed, at this most critical time in the Earth's evolution, whilst it does present a great opportunity for learning and spiritual advancement, it is also a time of great testing. Because of this many of the young people of today will fall by the wayside, but there should be no recrimination, no blame, no feelings of guilt, for this is a time of testing which young people would normally not have to face.

All those people who are now in their youth chose to incarnate into these dramatic and turbulent times because they wished to experience that which is now unfolding upon the Earth. They saw in the changes which were to come lessons which they could learn. They recognised that there was a great opportunity for soul evolution. Because this rebirth of the Earth is to involve a cataclysm, and because Atlantis is to rise again in that moment of rebirth, so many of the souls who are here in young bodies are citizens of Atlantis who have come to transmute the evil of over twenty thousand years ago. Young people should therefore recognise that they live in this Age of their own choosing. They cannot say that it is not what they want, that it does not give them that which they desire from life, for it is they themselves who have chosen to be here: no one has forced this decision upon them. Indeed, they are privileged to be present on Earth at this time of great growth and evolution, for there are many souls still waiting on the higher planes of life for just such an opportunity. You are all probably aware that the decision to incarnate is taken on levels above the physical long before the moment of conception. Consequently all you young people who live in this turbulent Age be aware that it has a lesson for you. There is a lesson in this chaos and disharmony which you have to learn. There are obstacles which you have to overcome.

Because the vibratory rate of this planet is being raised, because the frequency of the Earth is being increased by the Lords of this Solar Body, so there is this apparent speeding up of time and of the rate at which you lead life. There is much disharmony and evil to be seen as all the erroneousness of Mankind comes to the surface. It is therefore a difficult time to learn the lessons of youth. It is particularly difficult for one main reason. Society, as you know it, is declining. It is collapsing. As you look around you may witness in almost every aspect of life the final demise of Western civilisation, for Man, having pursued the path of intellect without the balance of spirituality, has created a wholly materialistic society in which the aims are self and self-aggrandisement. As a result of this, what you are witnessing in the youth of today is a generation of young people who for the first time in this Age have been given the freedom to be idle.

In the centuries which have gone by it had been an essential part of life that young people worked from the moment they were capable of doing so, both to help feed the family and to ensure the survival of that family within society. However, with the onset of the industrial revolution and the subsequent great advances in Man's technology there has been a rapid increase in personal freedom, the results being that the young people of today have the opportunity of avoiding the work which they should be doing. They have, therefore, lost the essential discipline of work. Today young people go to school and then during their holidays have long periods of rest when, truly, it should be in those periods of rest that they really begin to work, that they should be taught to appreciate the true values of life, for such is the nature of the educational system at this time that they will not have been taught such values at school but only the lessons which will lead them to adopt the values of society as they exist today: those of materialism, of providing only for the self, of obtaining personal possessions and power for the self.

Young people today are growing up with the freedom and with the time to pursue whatever they desire, but they have not been given the essential guidance to motivate themselves correctly. They are searching. They are looking for something to motivate their lives so that they may spend their hours of freedom profitably. You have only to look around your World today to see the many paths which young people have followed in their desperate search to discover a meaning to their lives. They have adopted many beliefs, created many dogmas, formed many cults, and lived their lives in ways which seem extraordinary to the older generation who did not have the same amount of freedom when they were young. The older generation cannot understand why young people need to pursue such aims, but they are not aware of the lack of motivation within the young people of today.

As I look at the lives of many of the young people of today I have to say that their basic motivation, and it is one which has been caused entirely by their parents and by the society in which they have been brought up, is that of self-gratification. Many of them also lack awareness for, basically, unawareness is selfishness: it is ignorance of the needs of other people, it is thinking only of the self to the exclusion of all those around. Young people today are for the most part selfish. They have not been taught the values of living in a true family union. They have not been taught the values of living in a true group or society. They have only been taught to imitate their parents and society around them which teaches that they should look first to the self, next to the family, next to the country, and only then to the World.

Hand in hand with this breakdown of modern civilisation has come the decline of organised religion. This in itself was destined to happen, but nothing has come to replace it, and because of this the spiritual guidance which is the essential birthright of every young person has been missing. You therefore have the young people of today living in an affluent age, which supports their whims, searching around for a form of guidance and a purpose to their lives which appeals to the ego, to the self. Do not assume, however, that my words apply to all the young people of today, for they do not. There are many young people who have guidance, who have motivation, who are fulfilling their destinies, but equally so there are many lost souls who do not possess that guidance, who are not on their destiny paths and who give cause for much concern, for it is the young people of today who are to be the founders of the New Age. Amongst them are many souls of great wisdom and evolution but because, as children, they have not been stimulated and encouraged in the right way, they have allowed their personalities to take over their very beings to the extent that they think only of their personalities and not of their higher selves. It is to these young people that I speak in this lecture.

Being of aged evolution, many of you have experienced levels of life in past incarnations on the Earth which were far removed from the ones in which you find yourselves today. You look back to the Ages when true spirituality existed on the Earth, to the great days of Atlantis, when Man did not live in so dense a body, when the Earth was not so wrought with devastation, disease and disharmony and, once more, you desire to experience that stage of evolution. That is why so many of the young people of today are turning to drugs, for within their soul memory is the knowledge of the use of drugs in those days of Atlantis. Drugs were used in Atlantis by the priests of the temples, but I would stress that they were used only by evolved souls who had passed many testing physical and spiritual initiations, and who were using them under the strictest guidance and control, with the purest of motivation. Today, young people use drugs as a form of escapism, to avoid the realities of physical life. If they cannot understand the nature of life around them, if they cannot find a purpose in life around them, then they try to reach another plane of existence and hope that there is one there.

I cannot stress too much the dangers inherent in this. Drugs can lift you, drugs *will* lift you, onto a higher plane of consciousness. That cannot be denied, but by so doing you are overcoming the inherent defence mechanism of your physical bodies which your Creator has wisely provided for you. Until you are in perfect harmony and balance, until you possess the wisdom, the understanding and the knowledge to recognise what exists on those higher planes of life and know how to handle what you will meet there, all that you are doing is putting your total incarnations into jeopardy, for you will so unbalance yourselves that you will be unable to fulfil your destinies. What is the point of experiencing the higher planes of life if you cannot understand them? What is the point of experiencing the higher planes of life if you cannot bring those experiences back to the physical level in an understandable and definable form, for how can you describe the colours and shapes of the astral in terms of the colours and shapes of the physical plane? Moreover the effect of drugs on the physical body is most damaging. Medical science has yet to discover this fully — and I will not at this time go into specific illnesses — but even the drugs that are considered harmless have a permanent and lasting effect on Man's physical body, for they are creating disharmony between Man's higher bodies. Moreover, if Man could but see the effect that drugs have on his etheric body, the energy giving body, he would be amazed. Drugs reak havoc with this particular body, leading to a loss of energy and subsequent apathy or ill health.

You have come onto the Earth to learn the lessons of the physical, not the lessons of the astral, the emotional or the mental planes: you have incarnated on the physical plane of Earth to learn the physical lessons of Earth at this moment in time, and only if you are of great evolution and know exactly what is taking place as you rise onto those higher levels of existence should you use drugs. Let the great Masters who have incarnated on the Earth be an example to you, for at no time did they advocate, or indeed practise, the use of stimulants to achieve higher levels of consciousness. They taught always that Man must reach these levels through his own inner development, and that he must work and strive with all that he possesses to achieve the knowingness of his Creator. But to many of the young people of today who have known only idleness it is the easy way, the quickest way, to get what the self wants, which appeals.

When I refer to drugs I am not talking only of the drugs which young people are using today but also of the many other forms of stimulants which are used by Man, for all of them do damage to Man's higher bodies. Medical science has been able to point to a few specific diseases of the physical body which can be attributed to alcohol, to cigarettes and to other herbal stimulants, but it has yet to discover the real damage that they cause. It is the disharmony which stimulants cause to his higher bodies that Man cannot see. The more Man takes these stimulants the more he disharmonises himself and the more he places himself in a position when he will never be able to make a correct decision with regard to his life. Today, therefore, the danger is that many young people have so abused their bodies that they stand little chance of ever regaining their destiny paths, not only because of the damage done to their physical bodies in terms of the nerves, the brain and the link between the brain and the mind, but also because they have placed themselves in a position where they will never be able to regain a state of normality and to see the condition in which they really exist. It is difficult to tell a man who is drunk that he is making a fool of himself, because he will never accept it. It is the same with a person using drugs or cigarettes. The ego is so in control that it will not be controlled.

The time is now long passed for the young people of today to pursue the ways of idleness. It is a time for action. It is a time for work as Man has never worked before. That is not to say that he must work around the clock without rest, without time for spiritual development and upliftment, but that the whole concept of work today is incorrect because of the way in which Man lives. If you look back at the lives of many of the great Masters you will see that they led simple, yet active, lives and that they followed trades which employed their hands as well as their brains. They did not incarnate into what, no matter what the Age, one would call the top technological or political jobs of the time. They chose simple tasks of humble work, for it is in such work that you can best harmonise your being. Indeed, it can perhaps be said that the simpler the work, the easier the path to bodily harmony.

Today there are many jobs which the old souls now incarnating in physical bodies will not, and should not, accept. Those which involve the prostitution of the Animal, the Vegetable, the Mineral and the Human Kingdoms should, of course, be rejected, but what the young people of today do not always realise is that they change society not by avoiding it, not by shunning it, not by establishing in isolation their own way of life, but by mixing with society expressly to demonstrate their own way of life. Society can only be changed from within, and that is the primary purpose for which the young people of today have incarnated. They have incarnated to change society. As I look around the World today I can see the influence of young people in many fields. They have brought a breath of fresh air to many of society's institutions and formalised ways of life. Young people today are not prepared to accept automatically the judgements and standards of their elders and, supposedly, betters. They bring with them the knowledge and the wisdom which they have acquired over many incarnations and, slowly, they are changing society. But the change is not occurring at the rate at which it should because so many of the young people of today are ignoring their duties and are denying their responsibilities not only to themselves but also to their Creator.

How then are the young people of today to change themselves so that they may become responsible members of society and fulfil the destinies to which they have agreed? Firstly, remember that it is in the simplicity of life that you will advance. Secondly, you must learn to become balanced, to control your emotions. You must realise that there is no reason whatsoever for sickness or disease within the physical body. Recognise it as the temple of the soul, and harmonise it with all that is around you. You must learn through meditation, concentration, and above all, perfect inner balance, to control your body, to dissolve sickness, to eliminate weaknesses of the flesh, to eat and enjoy the fruits of the Earth which are your birthright to enjoy, but not to make food and drink your master. Thirdly, you must harmonise yourself with Nature. You must become at one with her. Be aware of the wind, of the mountains, of the rain and of the trees. Grow to listen to them. Grow to communicate with them, to recognise the elementals and the devas, and to know that they too have a function to perform which you must respect. Fourthly, learn to commune with yourself and with the God within you, so that in times of crisis you know what to do and there is no doubt, no uncertainty, no waiting: there is only the certainty of your soul evolution which tells you what to do, so that when disaster looms nigh you will not be there, so that when disease threatens you will not suffer.

Obviously, if you are to achieve these four objectives it will mean that you will have to lead a life very different from that which society advocates today. So be it. It is by leading such a life that you will change this World, but remember that that way of life has to be seen by others, that it has to be lived amongst the peoples of the World, and that you have to work alongside those who do not understand in order to teach them. How are you, with your knowingness, for example, to convince those who are destroying present-day society through their political and financial views if you are not in a position to influence them? It must be amongst men that you work. It must be amongst men that you demonstrate. It must be amongst men that you teach.

So I say to the young people of today: the future of this planet lies in your hands. There are many evolved souls still to incarnate who will play a great part in the cataclysm which is to come, but it is you who are now approaching the age of thirty who will be responsible for the period of transition, who will have to face the death, the disease and the destruction. If, at this present time, you do not establish the way of life that you have known before then you, too, will suffer the fate of many less evolved souls, and will perish. As always, the choice is yours, but remember that many of you died in the cataclysm of Atlantis for the same reason: you were not prepared to subjugate that ego and to look beyond the self to the common purpose of life on this Earth. You are faced now with that same choice. The Lords of Karma have decreed. How will you answer?

MEDITATION

In the Western World today there has been an upsurge in the practice of meditation. Many people have gone to the East, have learnt varying methods of meditation there, and have brought them back to the West. There have also been visits of so-called 'gurus' who have come from the East to teach western Man how to meditate. May I therefore take this opportunity of presenting to you a view of meditation from the higher planes of life.

Meditation is very similar to prayer. If, when you go on your knees, you say: "Father, I pray that you will give me this or that, that you will lift my burden, that you will make me healthy, that you will make my path in life smoother", then you are limiting the whole concept of prayer. Similarly, if you enter into meditation with the idea of advancing only the self, of accruing benefits for the self so as to lead a better life, to progress further in life, then you are limiting the whole concept of meditation, for just as the motivation for prayer should be selfless so should the motivation for meditation. As I look at Man on the Earth today and see him praying selfishly for his own desires, so I see him meditating selfishly in just the same way to further his own objectives. This is not the path of true prayer, or of true meditation.

Just as when you go on your knees and pray you pray as befits your point of consciousness, so similarly with meditation you should meditate according to the knowingness within you, and therefore for anyone to come and impose a system of meditation upon you is most wrong. Meditation should be a wholly personal form of communion. How one person meditates will be different from another, and if you are led into a fixed system of meditation then you are truly limiting the very nature of your being, for everyone vibrates at a unique frequency. Therefore it is most wrong to go and adopt any of the methods of meditation practised in the East, for not only are these methods suited to a different race but their usefulness is limited according to the point of evolution of the individuals who developed them. Some of the teachers of meditation have come to the West with the highest motivation, but others have proved to be false prophets who seek only the adulation of their followers and who take pleasure in the belief that their way, their system, is paramount all over the Earth. It is the wise man who recognises that meditation is an individual, a personal, affair, and that what one man has discovered cannot be handed on to another.

If we analyse meditation it can broadly be defined as having two aspects, which I will call the horizontal and the vertical planes. The horizontal plane is concerned with the kingdom of Man, and the vertical plane with the kingdom of God. The horizontal plane of meditation is that with which Man usually concerns himself first, for he meditates to find the answers to the problems of the World in which he lives. He seeks to calm himself, to quieten his personality consciousness, to discover answers for all the problems with which he is faced, to decide on a plan of action and thus to help himself to lead a more harmonious life. Now it is obvious that this form of meditation is a desirable practice, for you have to solve the problems with which you are faced whilst you dwell in the physical. You have to plan your day, you have to organise your life, for if you enter the day without planning then much of that day will be wasted, but if you enter the day after an early morning meditation with your mind and body aligned in common purpose then much will be achieved.

When you are faced with the problems of the physical it is correct that you should withdraw into the silence and meditate upon them, to consider all the aspects as impartially as you can, to try and for once silence that personality consciousness which speaks so loudly and to seek the answer, the path which you should take. It is also correct that you should attempt to draw some knowledge of the purpose of life from your experience of it, that you should see the lessons in it for you, that you should consider the events of the day — your thoughts, your words and your deeds — and perhaps see if there is not something in them which will advance your knowingness of life. In all these things, therefore, the horizontal plane of meditation is important, but as you evolve you will soon rise above that plane and desire to know more of the Cosmos and of the true nature of God. You will then begin to meditate upon the vertical plane, the cosmic aspect. You will seek to move vertically instead of horizontally. You will seek the kingdom of God instead of the kingdom of Man.

When you sit in meditation on the vertical plane you are seeking solely to attune yourself to the God-head. It is important therefore that in this state of meditation you have a clear mind, that your physical brain containing the memories of the day and all that has gone on is stilled, so that in the quietness of your mind you can truly communicate with your higher self, for your higher self is your link to the God-head. The purpose, therefore, of this form of meditation is to link yourself to your higher self so that all the knowledge, all the knowingness of life that you have ever acquired, together with the knowledge of the cosmos, is available to you.

The very nature of this form of meditation is that you meditate to give rather than to receive. You sit to send the power of your being into the cosmos. Therefore do not enter into this form of meditation with thoughts centred on the lower self, on what you can obtain, on how you can increase your consciousness. It is by your meditating and offering, by your sending out, almost in a form of prayer, the very power of your being into the cosmos for the use of those Higher Beings who control the destiny of this planet, that you in turn will receive the knowledge of the cosmos.

There are many ways in which meditation can be done. It is up to you as an individual to discover the way which is most suited to yourself. As I said earlier, beware of those who teach systems, for meditation is a wholly personal link to your God-head which cannot be imitated. It is for you alone to establish that link to the God-head. Obviously you can be helped and guided by greater souls along the path towards your own form of meditation, but it is the wise teacher who knows that the student has to learn the way most suited to himself, and therefore encourages him to bring out from within the way that is best suited to his consciousness.

Meditation can be done individually and in a group. It is important that both forms are adopted, particularly group meditation, for when two or three are gathered together in meditation to offer the power which they possess up into the cosmos then that power links with similar powers all over the World and has great effect in the transformation of this globe. There are organisations, divinely inspired, which seek to get Man to meditate at fixed hours so that at such times great power can be generated. This is good, for the great Beings of the Hierarchy are able to use that power. It is also important that you as individuals sit and meditate alone, that you harmonise yourselves to the God-head, for unless you do that you will be in no position to change this World.

Let me give you a practical example. If you are faced with a difficult relationship on the physical level it is through attuning yourself, so that you reach up into the cosmos and contact on the higher levels of life that person with whom you are having a problem, that the problem can be solved. You may of course attempt to eliminate the problem purely on a physical level, but how often due to the personality consciousness is that way doomed to failure? It is through this process of going upwards and then downwards that the power of your true being can be conveyed and the true nature of your thoughts can be transferred to the person with whom you are in conflict. But until you have harmonised your true being you cannot attempt to heal such wounds in this manner.

When you meditate regard it as if you were praying, for meditation is a holy form of communication. It is an act of supplication, an act of giving. It should not be a method of obtaining, of receiving, although today many use it in this way. It is true, of course, that in meditation you can obtain personal solace and quietitude, and perhaps arrive at a more harmonious way of life, but these are side effects, not primary aims of meditation. All of you should attempt to meditate in the morning and in the evening, concerning yourselves with the horizontal plane in the morning and with the vertical plane in the evening. However, be aware that meditation is not something which need be entered into only once or twice a day. It is a continual act of being, and once you have raised your consciousness to these higher levels then you will find that meditation exists every minute of the hour, every hour of the day, and that within you is a continual link with your Creator. As you walk your path in life, as you meet your fellow men, as you experience the trials and tribulations of life, you will be so in tune with that higher self that you will lead a life of perfect harmony and love.

So whilst at present you may meditate once or twice a day try to realise that meditation should exist throughout your whole waking day. That is not to say that you should drift off into a dream world, but that as you are faced with the problems of the day you should consciously tune into the higher self. Your consciousness goes upwards into the realms of the Higher Beings rather than downwards into the vibrations of your fellowmen. Truly, if you are to bring out from within your very being that which you have discovered over many lives through much turmoil, pain and suffering, then you must begin to attune yourself to that higher consciousness. What is the purpose of incarnating on this plane of Earth if you ignore the inherent wisdom of your true being? What is the purpose of incarnating if you have within you the destiny of your life, the purpose for which you have come, the lessons which you are to face, the knowingness of your true being, and yet you deny this source?

You may now begin to see why meditation is the key to your evolution. It is the only key, for until you have unlocked the door to your higher consciousness truly you will not discover the meaning of life on this Earth. Therefore if all of you will only make great efforts to improve your ability to meditate, to contact your higher selves, you will have raised yourselves onto a level of evolution from which you will never fall, and in your incarnations to come you will always retain that awareness of life.

As I close, I would ask you all to cast a fresh eye on meditation. Examine the motivation behind your own meditation. Do you meditate to give or to receive? Do you project your mind horizontally or vertically, for it is by the very nature of your projection that you will control your meditation. If you cast your eyes upwards then truly you will rise upwards, but if you only cast your eyes downwards to the kingdom of Man then you will remain on the level of Man. As always, the choice is yours.

THE DESTINY OF BRITAIN

To many of her inhabitants it would appear that Britain is a declining country, that the qualities which led her to heights of power when she controlled almost half of the Earth's surface have disappeared and that the glory of Great Britain has gone. Indeed, at the present time, as she is faced with crisis after crisis, it would appear that Britain is set upon a path towards economic and moral collapse from which she will never recover. My purpose in speaking to you is to reassure you of the destiny of this truly great country, to show you why she is indeed still great and to tell you of her purpose in the destiny of the Earth.

Britain contains some of the most sacred and holiest points of divine power on the surface of this planet. Indeed, at the beginning of Creation Britain was a land inhabited solely by the angels and devic forces. When the first civilization of Man came into being in the area around the Dead Sea, the civilization which we know as Cordemia, the angels still walked the surface of Britain, and it was the power flowing through the receiving centres of this land that inspired, motivated and empowered the first tentative steps of Man in the civilization of Cordemia. To those of you who are familiar with the history of ancient Britain it is evident that significant events took place long before the records of Man began and that certain centres of power had been in existence before Man came and used them himself on the physical level. Great beings of the Angelic Realm, whom Man cannot see because of the frequency on which he operates, did indeed dwell on the surface of this land, and many of the ancient legends which exist today are the stories of their doings, of their administering to this planet's needs.

Britain, therefore, has always been the holiest of lands. It has been kept apart, separate, from the other land masses of the World even through the cataclysmic changes that have taken place, for it is, truly, a dwelling place of the gods. There are three

279

great centres of power on this Earth, and through these centres the love of your Creator is grounded. One of them is situated in Tibet, one is situated in the Holy Land, and the third is in Britain. The triple aspect of the Trinity — the Father, the Son and the Holy Ghost — rains down upon the Earth through these centres. The Father is grounded in Tibet, the Son in the Holy Land and the Holy Ghost in Britain. Therefore at varying stages in the Earth's history great souls have come to this land to tap into and to use the power of the Holy Ghost, and it is true when it is written that the Nazarene came to Britain as a young man in order to prepare his physical body for overshadowment by the Christ. It was by his physical presence in Britain, and in particular in Glastonbury, at this centre of great power, that he was preparing himself for the work that he was to do. Many other great Masters have also visited Glastonbury, although this fact is largely unknown to Man today.

Britain, therefore, is one of the great spiritual centres of the World. I cannot at this time go too deeply into the cosmic evolution of the Earth except to say that it is decreed that during a coming of the Christ in order to fulfil the Divine Plan for evolution the seeds shall be sown for the next coming, and that as the next coming of the Christ has indeed been destined to take place in Britain the Nazarene's visit to this land was intended to symbolise the next place of incarnation of the Christ Light. Those of you who have understood the significance of the Christ, who recognise that It is a light, a force, an illumination, not, as the religions of today would have you understand, a man, and that the Nazarene was indeed only an instrument through which the Christ operated, will understand that the next visitation of the Christ will manifest itself in similar form.

The history of Britain as you know it might appear on the surface to be somewhat chequered. It is true that there are events in the history of this land of which no nation would be proud, but throughout its long history Britain has truly been preparing itself for the role which is to come. Indeed, through the establishment of the British Empire Britain was unknowingly creating a federation of countries which are to be the backbone of the New Age, for though you may think that at the present time the links are weak, that the British Commonwealth no longer exists, truly the links are still there on a higher level of existence and there are, above all, the common factors of language, of justice, of government and of a sense of values which are peculiar to the British alone. Nations have changed and evolved, but the basic gifts of this country have been bestowed upon a large part of the World.

At the present time it would appear that Britain is on the verge of collapse. Certainly the way of life that has been pursued by the British is to change. The industrial and political systems which control this country are to disappear and from this situation there will arise a new British consciousness, a consciousness which possesses spiritual rather than material and political values. It is in Britain that the light of renaissance for the Aquarian Age is being kindled. Nowhere else in the World today is there so much activity on the spiritual front as there is in Britain, and if the progress which is now being made is maintained it will be to this country that the other nations of the World will look in the future. Indeed, it will be in Britain that there will be the first physical, and planned, manifestation of your brothers from outer space. There are many men of good-will in this country who, whilst not operating in public and making their beliefs and views widely known, are quietly acting as beacons, sending out the signals which will attract them.

Britain is to be the leader of the World, but not in the sense that she has led the World in the past, through force of arms, through the conquering of countries, but rather in the sense of a spiritual leader to whom other countries will look for guidance, for a source of knowledge and wisdom which they themselves do not possess. It has been written that Britain and America will be one. This is true. At the present time Man cannot conceive of the situation whereby this could occur, but a union of these two countries is to come about in preparation for the new Root Race which is to establish itself on the western coast of North America. In the U.S.A. today you have much potential, much power, with the gathering together of many races within its boundaries, but also a lack of wisdom and a need for guidance. It is this which Britain will provide, for being prepared within this country now are the teachers and the Masters of the New Age.

Look upon the transformation of Britain and upon what is to take place within the next five years not as a disaster but as a blessing. Liken it to the process of child-birth which, whilst painful on the physical level, brings new life, new expectations and new hopes. What this country is now experiencing is a time of re-birth. It is therefore unfortunate that at such a time Britain should have chosen to attach herself in federation to other countries in Europe. As a nation she has free choice and may do as she pleases, but through attaching herself to Europe she has delayed the destiny which she has to fulfil. She will in time overcome this obstacle, and find release from that federation, for Britain has first to develop herself individually, just as do all the other countries of Europe before they are able to federate themselves into a true European Community. In the years to come you will see that the Common Market is not what you think it is, that, truly, the individual countries concerned have not yet learnt to sacrifice and to place other countries before themselves, and that the motivation for entry into this union was not one of sacrifice but one of self-aggrandisement. Indeed, the motivation for Britain's entrance was not one of giving but one of receiving, of trying to avoid that which was written in the economic future of the country. Nevertheless, in spite of this union having taken place Britain will not avert an economic collapse. In Britain there exists a standard of civilisation, if I may call it that, which is unparalleled in any other country. All over the World there is admiration for British standards of justice, compassion and tolerance. These are some of the inherent qualities which Britain can give to the World, but she will not be able to demonstrate these qualities fully until after she has harmonised herself.

At the present time Britain is preparing herself for her future role, and preparing with her are many levels of consciousness above the physical. Those of us of the Hierarchy who seek to forward the plan for this Earth are drawing very close to Britain at this time. Many powers are manifesting themselves upon the surface of this little country. You are present at one great power point — Glastonbury. For the most part Man today does not understand the significance of this power-point. Intuitively he recognises the holiness, the sanctity, of this place, not because of that which has gone before, the legends, the fables and the tales, but because of that which he feels today. He senses the magnetic aura of this place, and that is why the young of today come here, for they are intuitively feeling the power which comes through this centre.

Some of you are aware that within Man's physical body there are seven centres of power, of cosmic energy, which are known as chakras. Countries have chakras similar to Man's, and

Glastonbury is one of the chakras of Britain. Other centres are London and Iona, and the remainder you may discover for yourselves through your own investigation. It is through these centres that the Earth's higher spiritual bodies are manifested onto the material or physical plane, and it is through this great power point of Glastonbury that, as I mentioned earlier, the power of the Holy Ghost flows. All those who come to this place are linking themselves with this energy, so that when they have departed, even when they are living in other countries, that etheric link will still be there, and at the right time, as the power is increased, as the transformation of this Earth takes place, they will be vitalised by that power. Those who come to Glastonbury, and this is true of any pilgrims who visit points of power, come not for the saintly men or women who lived here, not for the deeds that have been performed here, but to link themselves to this source of cosmic energy and power. This linking is not for the past, but for the future. It is for work which is to be done.

So, remember that Britain has had a glorious past and is a most holy and sacred land. Truly the angels have walked, and still do walk upon England's green and pleasant land. In the future Britain is to play a role which is without parallel, for which the people who now inhabit these shores have to undergo a period of transmutation, of transformation, so that in this change of the Earth that is to come, in this cataclysmic rebirth at the turn of the century, she may be ready to fulfil the true purpose of her being: the resting place of the Christ Light.

THE AQUARIAN CHRIST

As you look around the World today you can recognise many false religions, many false dogmas, many false prophets, the idols of clay to which Man clings to avoid the reality of his personal responsibility for recognising the Christ in him. Man has been led by his many earthly teachers and religious leaders into believing that he must always look outwards, that he must look to them for the spiritual sustenance of his life and for the instruction as to how he should think and what he should believe. Nowhere is this more evident than in the religious attitude today towards the Christ-Mass. You have a single religion which has taken upon itself the responsibility of representing the Christ and has spread its doctrines all over the World, professing infallibility and stating that if Man is to know of the Christ he must believe in the Church's interpretation. That interpretation is incorrect and is, indeed, responsible for misleading millions of souls who have followed its doctrines. The Christ is a light, an illumination, a principle for all men, for all religions, for all creeds, for all colours, for all races. It does not belong only to the Christian religion. The light of the Christ is instilled within every being on this Earth, and it is through understanding that light and following it that Mankind all over the World will be redeemed.

In the Age in which you live it is only natural that Man should regard physical form as an essential part of life. Having just lived through and experienced the Piscean Age Man is concerned mainly with the physical aspects of life and with the limitations of life as defined by his five senses. Therefore unless a cosmic power takes physical form on the surface of the Earth Man is reluctant to understand or to realise its significance. It is for this reason that great Beings have appeared on the surface of the Earth in physical form.

The form of the Christ was last manifested on the Earth by the Nazarene. It was through his physical form that the Christ was grounded and expressed. He expressed the Christ Principle for the Piscean Age to come, and his teachings have governed and illumined the lives of many people throughout this Age. Man has, of course, wrongly interpreted many of the Nazarene's teachings, indeed some have actually been changed to further Man's own ideas of life, but the vibration of cosmic spirit still lives with his words. You are now entering the Aquarian Age, the Aquarian Christ is soon to come and therefore in this lecture I seek to prepare you and to lead you into an understanding of the Aquarian Christ. That is not to say that the Christ of the Aquarian Age will be different from the Christ of the Piscean Age, but that the form which It will take on the Earth will be different, for no longer does the Piscean Christ have an appeal, especially amongst the young of today, in this, the Aquarian Age.

It is an interesting fact that as you look up at the Moon, the Earth's satellite, you see there a body which has form but no apparent life, as opposed to the Earth which you know has both form and life. This is because the frequency of life on the Moon is different from that on Earth. However, if the frequency of life on this Earth was to change, as it will in the years to come, you can appreciate that there could be beings on the Moon who would look down upon the Earth and would not see the expression of life as it will be then. They would regard the Earth as being a desolate planet, as you now regard the Moon. The expression of physical form can take on many appearances depending upon the frequency of matter and the vibratory rate of life on the planet. As you enter this, the Aquarian, Age the structure of matter on the Earth is to change. The vibratory rate of the Earth is to increase, the frequency of matter is to quicken, for the whole Solar Body is moving on an upward spiral of evolution. Therefore the physical form of life on this Earth will change, and as the Christ is within every form on this Earth so the appearance of the Christ will also differ.

The basic principle of the Christ, the principle which It illuminates onto this Earth, the principle which is to redeem both Mankind and this Earth, is that of sacrificial service in love. The Christ, therefore, is the spirit of service, of the sacrificing of the self, so that through the control of the lower elements of his being Man can rise to be an instrument of service. That, surely, was one of the main demonstrations of the Nazarene. He had so perfected his being through many incarnations, through many trials, tests and initiations that upon incarnating at that time he was capable of being Christed and of portraying the Christ in physical form. The Nazarene's life was intended to show what Man can achieve and what Man may do when he, too, is Christed. Do not think, however, that the Christ dwells only in a few beings of great evolution. The Christ expression exists in all of you, and the light which you shine, the Christ light, will vary only according to your points of consciousness, your soul knowingness, that which you have learnt both throughout your many past lives and, more especially, in this present incarnation at this critical moment in the Earth's history. You are all Christs in the making.

Christmas is not the time of the Nazarene's birth but the time when the higher beings of life celebrate, just as you celebrate a birthday, the birth of the Christ light. It is a time when all of you should look in particular to the Christ within you. It is a time for remembering that the Christ does exist within you, and that it is through the Christ that you will change this Earth and your very being. What does the Christ mean to you once you have outgrown and discarded the popular story of Christmas? What does the Christ mean to you, being souls of aged evolution, once it has been shown to you that Christmas is not as the Churches interpret it, that the Christ manifested thousands of years before the Christian religion was ever thought of and that It will exist for many more years after the Christian religion has died? How many of you have looked within yourselves to see there the light of the Christ? How many of you have recognised that the Christ light is the only light that you may follow to evolve both yourselves and this Earth on which you dwell?

Are you aware that the Christ light shines only on the Earth? Are you aware that there was a time on this Earth, when Man first dwelt in perfection, when the Christ light did not exist, when It was not needed? It was only after many aeons of evolution, after Man had been reborn on the Earth with the divine gift of free choice which led to his gradual downfall and degradation, that the Christ light was sent down onto the Earth by your Creator. Are you aware that the other planets within this Solar Body do not have the Christ? That, surely, is the significance of those three wise men in the Christmas story, for as they came to the birth of the Christ they came not only to pay homage but also to observe, for they had not seen the Christ before. Do you realise that on the three major planets of your

286

Solar Body from which those wise men came they had evolved to their level of evolution without knowing of the Christ, without the use of Its power? The wise men came bringing their gifts of gold, frankincense and myrrh which symbolised the gifts of their three planetary powers: truth, love and harmony. They came to welcome the Christ here on Earth.

Remember that the Christ light which dwells within you is the supreme gift of your Creator. It is a part of Himself. It is something which Man has been given as a privilege because of the nature of his being and his destiny in the evolutionary spiral of this Solar Body, for the creation of Earth and of Man who dwells on it is of a special significance. Each one of you has been created in imitation of your Creator: therefore you are gods in the making. You have within you the ability one day to become a god, a sun, to spread your illumination over a body as large as this Solar Body and to watch the growth and evolution of your very being as does your own Creator Whose spirit resides in the Sun. Therefore you are very special within the Solar Body in which you dwell. You incarnate into physical form on the Earth as a great privilege, yet there are so many who unthinkingly regard this school of life as drudgery, as boredom, as toil with little reward, who have not realised the great privilege which has been afforded to them: that of experiencing the Christ expression in physical form.

The Aquarian Christ is to appear in Aquarian form. Man will change the form of his physical body in the cataclysmic change which is to come at the end of this century, and likewise the form of the Christ will change. Within the Solar Body at this time there are the essences, or seeds, of two planets: one is within the aura of the Sun and the other is within the satellite rings of Saturn, that planet which sometimes Man knows as Satan, which is not the evil but the testing planet, the planet which holds the Sun in perfect balance and rhythm. At the correct time, to fulfil the Divine Plan both of that Being Whom you call God and of Beings, or Forces, beyond this Solar Body, these essences will take physical form and will become planets. When the planet within Saturn's rings comes into being it will release Saturn's pressure in the Solar System, and Saturn will no longer be the planet that tests and restricts. It will come into balance with the Sun after the Earth uprights on its axis and will form a complete trinity. It is in this trinity of Love, Creativity and Wisdom pouring forth from these three aspects that the Earth will know its thousand years of peace.

After Saturn has revealed her planet the Sun will throw its planet into orbit, and this will be, as it were, the son of the Sun. These two planets, the male and the female, the positive and the negative, will change the nature of life on this Earth. It is then that the Christ will come again, but instead of being grounded and exemplified by one man, as was the case with the Nazarene, It will be grounded by the perfect unison of a man and a woman, who will be the leaders of a new race of Humanity on Earth. You will therefore have a new aspect of the Christ, an aspect which will change your lives most radically, for no longer will the Satan side, the testing side, be present on Earth. No longer will Man have to master the influences under which he struggles to advance today with all the turmoil, the pain, the disharmony and the destruction that is prevalent on the Earth at the present time. He will have moved into this new Age of the Christ. His body will have changed, he will have extended his senses. He will be aware of life beyond the physical as he knows it today, and he will see the Christ too in another form beyond the physical. He will be led into a greater understanding of the Christ in him.

But all this will not be possible unless you have awakened the Christ in you so that when this great upliftment of the Earth takes place, so that when the Earth moves on its axis, as the Christ light changes within you, you will be ready for that change. The light of the Christ is the power which should motivate your lives. If you accept that light, accept that power, if you allow it to govern your whole being, then to you will flow the powers of the Cosmos, to you will flow the right to use the Natural Laws of the Universe and to perform 'miracles' as did the Nazarene. To you will come the gift of prophecy, the gift of knowledge beyond the realm of Earth, the union of life with worlds invisible. It all lies ready for you in the years to come, but it can come only to the form that is prepared, it can come only to those who have seen the Christ, who have known the true meaning of service, of love, of harmony, of goodwill.